Once There
Were Greenfields

Library of Congress Cataloging-in-Publication Data

Benfield, F. Kaid.
　　Once there were greenfields: how urban sprawl is undermining America's environment, economy, and social fabric/F. Kaid Benfield, Matthew D. Raimi, Donald D.T. Chen.
　　　p. cm.
　　Includes bibliographical references (p.　).
　　ISBN 1-893340-17-1
　　1. Cities and towns—Growth—Environmental aspects—United States. 2. Cities and towns—Growth—Economic aspects—United States. 3. Environmental degradation—United States. 4. Quality of life—United States. 5. United States—Environmental conditions. 6. United States—Social conditions—1980–I. Raimi, Matthew. II. Chen, Donald, D.T. III. Title.
HT384.U5B46　1999　　　　　　　　　　　　　　　　　　　　　　99-19928
307.76'0973—dc21　　　　　　　　　　　　　　　　　　　　　　　　CIP

Once There Were Greenfields

*How Urban Sprawl Is
Undermining America's Environment,
Economy, and Social Fabric*

F. Kaid Benfield
Matthew D. Raimi
Donald D.T. Chen

Natural Resources Defense Council
Surface Transportation Policy Project

The Natural Resources Defense Council is a nonprofit environmental membership organization with 400,000 members and contributors nationwide. Since 1970, NRDC's lawyers, scientists, and staff have been working to protect the world's natural resources and to improve the quality of the human environment. Visit us on the World Wide Web at **www.nrdc.org**.

40 West 20th Street
New York, NY 10011
212 727-2700

71 Stevenson Street
San Francisco, CA 94105
415 777-0220

1200 New York Avenue N.W.
Washington, DC 20005
202 289-6868

6310 San Vicente Boulevard
Los Angeles, CA 90048
323 934-6900

The Surface Transportation Policy Project is a nonprofit, public interest coalition of over 200 groups devoted to ensuring that transportation policy and investments help conserve energy, protect environmental and aesthetic quality, strengthen the economy, promote social equity, and make communities more livable. Visit us on the World Wide Web at **www.transact.org**.

1100 17th Street N.W.
Washington, DC 20036
202 974-5131

Production Supervision
Sharene Azimi

Copy Editing
Jon Swan

NRDC Director of Communications
Alan Metrick

Design
Jenkins and Page/NYC

Electronic Assembly
Bonnie Greenfield

Cover Photo
Chesapeake Bay Foundation (sprawl)

Ordering Information
Copies of this book are available for $20 each plus shipping and handling ($3 for the first book, $1 each additional book). Make checks payable to NRDC in U.S. dollars only and mail to: NRDC Publications Department, 40 West 20th Street, New York, NY 10011. California residents must add 7.25 % sales tax. For a complete publications list, foreign shipping rates, and bulk discount information, call (212) 727-4486.

This report is printed with vegetable-based inks on 100% recycled paper (text: 75% post-consumer content/cover: 50% post-consumer content). Using these papers instead of virgin fiber saves an estimated: • 61 Trees • 7.6 Cubic Yards of Landfill Space • 17,695 Gallons of Water • 11,783 Kilowatt Hours of Energy • 172 Pounds of Air Pollution.*

Compiled by New York Recycled Paper Inc., from the following sources: U.S. Environmental Protection Agency; Pacific Gas & Electric Company; Riverside Paper Company; American Paper Institute, Inc.
*Extrapolated from figures for groundwood papers.

Acknowledgments

This book is a product of **The Toolkit for Smart Growth**, a joint project of the Natural Resources Defense Council (NRDC) and the Surface Transportation Policy Project (STTP). The Project also has produced a white paper, "Another Cost of Sprawl: The Effects of Land Use on Wastewater Utility Costs," available separately from NRDC. A forthcoming volume will present practical advice to assist governments, businesses, and stakeholders in evaluating development options and pursuing alternatives to sprawl.

The Toolkit for Smart Growth is made possible by generous support and assistance from The Joyce Foundation, the Alliance for Transportation Research Institute, The George Gund Foundation, the Urban and Economic Development Division of the United States Environmental Protection Agency, and The J.M. Kaplan Fund, Inc. This book also has drawn extensively from research made possible by the support of The Nathan Cummings Foundation and The Energy Foundation for NRDC's Transportation Program, and by Matthew Raimi's term as The Helen W. Buckner Fellow at NRDC. In addition, the design of this book was made possible in part by support of The John D. and Catherine T. MacArthur Foundation. NRDC and STPP express their deep appreciation to these institutions for enabling this work to go forward.

As with all our organizations' work, NRDC and STPP would like to thank our members for their support.

The authors wish to thank a number of very special colleagues and friends whose work, advice, and insight helped us shape and finish this book: Tanya Washington, Susan Exline, and Stacey Justus, current and former NRDC program assistants, who not only produced and shaped the manuscript many times over, but also contributed insightful research and writing along the way; Sharene Azimi, our publications director at NRDC; Jill Kruse, STPP planner and analyst, who worked with us almost from the beginning in shaping the Toolkit for Smart Growth; former NRDC attorney Michael Fitts, who helped conceive the project in its infancy; and Frances Beinecke at NRDC, and Hank Dittmar and Roy Kienitz at STPP, whose patience we tested and whose indulgence we appreciate.

We also wish to thank a large number of friends both within and outside our organizations who provided research advice and/or comments on the manuscript, and whose wisdom improved the product: Reid Ewing, Florida Atlantic University and Florida International University; Ron Wilson, EarthJustice Legal Defense Fund (retired); Ken Adler, U.S. Environmental Protection Agency; Geoff Anderson, U.S. Environmental

Protection Agency; Constance Beaumont, National Trust for Historic Preservation; Tom Bier, Cleveland State University; Jennifer Bradley, the Brookings Institution; Diane Cameron, NRDC; Lee Epstein, Chesapeake Bay Foundation; Laura Gabanski, U.S. Environmental Protection Agency; Jacky Grimshaw, Center for Neighborhood Technology; Susan Handy, University of Texas School of Architecture; John Holtzclaw, NRDC; Rich Kassel, NRDC; Bruce Katz, the Brookings Institution; Peter Lehner, NRDC; Donna Liu, NRDC; Rob Michaels, Environmental Law and Policy Center of the Midwest; Marya Morris, American Planning Association; Tom Muller, Logistics Management Institute; Ann Sorensen, American Farmland Trust; and Frank Vespe, Scenic America. In addition, a number of individuals and institutions provided valuable assistance in helping us illustrate the text with photographs and other graphics: The Chesapeake Bay Foundation, Steve Delaney of the U.S. Environmental Protection Agency, Peter Haas of the Center for Neighborhood Technology, and Joe DiStefano of Calthorpe Associates. The conclusions we have reached are, of course, ours and ours alone.

It may assist some readers to know who, among the three of us, wrote what in the text. In fact, it was a group effort, which we conceived, discussed, and critiqued many times, and produced together. We all read and edited each other's drafts and contributed to each other's research. Nevertheless, there were some divisions of responsibility. Matt Raimi was primarily responsible for the research and drafting of the material on the fiscal impacts of sprawl, as well as for assembling the book's photographs, charts, and tables; Don Chen researched and drafted the social impacts chapter; Kaid Benfield was primarily responsible for the rest. Kaid also served as editor-in-chief. But we all subscribe to the book in its entirety.

F. Kaid Benfield
Matthew D. Raimi
Donald D. T. Chen
March 1999

Table of Contents

Tables and Figures

Preface
Of Fields and Dreams

In 1960, one of the most popular songs in America was a simple folk song by a group called The Brothers Four. Its opening lines evoked a youthful, sentimental memory of the best of the American landscape:

Once there were greenfields, kissed by the sun
Once there were valleys where rivers used to run
Once there were blue skies with white clouds high above
Once they were part of an everlasting love . . .[1]

In large part, this book is the story of what has happened to America's greenfields in the four decades since the haunting rhythms and minor chords of this song filled our nation's radio airwaves.

This is also a story about the so-called "American Dream." It is about astonishing rates of growth and about progress and prosperity, all of which are good and all of which we salute. It is about the United States of America at the beginning of the 21st century, and about our country's expanding population and economy.

But our story is also about the Dream's nightmarish twists. It is not so much about sensible, "smart growth"—patterns of development that are environmentally and economically sustainable, and socially equitable—as it is about, to put it bluntly, dumb growth. It is about landscapes lost, traffic congested, air and water polluted, public health endangered, and a potential energy crisis that could make those of the 1970s look mild by comparison. It is about how nearly all of the positive strides that we have taken in improving our environmental quality could be reversed if we do not change the way we grow.

Our story is also about economic waste, rising taxes, and the unfair burdens that dumb growth places on taxpayers and governments. And it is about the consequences for those left behind as

Greenfields, and other open spaces such as forests and farmlands, are an integral part of our human existence.

S.C. DeLaney/EPA

we place more and more of our investment and energy in new places—in our vanishing "greenfields"—rather than in the places where people already live.

Most of all, it is a story about our cities, the regions that surround them, and the people who live in these cities and regions. It is about Chicago and Cleveland and Fresno, about Loudoun County in Virginia and the Willamette Valley in Oregon. It is about what is happening to these places and their inhabitants as our development expands outward much faster than our population increases. It is about our houses and our yards and our workplaces and our stores and our schools, most of which are good, and where we have been putting them, most of which is not.

Ours is not, however, a story about villains. The only perpetrators are ourselves. And, we have allowed this to happen only because, until recently, we have known no better.

Nor is our story about nostalgia. We are 21st century environmentalists. We seek progress, not retreat. We seek a future for our great regions and for our children that, with smarter growth, will be more prosperous as well as more environmentally sustainable and socially equitable than will be the case if we continue down our present blind, dumb path. We believe that this brighter dream is well within our reach.

This book is organized into five chapters. First, we describe the basic facts and trends that constitute our current patterns of growth. Second, we discuss the consequences of these patterns for our environmental resources, including air, energy, land, and water. Our third chapter discusses the fiscal costs of inefficient development, and our fourth describes the social consequences of development patterns that ignore existing communities. Finally, we conclude on an optimistic note, presenting some strategies and examples that we believe hold promise for a more environmentally, economically, and socially sustainable future.

Our narrative is intended not only to tell this story, but also to constitute a reference volume that will present readers with a wide range of data and information, as well as citations pointing to a larger body of research. Our hope is that, by organizing the various findings contained in what others have written about this subject, we can help readers bridge the gap between broader books about sprawl, which make a compelling case but do not always provide detailed annotations, and academic reports and other more focused work, which detail parts of the story but do not attempt to illuminate the whole. We are not academics, and we acknowledge that we have come to this project with a point of view; but we have investigated the facts, and we are firm in our conviction that the problems we raise are real and serious.

In sum, we intend this book to tell why we should care about the way we grow, and to present some ways that we might do better. Now, in pursuit of a brighter American dream, we begin our story.

Spreading Out
The Facts of Contemporary Development

Our story begins with a description that, were it not so familiar, might itself seem sprung from a dream:

> What hath been wrought by 40 years of interstate construction, subdivision building and basically nonexistent regional planning?
>
> . . .
>
> [M]any metropolitan areas have evolved as suburban expanses with no real center of gravity. Growth is diffused. New commercial centers sprout up randomly, surrounded by jerry-built communities and upscale cul-de-sacs that often supplant the original central business district while competing with each other for tax base and infrastructure.

Two years later, the same author suggested how this familiar yet disturbing vision has developed:

> Suburbs struggle because they have let developers run amok, oblivious to traffic growth, sewer system capacity, or even recreational needs. . . . In many areas you need a car to get anywhere or do anything—from buying a quart of milk to jogging.

This is not the environmental community talking. Rather, these are the observations of the real estate industry, in its 1997 and 1999 annual reports, *Emerging Trends in Real Estate*, prepared by one of the nation's oldest real estate valuation and consulting firms,

3

in partnership with one of the nation's leading property managers and the world's largest professional services organization.[1]

To what extent should these observations, voiced so eloquently by the real estate industry, be cause for more widespread concern? Put another way, in the first half of the 21st century, the U.S. population is expected to grow by half. That anticipated growth of some 130 million people is equivalent to the current population of France and Germany combined.[2] What do present trends say about where these new citizens will live, work, and shop? Does the spatial form toward which we grow matter? If so, what should we do?

In this opening chapter, we present a compendium of factual, numerical information. In particular, we first present a range of basic population and settlement trends, both for the United States as a whole and for a sampling of places around the country. Next, we zoom in a bit, detailing individual components of these overall trends. In particular, we report what a number of observers have said about the characteristics of what has come to be called—sometimes a bit loosely, perhaps—"urban (or suburban) sprawl," and we present trend data and descriptions with respect to dispersal of residences, employment, and shopping. Because we hope our work will be useful as a reference volume, we have tried to be comprehensive (if inevitably a bit overwhelming) in our reporting of the facts.

Next, we zoom in closer still, presenting a case-study discussion of the facts regarding one of America's greatest metropolitan regions, Chicago. Finally, we close the chapter with a brief review of some of the reasons why sprawl predominates, presenting a few of the historical and cultural factors that have contributed to it.

We are writing this volume in the late 1990s, shortly before the decennial American census is likely to collect new information on many of these topics in the year 2000. We will look forward with great interest to additional data as they become available, but we do not expect the 2000 census to dispute the basic trends that we report here. Our judgment is that this story must be told now.

Metropolitan and Suburban Growth Trends

Population trends reveal that, notwithstanding our agrarian history, we have become overwhelmingly a nation of metropolitan citizens. At the same time, our metropolitan regions are exhibiting rapid rates of dispersal.

The Nation as a Whole

Eight of ten Americans now live in areas defined by the Census Bureau as "metropolitan."[3] More than half live in the 39 largest metro areas of one million or more,[4] which grew in population by an average of 44 percent between 1960 and 1990.[5] Since 1950, the combined population of U.S. metropolitan areas has more than doubled, and the percentage of our citizens living in areas defined by the census as "urban" has risen steadily throughout our nation's history.[6]

Low-density sprawl from the air—cul-de-sacs and single-family homes spread over the countryside.

Within these overall trends are some notable subsets, including the explosive growth rates of smaller cities. Those with populations from 50,000 to 100,000 and from 100,000 to 250,000, in particular, have grown some 50 percent faster than metropolitan regions as a whole. This is true not only for smaller cities but also for smaller metropolitan areas—i.e., those with populations from 250,000 to 500,000.[7] This rapid growth suggests that the small-city environments chosen by the people moving to these places are disappearing rapidly.

It will surprise few readers that the fastest-growing regions are located in the southern and western United States. Among the large metropolitan areas growing at the extremely rapid rate of 50 percent or more in the single decade of the 1980s were Riverside-San Bernadino, California (66 percent); Las Vegas, Nevada (60 percent); and Orlando, Florida (53 percent); several smaller regions in Florida also grew at rates well above 50 percent.[8] From 1960 to 1990, population in the West grew nearly six times faster than did population in the Northeast and Midwest, and population in the South grew about twice as fast.[9] By the mid-1990s, the rate of growth in the South had accelerated and begun to approach the rapid rate of growth in the West.[10] Eleven of the nation's twenty fastest-growing metro areas in the 1990s are located in the southern states of Texas, Florida, Arkansas, North Carolina, and Georgia.[11]

But the most striking revelation of recent population trends is the extent to which we are moving to the fringes of our metropolitan regions. Since 1980, suburban population has grown a staggering ten times faster than central-city population in our largest metro areas.[12] Meanwhile, as suburban growth has been booming, the shares

Table 1-1
The Fastest-Growing Areas in the United States, 1990–1996

Metropolitan Area	Percent Change in Population, 1990–1996
Las Vegas, NV-AZ	40.9
Laredo, TX	32.7
McAllen-Edinburg-Mission, TX	29.2
Boise City, ID	25.9
Naples, FL	23.7
Fayetteville-Springdale-Rogers, AR	23.7
Austin-San Marcos, TX	23.1
Phoenix-Mesa, AZ	22.7
Provo-Orem, UT	21.3
Brownsville-Harlingen-San Benito, TX	21.1

Source: U.S. Bureau of the Census, "Estimates of the Population of Metropolitan Areas," Washington, DC: 1997, MA-96-9.

of employment and population claimed by central cities have been declining; in many central cities, absolute population has declined.[13] Indeed, in each of the eight years between 1988 and 1996, central cities taken together suffered a net outmigration of between 2.4 and 2.9 million people. During the same period, suburbs experienced a net gain of between 2.1 and 3.1 million people each year.[14]

The cumulative impact of this disparity in growth is that, as of 1990, suburbs held nearly 60 percent of the U.S. metropolitan population.[15] Under current trends, some four-fifths of the country's growth in the coming decades can be expected to locate in so-called "edge cities" and other suburbs that disperse development to the outer reaches of our metro areas.[16]

Such outward migration has obvious implications for consumption of land. The numbers bear out the supposition: from 1960 to 1990, the amount of developed land in metro areas more than doubled, while population grew by less than half.[17] According to the Department of Agriculture's National Resources Inventory, nearly one-sixth of the total base of land developed in our country's long history was claimed for development in just 10 recent years, from 1982 to 1992.[18] Some of the fastest growth is occurring beyond the areas now defined as metropolitan, in still-rural communities 60 to 70 miles from metropolitan beltways. Such "exurbs" already account for 60 million people and one-quarter of the recent population growth of the lower 48 states.[19]

Region-by-Region Examples

No part of the country has escaped decentralization. While it is beyond the scope of this book to report on every major metropolitan area, a sampling of recent trend data on a region-by-region basis sharpens our focus on the pace of sprawl.

The Northeast   From 1980 to 1994, the suburbs around Washington, DC, grew in population by a booming 18.3 percent, while the central city lost 17 percent of its residents.[20] In the first seven years of the 1990s, the city of Washington lost some 78,000 residents—more than one person every hour—even though the surrounding metropolitan area was one of the nation's fastest growing during that period. The population of central city Washington is now at its lowest point since the 1930s.[21]

Forty miles north of Washington, the city of Baltimore has lost some 250,000 people in the past 25 years.[22] Meanwhile, in nearby and once-rural central Maryland, population has soared by an additional 1.2 million people in the last twenty years.[23] The impact on the land is even greater than the population shifts by themselves suggest, because the number of people in an average Maryland household has been declining, while average residential lot size has been increasing.[24] The Maryland Office of Planning projects that, from 1995 to 2020, more land will be converted to

---

Figure 1-1
Change in Metropolitan Population and Developed Land Area, 1970–1990
Source: Henry Diamond and Patrick Noonan, *Land Use in America*, Washington, DC: Island Press, 1996.

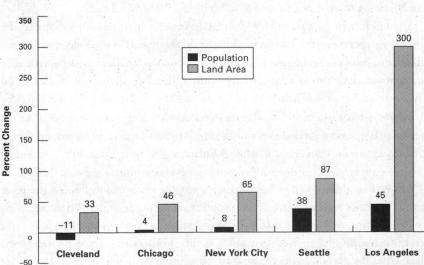

housing in the region than in the past three and one-half centuries.[25] In fast-growing Carroll County near Baltimore, students are now crammed into 109 portable school facilities to meet excess demands; 76 percent of the county's population has sprawled into the countryside, outside existing incorporated towns.[26]

Trend data from other parts of the Northeast are consistent with those in Washington and Maryland. From 1960 through the mid-1980s, the urbanized area around New York City grew by 65 percent, while the region's population grew only 8 percent; the farthest reaches of New York City now stretch into eastern Pennsylvania and across 100 miles of New Jersey.[27] In greater Boston, some 97 percent of the region's developed land area is now outside the city limits.[28]

The Industrial Midwest   In theory, one might expect the so-called "Rust Belt" cities to be relatively immune from sprawl, since as a rule their population has been growing slowly, if at all. In fact, precisely because overall growth has not been rapid, the statistics regarding suburbanization are particularly dramatic.

For example, in the two decades from 1970 to 1990, the consumption of residential land in greater Chicago grew an amazing eleven times faster than the region's population.[29] (Because we have chosen Chicago for our close-look case study, we examine that region in particular detail below, in a special section.)

In the past three decades, greater Detroit consumed land at an even faster rate, 13 times faster than its rate of population growth.[30] The city's outward sprawl has occurred, like Washington's, while the central city has been losing population; Detroit proper lost 44 percent of its population between 1950 and 1990.[31]

Among cities in the industrial Midwest, Cleveland merits special mention because it has been sprawling at a rapid rate even while the region as a whole, not just the urban core, has been losing population. In particular, from 1950 to 1990, the suburban population around Cleveland more than doubled, while that of the central city declined by almost half.[32] Since 1970, the regional population declined by 11 percent, while the amount of urbanized land grew by 33 percent.[33] Planners project that by 2010 greater Cleveland's population will decline another 3 percent, but developed residential land will grow another 30 percent.[34]

The Plains   Metropolitan Kansas City owns the distinction of being the most spread-out region in the country. In an excellent six-part series published in late 1995, the *Kansas City Star* reported that, over five decades, the location of the region's most expensive housing has moved two miles farther from downtown every ten years. Meanwhile, the portion of the region *losing* population swelled from 16 to 282 square miles. Despite these declines in the core, the overall regional population has grown at a robust 29 percent, and the amount of developed land has doubled. Today, not only does Kansas City have more average space between its homes than any other region in America, it also and not coincidentally has the most freeway miles and total road miles per person. The area's population density in 1990 was only one-fourth what it was in 1920.[35]

In the Minneapolis-St. Paul area, the impacts of ever-outward growth trends have been well documented. In the last two decades, for example, the region's core cities and inner suburbs declined in both public school enrollment and property values. In the same period, outer suburbs around the Twin Cities experienced growth in school enrollment and property values, and also enjoyed the greatest share of regional-job growth.[36]

The Sun Belt   As discussed above, no area of the country is growing and dispersing faster than the South and Southwest. As the authors of *Emerging Trends in Real Estate* put it, "the country's fastest-growing major metropolitan areas—Atlanta, Phoenix, Dallas—aren't really cities at all. They're suburban agglomerations—diffusions of subdivisions and horizontal development with no relation to the original urban cores."[37]

The numbers bear them out. The prototype "city" of the future, if present trends continue, may well be metropolitan Phoenix, which is reported to be developing open land at the rate of 1.2 acres per hour.[38] Indeed, the geographic reach of Phoenix is now said to be equivalent in size to Delaware.[39] Another Sun-Belt candidate to represent the metropolis of the future is Atlanta, which has grown in population at an average annual rate of 2.9 percent since 1950, with almost all of the growth in the suburbs; the growth rates are even higher for the numbers of jobs and households.[40] Real estate analyst Christopher Leinberger points out that the north-to-south reach of Atlanta stretched 110 miles in 1998, up from "only" 65 miles in 1990. Leinberger claims that "it is altogether probable that in terms of land area Atlanta is the fastest-growing human settlement in history."[41]

Meanwhile, in Texas, metropolitan Dallas grew by 30 percent in the single decade of the 1980s; some outer suburbs north of Dallas grew explosively by 80 percent in those ten years.[42] The state of Texas had four of the ten fastest-growing metropolitan regions in the country in the late 1990s.[43] In Florida, home to the nation's most rapidly growing smaller metro areas, developed land grew by a whopping 80 percent in one decade, from 1974 to 1984, twice as fast as the population.[44]

The Far West   If Kansas City is the best statistical example and Phoenix a vision of the future of dispersed growth in America, surely the best-known example of sprawl is Los Angeles. Some 89 percent of the land described by the census as constituting metropolitan Los Angeles lies outside the central city, as does over three-fourths of the

population.[45] In the last two decades, the geographic reach of Los Angeles nearly tripled, while its population grew by slightly less than half. Greater Los Angeles is now said to occupy space equivalent in size to Connecticut.[46]

Even the Pacific Northwest is suffering from rampant sprawl; the Puget Sound region, which includes Seattle, grew two and one-half times faster in developed land than it did in population from 1970 to 1990.[47] The Northwest is also home, however, to the country's most celebrated exception to these trends—Portland, Oregon, which has prospered and grown in population largely without claiming new land for development. (Because Portland's experience did not occur by accident, and because its success in managing growth is so instructive, we discuss it in detail in Chapter 5.)

In metropolitan Los Angeles, 89 percent of the land and over 75 percent of the population lies outside the central city.

Putting a Face on Dispersed Development

What does our new landscape look like? Consider the drive-by view, as articulated by *Washington Post* writer Todd Shields in his description of modern real-estate advertising:

> Each Saturday, developers plant the roadsides with waist-high signs that tell us why [sprawl development] is happening. In neon shades of orange and green, the ads stand in thickets by tobacco barns and produce stands: "From the 180s," "$5000 Closing Help," "From the 150s," "$107,995," "Free Basement."[48]

Or, consider the satellite view. Philip Lewis, a researcher at the University of Wisconsin, has used nighttime satellite photographs of electric light patterns to identify an emerging, doughnut-shaped, 400-mile-wide mega-city in America's heartland, comprising Chicago, Milwaukee, Madison, the Twin Cities, and Mason City, Cedar

Rapids, and Davenport in Iowa. The hole in the doughnut is, for now at least, mainly Wisconsin farmland.[49]

Characteristics of "Sprawl"

A number of observers have attempted to characterize late 20th-century patterns of development. Professor Reid Ewing of Florida International University notes that what we have come to describe as "sprawl" is hard to define precisely by geographic features, although it includes so-called "leapfrog" or scattered development, commercial strips along roadsides, and large expanses of low-density or single-use development that isolates living, working, and shopping places from each other. Ewing believes that sprawl is best identified by its impacts or indicators, including poor accessibility between residences and other destinations and a lack of functional open space.[50] Attorney Lee Epstein of the Chesapeake Bay Foundation concludes that, "in general, recognizable sprawl takes the form of large expanses of low-density, single-use development, married with strip and auto-oriented commercial land uses, at the very edges or beyond the fringes of existing urbanization."[51]

Professor Rutherford Platt of the University of Massachusetts colorfully describes much recent development as "mushburbs," pointing to a characteristic lack of integration of planning and design among their various components. Professor Platt notes that these patterns are typically characterized also by a shortage of affordable housing, a lack of educational, cultural, and aesthetic amenities, and an absence of civic traditions and a sense of community.[52]

A somewhat more charitable view is taken by Brookings Institution economist Anthony Downs, who concedes that much of what we consider to be sprawl is, in fact, an expression of the American Dream: ownership of detached, single-family homes on spacious lots, ownership and convenient use of automobiles, employment in low-rise workplaces with free parking, residence in small communities with strong local governments, and an environment free from the signs of poverty. Downs notes, however, that "the results are inconsistent with the high quality of life that this vision promises," and that they include excessive travel, traffic congestion, lack of affordable housing, debates about the costs of infrastructure and services, and deteriorating open space, among other problems. Downs notes also that most Americans do not realize their responsibility in causing these growth-related problems.[53]

What is undeniable is that the new growth has taken a very different form from the old. Although settlements have been growing and evolving since colonial times, until the middle of this century we tended to locate in recognizable cities and towns. Our changes were much more gradual and reflective of customary patterns of town lay-

These photos contrast automobile-dependent sprawl (above), with a traditional urban community that facilitates walking and transit use (below).

out and structure, with little significant departure from established principles of lot size and street geometry.[54] Today, despite the desire for strong local communities noted by Downs, the result is likely to be much more chaotic. Urban writer Joel Garreau, for example, describes a typical edge city in New Jersey called "287 and 78" (named for the intersection of two Interstate highways). The community, if one can call it that, has no political boundaries, no elected ruling structure, and no overall leader; instead, it is "governed" by a patchwork of generally uncoordinated and conflicting zoning, planning, and county boards.[55] "287 and 78" represents not the dream, but the reality in today's America.

How Spread Out Are We?

There is no question that, as our dispersal outpaces our population growth, we are becoming much more spread out. In 1920, the average density of all of the Census Bureau's urbanized areas, which include cities, suburbs, and towns but not farms, was 6,160 persons per square mile, a little less than 10 persons per acre. By 1990, that figure had diminished by over half—to 2,589 persons per square mile, about four persons per acre. Most telling, however, is that the average density of our recent development—that built since 1960—is only 1,469 persons per square mile, a little over two persons per acre and less than one-fourth the average in 1920.[56] The impact on our landscape is compounded by the fact that, as we were spreading out during this period, we grew fourfold in population.[57] The result is that today we are occupying some eight times more developed land than we did in 1920.

As more and more land has become "urbanized," we have lost rural land.[58] But even land that still qualifies as "rural" under the Census Bureau's definition is less so than it once was. The average population density of rural land has increased 16 percent since 1950.[59]

> ### The International View
>
> Metropolitan regions in America are much more spread out than they are in many other parts of the world. Newman and Kenworthy's research reveals that, for example, metropolitan areas in Europe are on average three to four times more dense than typical American cities. This holds true even in the outer, newer suburbs; although European regions are similar to those in the U.S. in that their new development on the fringe is less dense than that in the core, their outer suburbs nevertheless have four times the density of those in America. U.S. cities are also the world's least centralized in terms of employment.[60]

Two trends within this larger framework have particular relevance for land development: a decline in the average number of persons per household and a rise in the amount of land claimed per household. In particular, as our society has evolved to include higher shares of singles, single-parent households, smaller families, and so-called "empty nesters," the size of the average U.S. household declined from 3.28 to 2.63 persons from 1940 to 1990. It is expected to decline further, to 2.48 persons, in 2000.[61] This means that, as the population increases, the number of households seeking space is increasing faster. And many of them are seeking more space than ever: illustrative of the changes in the average consumption of developed land per new resident is the trend in western Massachusetts, where overall consumption of land (including roads, parking lots, and public and commercial land, in addition to housing) increased from around half an acre per person in the 1950s and 1960s to 1.83 acres per person by 1985.[62] In Maryland, large-lot development of one acre or more per household is the fastest-growing category of land use, constituting some 20 percent of all residential units developed and over three-quarters of all land converted to housing in that state in the 1980s.[63]

There are, of course, marked differences in city densities among different parts of the country. Cities in the Northeast, which are older and predate the automobile-oriented building boom of the last 50 years, tend to have three times the density of cities in the Midwest, and six times the average density of cities in the West, Midwest, and South taken together.[64] The Australian researchers Peter Newman and Jeffrey Kenworthy, who have been tracking land and transportation data in cities around the world for decades, have observed that metropolitan New York has five times the density of metropolitan Houston and Phoenix. Newman and Kenworthy are careful to point out, however, that such differences are concentrated mainly in the central cores of these metropolitan regions; the newer, outer areas of U.S. cities tend to have uniformly low densities, regardless of their location.[65]

Business on the Move

Workplace trends are just as dramatic as those for where we live, if not more so. The 200 or so "edge cities" of offices and shopping, located along freeways on the suburban fringe of our metropolitan areas, now contain some two-thirds of all U.S. office space.[66] This reflects astounding job growth on the fringe; suburbs of all types held only 25 percent of the country's office space as recently as 1970.[67] Around 95 percent of the 15 million new office jobs created in the 1980s were created in low-density suburbs.[68] (As discussed in detail in chapters three and four below, some suburban job "growth" can be illusory when placed in a broader context; in fact, many "new" jobs are really only displaced from other locations.)

For the manufacturing sector, the numbers are even more dramatic. In the 1980s, suburbs and exurbs captured 120 percent of net job growth in manufacturing. The number exceeds 100 percent because cities were losing manufacturing jobs at the same time that new ones were being created in suburbs. Two-thirds of the net growth in employment in all sectors in our metropolitan areas in the 1980s went to suburbs.[69]

These trends, too, show up in specific locations in regions around the country. Once again, the fast-growing Sun Belt leads the way, with over 80 percent of total office space in greater Phoenix and Houston now located in the suburbs.[70] Beyond the Sun Belt, there is more office space now in the edge cities of New Jersey than in the financial district of Manhattan, home of the 120-story World Trade Center and one of the densest concentrations of office space in the world.[71] In Boston, the share of suburban office space grew from 20 percent to 60 percent in the 1980s.[72]

For the greater Washington, DC, area, *The Washington Post* has reported that in the early 1990s the central city lost 45,000 jobs, while the Maryland and Virginia suburbs gained 174,000.[73] The locations with the greatest shares of regional job growth were Fairfax and Prince William counties in Virginia, some 20 and 35 miles, respectively, west of downtown.[74] Of the 27 companies on *Inc.* magazine's mid-1990s list of fast-growing businesses in the Washington region, all but two are based in the suburbs.[75] The pervasiveness of contemporary job dispersal is illustrated plainly also in Los Angeles, where the 19 largest geographic job centers, even taken together and including Los Angeles's downtown, hold only between 17 and 18 percent of the region's jobs.[76] And it is illustrated in Ohio's 7 major metropolitan areas, where suburbs captured 90 percent of the job growth in the mid-1990s and now hold nearly two-thirds of all jobs.[77]

Across the country, many of these businesses are choosing not only sprawling locations but also a sprawling form. The Bishop Ranch development, thirty miles east of

San Francisco, contains a "landscraper" three stories high and over half a mile long.[78] The building that houses Ameritech's headquarters, west of O'Hare Airport near Chicago, is also more than half a mile long. And cars can claim more space in such developments than people: a typical suburban office park might provide 1,400 square feet of parking, usually in surface lots, for every 1,000 square feet of floor space.[79]

Moreover, each suburban office building is characteristically much more isolated from services and shopping than are offices in the typical downtown business district. Although the degree of mixture among possible uses varies from one location to another, many outlying office properties are functionally single-use, with 90 percent or more of floor space devoted to offices.[80]

Suburban Retail Trends

The same trends are evident in retail development. A single shopping mall, the South Coast Mall in Orange County, California, now does more business per day than all of downtown San Francisco.[81] And San Francisco, which has retained its retail core, is luckier than most American cities; much more typical is the smaller city of Huntsville, Alabama, reported in the early 1990s to have lost every one of its traditional downtown stores to the strips and malls on the city's edge.[82]

Many other activities have moved with them. The ironically named Towne Center mall outside of Waldorf, Maryland, in the Washington, DC, region, now hosts charity balls and children's and seniors' activities, in addition to some twelve million shoppers per year, in its nearly one million square feet of

Suburban shopping malls and strip malls have pulled business away from traditional downtown areas.

space. Inside are placed pine trees similar to those that once grew on the site, along with sculptures of the region's native great blue herons. As one Towne Center patron put it, "Where else do you go around here? This is it. The mall is our lives."[83]

Another highly visible trend in American retailing is an increase in scale. The typical supermarket is now pushing 60,000 square feet, and discount stores may claim twice that much or more.[84] These enterprises also tend to locate where there is a lot of cheap land on which to build. In the single jurisdiction of Lancaster County, Pennsylvania, famous for its historic Amish farms, developers teaming up with retail giants proposed in the mid-1990s to construct four immense retail facilities: a 500,000 square-foot "power center" of several adjacent superstores on the edge of the city of Lancaster, and three 200,000-square-foot Wal-Mart stores in other parts of the county, all within 15 miles of each other. Wal-Mart even filed a lawsuit challenging a Lancaster township's authority to require compliance with open-space preservation and traffic mitigation measures deemed necessary to accommodate one of the stores.[85]

These so-called "big-box" stores and centers are coming to dominate the American shopping landscape. They represented more than 80 percent of all new stores built in 1994, according to at least one article,[86] and surely constitute a major reason why in 1998 there were 19 square feet of retail space for every American, a 30 percent increase since 1986.[87] Moreover, the new stores shape the landscape not only when they are thriving but perhaps even more so when they are abandoned. As of the late 1990s, retail sales had slipped from the rates of growth noted earlier in the decade; some large chains had announced the closure of many stores, and continued growth in mail-order and Internet sales threatened further inroads into superstores' on-site business.[88] The real estate industry's *Emerging Trends* report for 1999 observes that there are already too many shopping centers for the number of tenants and that a fifth of the regional malls existing in 1990 will "be nonfunctional by 2000."[89]

A Case Study: Sprawl in Greater Chicago

Neither eastern nor western in its geographic orientation, yet world-class in its population, industry, and culture, Chicago is in some ways the quintessential American metropolis. It has often been the subject of urban research designed to discover what is typical or representative of our society as a whole. And, indeed, its trends with regard to population and land development are typical. In this section, we look at them in some depth, to provide a case-study illustration of how these changes in the American landscape are reshaping one of our country's most important regions. We believe the illustrations will strike a familiar chord in many readers.

Facts and Trends: Chicago by the Numbers

Chicago was incorporated in 1833 as a mere three-eighths of a square mile on the western shore of Lake Michigan. The city experienced rapid growth in the second half of the nineteenth century, largely because of the rising importance of the grain and timber industry in the upper Midwest. By 1900, the city proper had reached 90 percent of its present area of 222 square miles.[90] Chicago's citizens have a long and proud tradition of striking accomplishments in architecture and planning, and the city has been blessed over the years with some of the best work of such giants in the field as Louis Sullivan, Frank Lloyd Wright, Daniel Burnham, Frederick Law Olmsted, and Harry Weese.[91]

Today, however, the city of Chicago accounts for only 6 percent of the land area of its metropolitan region and houses about one-third of the region's population of around eight million people. The metropolitan governing structure is chaotic, with some 267 municipalities and counties identified in 1994, and an incredible total of 1,250 local "governments" of one sort or another, including various school and service districts and regional authorities.[92] Cook County, in which the city of Chicago is located, is overlaid by an average of 4.8 special districts at any given location, and hundreds in all.[93]

Metropolitan Chicago, or "Chicagoland," as it is sometimes called, comprises the city proper and six nearby counties: Cook County, surrounding Chicago itself to the north, west, and south; Lake and McHenry Counties, farther to the north and northwest, respectively; DuPage and Kane Counties, farther to the west; and Will County, farther to the southwest and south. Chicago is bordered on the east, of course, by the waters of Lake Michigan. Beyond the six-county region in Illinois, Chicago's influence extends to developed areas to the far southeast, in the state of Indiana, and to the far north, in Wisconsin.

Like that of other older cities, the population of central-city Chicago has been declining steadily in recent years, while the suburban population has nearly tripled since the 1940s.[94] Masked within this larger trend of inner-city decline and suburban growth, however, is the fact that the inner suburbs of Chicago also have begun to lose population. By the 1990s, townships losing population included most of those in suburban Cook County, as well as some of the older settlements in neighboring Will, DuPage, and Lake Counties. Meanwhile, the far outer suburbs in McHenry, Kane, and northwestern Will Counties, as much as 50 miles or more from Chicago's downtown ("the Loop"), were experiencing rapid growth.[95] In his book *Metropolitics*, researcher (and Minnesota legislator) Myron Orfield cites seven rings of declining suburbs on Chicago's south side and five rings of decline to the west, all in contrast to the booming outer suburbs to the city's northwest.[96]

Overall, between 1970 and 1990, 165 Chicagoland municipalities, mostly in outlying areas, gained over one million residents combined. Ninety municipalities, mostly at or near the region's center, experienced a combined net loss of 771,000 residents.[97] The net effect is that the Chicago region as a whole has been experienc-

Figure 1-2
Map of Chicago and Refererenced Jurisdictions
Source: Peter Haas, Center for Neighborhood Technology

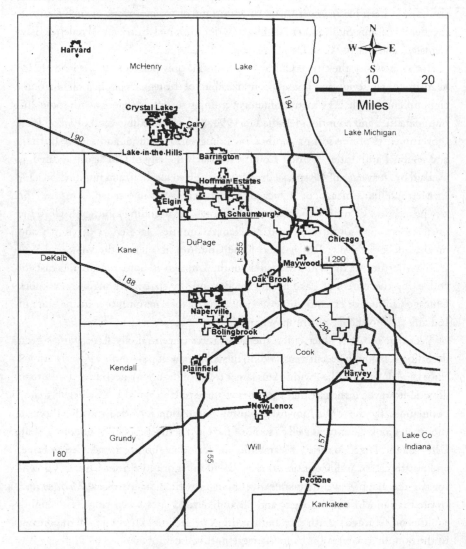

ing only modest population growth, a total of 4,1 percent from 1970 to 1990. But during the same period the amount of developed, residential land has increased more than 11 times faster, by some 46 percent.[98]

These trends are having a predictable impact on regional density characteristics. At some 12,254 persons per square mile, about 19 persons per acre, the city of Chicago is relatively dense, about the same as Boston and Philadelphia. In comparison to other U.S. cities, central-city Chicago's density is less than that of New York, San Francisco, and East Los Angeles, but greater than that of Miami, Minneapolis, Detroit, and Seattle, and much greater than that of other western cities.[99] But both central city density and outer area density have been declining since 1960; overall regional density for Chicagoland's "urbanized" areas is now under seven persons per acre, even including the dense central city, and about one-third less than it was in 1960.[100] Chicago's suburbs have even lower population density than some in the Sun Belt, including suburbs in Los Angeles and Orange Counties in California and Dade County (Miami) in Florida.[101]

A lot is at stake for Chicagoland's future. Suburban northeastern Illinois is projected to grow by nearly 600,000 additional persons, a 15.5 percent increase, between 1990 and 2010. Reflecting the national trend toward smaller households, discussed above, the number of suburban households is expected to increase faster than the suburban population, by 25 percent (adding a total of 400,000 new households), during the same period.[102] Some estimates for the region as a whole suggest that, by 2020, Chicagoland will add 1.8 million more people and 1.4 million more jobs than it contained in the 1990s.[103] How this growth is accommodated will have a tremendous impact on the region's character as well as its landscape.

The Hot Development Scene: Metro Northwest
The most dramatic development changes in metropolitan Chicago, as elsewhere, are occurring on the outer fringe of the region. They are occurring particularly in places like the northwestern corridor extending to McHenry County, some 35 miles northwest of the Loop and beyond. As *Edge City* author Joel Garreau has said, "This competing vision of what progress means is being fought all over America and no place more than in McHenry County and places like it."[104]

On the way to McHenry, one might drive through the outer Cook County community of Schaumburg, 25 miles northwest of the Loop. Described by Professor Platt as once a "sleepy farm village," Schaumburg experienced its first building boom in the 1960s, as a result of new highways and westward development generated by expansion of O'Hare International Airport. By 1970, Schaumburg already was home to the world's largest indoor shopping mall and, by the 1990s, the village (as its boosters still prefer to call it) housed more than 30 million square feet of office, industrial, and commercial development, including the corporate headquarters of Motorola.[105] The adjacent suburb of Hoffman Estates, which is mostly surrounded by Schaumburg, now houses the world headquarters of Sears, Roebuck and Co., no longer in the landmark Sears Tower in downtown Chicago.[106]

Motorola is already on the move once more, with a new plant in Harvard, on the far reaches of McHenry County and only eight miles from the Wisconsin border. Motorola also is constructing a 132-acre campus facility, housing 1,000 jobs, on the fringe of Elgin in neighboring Kane County, some 40 miles northwest of the Loop. The company was lured there by the City of Elgin, Kane County, and the state of Illinois with generous financial incentives and free infrastructure.[107]

In fast-growing McHenry, once-separate communities are now losing their distinctive character and even their boundaries. Some of the most explosive growth, for example, has occurred in the community of Crystal Lake, whose population increased 60 percent between 1980 and the mid-1990s, and whose local government was reported as of this writing to be seeking more development still.[108] Crystal Lake's boundary will soon touch that of nearby Cary and Lake in the Hills, as Schaumburg's has already touched that of Hoffman Estates. The issue of local political boundaries can be touchy in other ways, too, as localities in greater Chicago's complex jurisdictional mix wage aggressive annexation wars, in some cases extending their limits by as much as eight miles at a time, in order to grab unincorporated land that is ripe for development.[109]

The sprawling growth of Chicago's metro northwest has brought with it growing pains. Crystal Lake's public schools, for example, began in the mid-1990s to use split shifts in an effort to shoehorn the community's rapidly growing student population into existing facilities.[110] In Barrington, located between Crystal Lake and Schaumburg, residents of new, large-lot subdivisions on once-rural land have now themselves become worried about growth, opposing condominiums, apartments, theaters, restaurants, and shopping malls near their new homes.[111]

Haphazard growth is occurring in McHenry and other northwestern Chicagoland counties, notwithstanding a desire on the part of some local officials for a more orderly, rational pattern. McHenry County itself has a carefully structured land use plan (as does a metropolitan regional authority, the Northeastern Illinois Planning Commission). The county's plan emphasizes cluster development and incremental growth in and adjacent to existing towns, rather than in a scattered, "leapfrog" fashion; it provides for pedestrian and bicycle-friendly environments and for the protection of open space. But the McHenry plan—like that for the region as a whole—is to little avail, because is backed by no authority; in Illinois, as in much of the country, decision-making authority rests, not with the county, but with its municipalities, which may annex and develop at will.[112]

Development to Chicago's South and Southwest

Meanwhile, the region's southern and southwestern fringe is also developing rapidly. Characterized in the 1990s as Chicagoland's largest new residential development in years, Lakewood Falls was being constructed on 650 unincorporated acres in Will County, between the already burgeoning suburb of Naperville and the town of Plainfield, some 30 miles southwest of the Loop. Lakewood Falls will comprise more than 2,000 new homes.[113]

In Naperville itself, in the western reaches of DuPage County, massive population increases were reported in 1995 to have caused the construction of fourteen new elementary schools, four additional middle schools, a new high school, and an expansion to an existing high school. Meanwhile, DuPage County as a whole, including older settlements closer to the urban core, was experiencing a sharp decline in public school enrollment.[114] Twenty miles south of Naperville, in the Will County town of New Lenox, school enrollment jumped 35 percent in 1995 alone, prompting officials to seek a 50-percent increase in the educational tax rate, as well as an increase in construction debt. Similar pressures are being felt by school districts all over the Chicago southwestern fringe.[115] Will County, projected to be the region's fastest growing, is expected to double its population of residents, from 357,301 in 1990 to 727,464 in 2020.[116]

Growth in the metro southwest will only accelerate if two controversial projects on state drawing boards in the late 1990s are realized. First, massive expansion of the Chicago region's system of tollways has been proposed, including the extension of I-355 from Bollingbrook, on the corner where DuPage, Will, and Cook Counties meet, to New Lenox, some 12 miles farther south. As of this writing, that road has been blocked by litigation.[117] Second, a third major airport for the Chicago region has been proposed for the now-rural community of Peotone, in southern Will County 40 miles south of the Loop and halfway to the downstate Illinois town of Kankakee. (The airport proposal is accompanied by an additional proposed extension of I-355.) Although the airport would likely spur development well south of the existing developed region, in the fringes of Will and Kankakee Counties, it is being touted by its proponents as an antidote to continued suburban sprawl.[118]

Where Chicago's Jobs Are Going

In greater Chicago, as elsewhere, jobs and civic institutions are sprawling into the suburbs and countryside. Sears and Motorola, discussed above, are not the only com-

> ### Meanwhile, in the Inner Suburbs...
>
> Almost exactly halfway between the Chicago Loop and Peotone lies the struggling southern Cook County suburb of Harvey. In the 1960s, Harvey proudly opened what at the time was a virtual showcase of state-of-the-art retailing: the Dixie Square Mall, anchored by Montgomery Ward and other major tenants. As this report was being researched, however, Dixie Square had become a decaying eyesore, abandoned to development farther south and being targeted for redevelopment by anxious community leaders.[119] Myron Orfield describes "the empty malls and abandoned buildings" of Harvey and other inner southside Chicago suburbs as comparable to "some of the third world's less favored areas."[120]

panies lured by lucrative incentives to abandon the city. Overall, over twice as much office space in the region is being constructed outside the city limits as within. Although Chicago's central business district remains relatively strong among major U.S. cities, the downtown share of the region's inventory of office space declined from 91 percent in 1970 to 68 percent in 1986 and has continued to decline. Researcher Robert Cervero notes that the jobs have been going, as noted above, to places like Schaumburg, the I-88 corridor between Oakbrook and Naperville, the O'Hare Airport area, and the Lake-Cook County border on the north side of the region.[121] Indeed, Orfield reports that 80 percent of the region's new jobs are going to the northwestern suburbs.[122]

As a result, the region's employment density, measured in jobs per unit of land, has been declining steadily. This is especially the case within the boundaries of the city of Chicago. Despite the fact that the number of jobs in the central business district has been increasing, the share of regional jobs located downtown has been declining slowly, and the share of regional jobs located within the city as a whole has been falling sharply.[123] The suburban share of the region's employment, on the other hand, grew by one-third, from approximately 44 percent to 61 percent, between 1970 and 1990.[124]

Cervero characterizes suburban Chicago's new workplaces, including those in the I-88 corridor between Oakbrook and Naperville, as having a strikingly—if typically—different design and form from those in the inner city. Characteristics include the following: linear development along thoroughfares; little coordination among individual projects; disconnected office complexes that emphasize traffic circulation within rather than between them; a prevalence of low-density, single-use structures;

vast parking lots; and few if any pedestrian or transit amenities. Cervero notes also that there is insufficient housing near the areas of job growth, especially for lower-salaried workers.[125]

Overall, the impact of suburban commercial growth on the region's landscape is staggering. From 1970 to 1990, greater Chicago's consumption of land for commercial and industrial uses grew 74 percent, eighteen times faster than population.[126]

Along with businesses and their employees, a range of other institutions have also proliferated beyond what were once the boundaries of metropolitan Chicago. DuPage County, which lies from 15 to 30 miles west of the Loop, has seen the construction of a reported 41 new government facilities and 50 church facilities and related projects just in the last six years, all raising the same controversial issues of traffic, access, and parking as does residential and office development.[127] More than a dozen multi-million-dollar suburban arts centers now ring the Chicago area; patrons wishing to see such performers as the American Ballet Theatre and the Lincoln Center Theatre Company, as well as such popular musical acts as David Grisman and Chick Corea, are now as likely to do so in the suburbs as in Chicago proper.[128]

Figure 1-3
Percent of Chicago Region's Employment by Jurisdiction, 1970–1990
Chicago Area Transportation Study, *Status of Transportation Planning of Northern Illinois*, Chicago, IL: 1997.

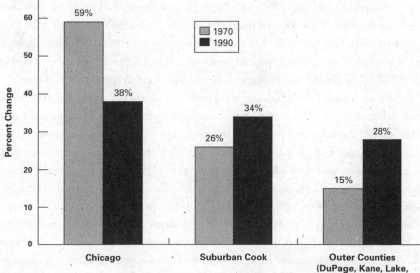

We believe Chicago's patterns to be typical, in many ways, of those facing most regions and communities across the country. We will return to the Chicago example periodically in this book's later chapters, as we examine the impacts of our nation-wide development patterns on several indicators that are important to the health of our environment, economy, and social fabric. First, however, we take a brief look at some of the reasons for these typical patterns of development.

The Reasons Why

This book is primarily concerned with the results rather than the causes of current development patterns. Nevertheless, we believe it worthwhile to discuss at least a few of the reasons why. They are many.

Traditionally, people have gathered in cities for economic reasons, clustering social and business functions to reduce transportation costs and to take advantage of economies of scale in large production enterprises.[129] Since World War Two, however, the combination of intensified roadbuilding, cheap gasoline prices, and a shift to an infor-mation-based economy have all weakened these traditional incentives in America. Some observers contend that, in today's economic circumstances, low-density living is simply an expression of consumer choice; survey respondents asked to explain why they live so far from work most often point simply to "good schools" and say that they "like their house."[130] Given the low cost of automotive travel and the relatively high cost of housing in today's marketplace, consumers can benefit greatly by moving farther out in order to lower the cost of housing, even if they have to spend more on travel.[131]

For the segment of the housing market with school-age children, the lure of sub-urban school districts can be especially powerful. Indeed, there is little question that urban public schools, burdened with the challenge of educating disproportionate shares of poor and minority pupils, on average exhibit inferior educational performances in comparison to suburban schools. Although there are exceptionally effective urban schools (including both public and private schools), suburban students tend to outscore their urban counterparts on basic tests of academic proficiency across all subjects. Urban schools also lag behind in the upkeep of facilities and in teacher credentials.[132]

The desire of homebuyers to choose locations with good housing and good schools is understandable and cannot be underestimated. Moreover, for those with means, the choice can become a self-fulfilling prophecy: as middle- and upper-income taxpayers flee cities and inner suburbs, the places to which they flee soon become the only places with sufficient tax bases to support a good public school system. The prophecy may not be fulfilled indefinitely, however, since eventually the new communities mature and begin to take on the problems previously associated only with the original, "old" communities. As those with the means move even farther out, the pattern repeats. Moreover, as the cycle of decay and escape manifests with respect to education, so it does also with respect to perceptions of crime and race, which also fuel outward residential flight.[133] The social issues fueling sprawl are discussed in some detail later in this book, particularly in chapter four.

Beyond residential preferences, many businesses seek suburban locations, too, often in search of the potential customers and employees who have migrated nearby. Other businesses seek suburban locations in pursuit of lower land costs and proximity to freeway interchanges. Some simply want to escape the same urban problems that are troubling renters and homeowners.

It is not as simple, however, as the free market in action. While many Americans who can afford them do tend to prefer single-family homes with yards, in safe neighborhoods with good schools, this does not mean that they necessarily want them in sprawling communities. These and other desirable housing types and environments can, in fact, exist in non-sprawling communities, just as apartments, cluster housing, and other higher-density types can exist within sprawl. Survey data indicate that most Americans would prefer to live and work in a small town or an older suburb rather than a new, sprawling one. Images of traditional housing and community types elicit more favorable responses than sprawl types by very high margins; moreover, fully three-fourths of survey respondents in New Jersey want to see development occur within existing cities or older suburbs, not on land currently in open space or rural uses.[134]

Clearly, forces in addition to simple consumer preference are at work. The pattern of development is, in fact, created by a more complex mix of participants, including not only consumers but also financial institutions, large and small businesses, large and small developers and speculators, and local, state, and federal governments. Notwithstanding the existence of local land-use plans, patterns of development occur not so much as the result of any grand deliberate scheme as from the many separate decisions made by these single-purpose actors, whose motives are quite remote from the pattern that they shape. Public agencies typically are reactive participants at best, forced to carry out their roles with haste, poor information and resources, and little theory behind their actions.[135] This complex dynamic was summed nicely by Tony Hiss in *The Experience of Place*, published in 1990.

The places we know are the product of thousands of small decisions—let's buy a house, let's start a business, let's put up a new office center, let's bring more tax dollars in. . . . What is new is that our switch of transportation systems [to automobiles and Interstate highways] has spread these individual decisions across huge regional expanses, on the optimistic assumption that things would continue to work out."[136]

Indeed, to the extent that government has been a direct participant in the process, its contribution has generally encouraged low-density, dispersed development. In particular, planners working for municipal and county governments have developed a body of practice that rests on what Lee Epstein calls "chiefly spatial solutions to urban problems," such as the separation of land uses thought to be incompatible and the relegation of green space to individual lots rather than its integration into the community at large. Over time, this planning practice has been endorsed by land-use lawyers and the courts, producing the byzantine systems of plans, categories, codes, standards, and variances that are in use in one form or another across the country today.[137]

It is now common practice, for example, for local governments to prescribe minimum residential lot sizes, as well as setbacks and parking requirements that make businesses hostile to pedestrians and city environments but a perfect fit for strip corridors along highways. Prescriptive zoning may prohibit not only a mix of housing types but also walkable access to in-neighborhood services, such as day-care centers and convenience stores. Generous tax subsidies are provided for housing, transportation infrastructure, and extensions of public services to fringe locations.[138]

To make matters worse, suburban and exurban governments often compete aggressively to lure large businesses to fringe locations in a vicious cycle of tax-dollar pursuit. As new suburban residents in formerly rural locations demand expensive schools, roads, and improvements in public safety and social services, jurisdictions chase businesses to provide additional revenues. The businesses, in turn, work the jurisdictions for all they can get, in the process reducing their net value to the communities.

We presented some examples of this practice in our discussion of Chicago.

Prescriptive zoning, which often requires minimum setbacks and large lots, has generally encouraged low-density, dispersed development.

CALTHORPE ASSOCIATES

NIMBYs Can Cause Sprawl, Too

New construction proposed near existing neighborhoods is often met with staunch opposition by residents who fear that it will increase traffic congestion, raise taxes, overcrowd schools, and generally reduce the quality of life. This opposition now has its own acronym—"NIMBY," for "Not In My Back Yard." Indeed, the ubiquity of such opposition has spawned a number of additional parody acronyms, including LULU ("Locally Unwanted Land Use"), BANANA ("Build Absolutely Nothing Anywhere Near Anything"), CAVE ("Citizens Against Virtually Everything"), and NOPE ("Not On Planet Earth").

Although sometimes well-intentioned, NIMBYism has inadvertently contributed to sprawl by pushing new developments farther and farther away from the city center. The reason for this is relatively simple: because developers often want to avoid conflicts with citizen groups—conflicts that increase project time and reduce profits—they choose to build where there is little opposition to the proposed developments. In many instances, these new locations are cornfields or cow pastures (after all, corn and cows are not invited to public hearings) on the suburban fringe—locations removed from other developments and where land is relatively inexpensive.

In some respects, citizens cannot be blamed for their strong reactions to growth—they have been plagued by so many poorly planned and ugly developments over the years that they have come to distrust all new development, even well-planned, "smart growth" proposals that could generate benefits for their communities. Still, NIMBYism now contributes to the very impacts that typically form the basis for citizen opposition: more traffic congestion, higher taxes, and overcrowded schools across an entire metropolitan area.

Another example can be found in suburban Manassas, Virginia, once famous primarily for its rural, historic Civil War battlefield but now well inside the Washington, DC, metropolitan area. Manassas recently offered a semiconductor manufacturer a package of incentives, including favorable water and electricity rates, a 50 percent cut in the tax rate on manufacturing equipment, and an accelerated depreciation schedule; the state of Virginia chipped in state income-tax credits, $38 million in grants, and a job-training program. To lure the controversial Disney's America theme park that was proposed (although subsequently withdrawn) for rolling farmland just west of Manassas, then-Governor George Allen offered a $163 million package of incentives.[139] The bidding can get especially fierce when states and fragmented local jurisdictions within metropolitan regions compete with one another for these businesses.[140]

Multi-million dollar highways, largely paid for with federal subsidies, have made outlying areas more accessible and have contributed to sprawl.

Indeed, local governments interested in attracting new development do not hesitate to override growth management plans, even the ones they themselves have created. In Loudoun County, Virginia, north of Manassas, civil servants won a prestigious award from the American Planning Association for their comprehensive land-use plan and another award for a local ordinance designed to maximize open space in rural areas by encouraging cluster development. But the county's prodevelopment Board of Supervisors nevertheless approved large-scale developments in areas of the county planned for preservation, rejected a study of the costs and revenues associated with growth, and chose not even to evaluate a conservation organization's proposal to preserve the county's rural character with transferable development rights. In the late 1990s the board approved rezonings to accommodate over 50,000 new houses and a doubling of its population over fifteen years. Four Loudoun County planners resigned in a single year amid these controversies.[141]

Federal policies, too, have encouraged sprawl development. Substantial federal subsidies for the Interstate Highway System unquestionably made outlying areas more accessible, at least for those able to drive, and more attractive to investors, developers, and their customers. Some analysts argue that federally backed insurance for home mortgages also has contributed to sprawl, along with a variety of federal tax subsidies, including deductibility of mortgage interest, accelerated depreciation, five-year amortization, and deductibility of so-called "passive" real estate losses. State and local subsidies for suburban and exurban highways and other public infrastructure and services also have played a large role.[142]

As these examples illustrate, and as Anthony Downs has concluded, "unlimited low-density development has dominated nearly all American policies affecting metropolitan area growth for more than four decades."[143] No wonder the result. We turn now to the consequences.

Paving Paradise
Sprawl and the Environment

The changes in American land use patterns in the latter decades of the 20th century have been dramatic. The impacts that these changes have brought to our quality to life—to our environment, our economy, and our social fabric—have been equally dramatic. In this chapter, we specifically document the impacts of sprawl on the American environment.

In many ways, recent decades have marked a period of tremendous environmental progress in our country. Since 1970 we have enacted and strengthened an impressive honor roll of national environmental legislation, including the National Environmental Policy Act, the Clean Air and Clean Water Acts, the Endangered Species Act, the National Energy Policy Act, the "Superfund" hazardous waste law, and the Intermodal Surface Transportation Efficiency Act. Additional laws and programs, many of them ambitious and innovative, have been adopted at the state and local levels.

These laws have made a difference. Many of our industries—and our cars, too—are less polluting today than when "Greenfields," quoted in our title and preface, was a popular song. Some formerly declining species are now recovering. Abandoned waste sites are being cleaned up. Noted author and self-described "ecorealist" Gregg Easterbrook has made the case that things are, in fact, getting better, in his best-selling 1996 book of "environmental optimism," *A Moment on the Earth.*[1]

Are the environmental optimists right? Given the evidence of progress, do we have any environmental reason to be concerned about the rapid consumption of land and dispersal of our activities documented in chapter one? After all, use of land can be productive. Dispersal can reflect increased personal mobility and even a higher standard of living.

Unfortunately, we do indeed have cause for concern. The impacts of unmitigated, ever-outward urban sprawl threaten to undermine much of the environmental progress that our American society has made and must continue to make in order to secure a sustainable, healthy, and productive future for our children and our country. In particular, those impacts threaten our progress in addressing automobile dependence, conserving energy, reducing air pollution, protecting farmland, wildlife habitat and scenic resources, and improving water quality. We discuss each of these issues below.

Driving Ourselves Crazy

I've been driving from one meeting about sprawl to the other for the last fifteen years, and the only thing that's changed is that now it takes a lot longer to get there.

—ROB MELNICK, ARIZONA STATE UNIVERSITY.[2]

As we spread ourselves farther and farther apart, it becomes inevitable that we must travel longer distances to work, shop, enjoy recreation, and visit family and friends. The convenience store and even the playground may no longer be within walking distance. The bus stop may be farther away, too, even if we are fortunate enough to have a bus that goes anywhere close to our destination; in some places, there may be no bus service at all. Work may be on the other side of town or even in another town altogether. The Chesapeake Bay Foundation's Lee Epstein describes the phenomenon:

There still is "quiet" in far suburban streets, but the cost to the rest of metropolitan areas' regional transportation systems from miles of curlicue cul-de-sacs, the absence of a true network of streets, low densities that are nearly impossible to serve with cost-efficient transit, and isolated "pods" of segregated office, commercial, and residential uses, has been inordinately high; the cost to real mobility may be higher still.[3]

The only good choice for most suburbanites is to drive, and to drive a lot. And that is exactly what we are doing.

The Astonishing Growth in Traffic

Traffic is growing at an alarming rate. Motor vehicle use in America doubled from one to two trillion miles per year between 1970 and 1990.[4] Over a longer span, from

1950 to 1990, passenger vehicle miles traveled increased at an average rate of 4.2 percent per year; more recently, in the 1980s, passenger vehicle usage grew at the faster rate of 4.7 percent per year, and total miles traveled by all light duty vehicles grew at a staggering rate of 5.5 percent per year.[5] Traffic growth in the United States has considerably outpaced that in the developed world as a whole, where automobile use has been growing at the slower (if still troubling) rate of 3.3 percent per year.[6] Overall, the U.S. Department of Transportation's National Personal Transportation Survey (NPTS) has reported that vehicle miles traveled grew by 40 percent in only seven years, between 1983 and 1990.[7]

There are a number of troubling factors associated with this growth in vehicle use, all pointing to increased inefficiency in travel patterns. These include growth in average trip length, growth in the number of vehicle trips taken per person and per household per year, a decline in all modes of travel other than single-occupancy driving, and a decline in average vehicle occupancy.[8] As a result, from 1975 to 1990, vehicle use would have grown just over 50 percent even if there had been no population increase at all.[9] In fact, in the 1980s, vehicle miles traveled grew more than four times faster than the driving-age population and many times faster than the population at

Figure 2-1
Total Vehicle Miles of Travel Per Year, 1960–1995

Source: Bureau of Transportation Statistics, U.S. Department of Transportation, *National Transportation Statistics, 1998*, Washington, DC: 1998, Table 4-12.

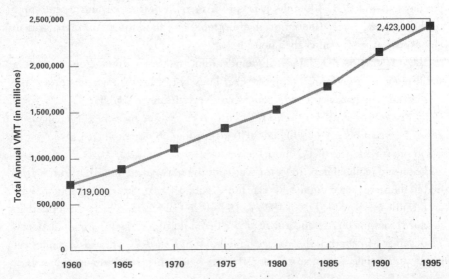

Figure 2-2
Vehicle Miles Traveled (VMT) Per Capita, 1960–1995

Source: Bureau of Transportation Statistics, U.S. Department of Transportation, *National Transportation Statistics 1998*, Washington, DC: 1998, Table 4-12; U.S. Bureau of the Census, "Historical National Population Estimates," Washington, DC: April 2, 1998.

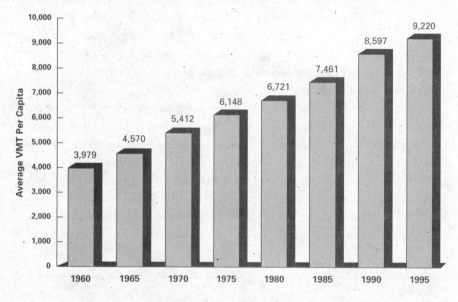

large.[10] Our typical new suburban household owns 2.3 cars, takes 12 automobile trips per day and drives 31, 300 miles per year.[11] American households now spend more of their income on transportation than on food, and more on transportation than any expense category other than housing.[12]

Because of expected changes in demographic and economic factors, including stabilization of growth in multiple-worker households, most forecasters expect the increase in vehicle travel to slow somewhat. Nevertheless, research at DOT's Volpe Center projects that miles traveled will continue to grow at an average annual rate of 2.2–2.7 percent between 1990 and 2030, depending on potential changes in population growth and the fuel economy of vehicles.[13]

Local and regional data are consistent with the national trends. Traffic grew five-fold in the Seattle region in the 30 years from 1960 to 1990.[14] In the Washington, DC, area, traffic nearly tripled from 1973 to 1994.[15] In California, vehicle use more than doubled from 1970 to 1990, growing more than four times faster than population.[16] The average *resident* (not the average household) of Kansas City travels 25 miles per day by automobile.[17] In metropolitan Atlanta, where traffic congestion is said to waste

Traffic in Chicago

Despite a public transit system that remains relatively strong by American standards, automobile traffic has taken over greater Chicago. From 1973 to 1990, private car usage increased 49 percent, about the same rate as the spread of developed land and many times faster than the region's population.[18] Since 1960, auto mileage driven per capita in Chicago has more than doubled.[19] More recently, regional vehicle miles traveled grew some 22 percent in only five years, between 1989 and 1994.[20] Between 1947 and 1990, the portion of the region's population who use the area's largest transit service, the Chicago Transit Authority, has declined more than 65 percent.[21] As of 1995, Pace, the suburban bus transit agency, had captured less than 2 percent of the commuting public in its first 14 years of existence.[22]

Driving to and from work around Chicagoland suburbs can now take an hour or even more. The Texas Transportation Institute, which has ranked the region as the third most congested in the United States, has estimated that the metro area loses more than three billion dollars per year to lost productivity and excess fuel consumption from traffic jams.[23]

Nevertheless, Chicago ranks second only to New York in transit ridership among the ten U.S. metropolitan areas surveyed by the Newman and Kenworthy research team, with 5.4 percent of total passenger miles, and around three times that share of total regional commuting trips, claimed by transit. (By comparison, transit claims a 10.8 percent share of total passenger miles in New York, a 5.2 percent share in San Francisco, and a 4.6 percent share in Washington, DC. Toronto leads the North American continent with a 23.6 percent share.)[24] The share of work trips into the city of Chicago taken on transit is significant indeed, at 29.7 percent.[25] As transportation writer Neal Peirce has observed, the loss of transit in Chicago would be catastrophic, resulting in as many as 700,000 new automobile trips per day on Chicago streets.[26]

But the shift of Chicagoland jobs to the suburbs, described in chapter one, has had a tremendous impact on the region's roadways. In the 1980s, for example, the number of workers commuting into DuPage county increased by 62 percent.[27] In the late 1980s, researcher Robert Cervero attributed this trend partly to the fact that DuPage had some 6,400 more service jobs than resident service-industry workers, chiefly because most could not afford to live there. Cervero also found that the DuPage community of Oakbrook, which had five times more jobs than residents, drew more than 60 percent of its 35,000 workers from more than 10 miles away. In suburban Cook County, two-thirds of Schaumberg's workers commuted from more than 10 miles away.[28] To deal with the changing patterns of the region's traffic, the Chicago Area Transportation Study released a 20-year plan in the late 1990s calling for some $34 billion worth of new roads and other transportation projects, many of them controversial.[29]

$1.5 billion per year in fuel and lost productivity, the average motorist drives even farther—34 miles each day.[30]

Changing commuting patterns have contributed significantly to the overall trends on vehicle use. In particular, as job growth has become more dispersed, the length of the average American trip to work has increased 37 percent, from 8.6 to 11.6 miles, from 1983 to 1995.[31] Average time spent on commuting to and from work also lengthened in 35 of our country's 39 largest metro areas in the 1980s.[32] The number and share of commuters carpooling to work declined, from over 19 million and 20 percent in 1980 to 15.4 million and 13.4 percent in 1990.[33] Of all commuting modes, only driving alone increased its share of workers (by 13.7 percent) in the 1980s.[34]

Within metropolitan regions, the number and share of suburb-to-suburb commuting trips has grown substantially, now claiming more than half of the total and an even larger majority in many regions.[35] The length of all commuting trips has grown, as noted, but the length of suburb-to-suburb work trips has grown much faster than the length of suburb-to-city trips.[36] Only 1.6 percent of suburb-to-suburb work trips are taken on public transit.[37] In some regions, the share is virtually invisible, less than 0.5 percent.[38]

The inability of public transit to capture a large share of travel in America's spread-out metro areas is striking. The Newman and Kenworthy team found that transit claimed an average share of only 3.6 percent of all trips (not just commuting) in 10 large U.S. metro regions.[39] For the country as a whole, the 1995 NPTS put transit's share at a paltry 1.8 percent of passenger trips and 2.1 percent of all passenger miles, albeit with much higher usage in urban areas, particularly in the Northeast.[40] Notwithstanding the exceptions, the situation has caused Professor Kenworthy to

Table 2-1
Change in Vehicle Occupancy Share for Work Trips, 1980–1990

Occupancy	1980	1990	Percent Change
Drive Alone	64.4%	73.2%	+13.7%
2-Person	13.8%	10.5%	−23.9%
3-Person	3.5%	1.7%	−51.4%
4+ Person	2.5%	1.1%	−56.0%

Source: U.S. Bureau of the Census, "Private Vehicle Occupancy for the United States: 1990 and 1980 Census," Washington, DC: undated.

(*Note:* The shares do not add up to 100 percent because the figures in the table do not include other modes of transportation, such as transit, bicycling, and walking.)

conclude that public transit has become "almost irrelevant in the overall transport task of U.S. cities."[41]

Transit usage in the United States is much lower than it is in other countries with advanced economies. In European communities, transit accounts for between 11 and 26 percent of all trips; walking and bicycling also claim large shares of the total. Even in Canada, where travel patterns might be expected to mirror those in the United States, public transit claims a 15 percent share.[42]

One result of all this traffic, as every delivery van driver and harried parent knows only too well, is overwhelming congestion. Seventy percent of peak-hour travel on urban interstate highways now occurs on congested roads operating at more than 80 percent capacity. As recently as 1971, only 40 percent of peak-hour travel was classified as congested.[43] The average speed of vehicles using Washington's Capital Beltway declined more than half, from 47 to 23 miles per hour, in the 1980s.[44] The Texas Transportation Institute has estimated that the economic cost of lost productivity

---

Figure 2-3
Mode of Transportation in the United States and Select European Countries (as a percentage of total trips)

Source: John Pucher and Christian Lefevre, *The Urban Transport Crisis in Europe and North America*, London, England: MacMillan Press, 1996, p. 16.

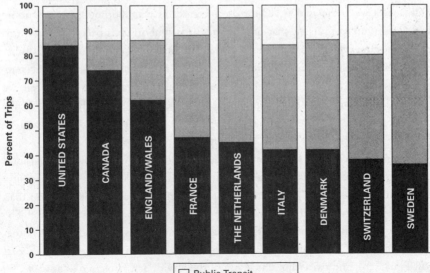

and other waste due to traffic jams in the nation's 39 largest metropolitan areas reaches some $34 billion annually.[45] The average American driver spends 443 hours—the equivalent of 55 eight-hour workdays—per year behind the wheel.[46]

We cannot build our way out of this congestion simply by constructing new roads, and widening existing ones, *ad infinitum.* Aside from the massive expense and accompanying emissions problems (see below) that would result from such a strategy, the approach does not work. Instead, congestion relief from new road capacity is almost always short-lived, because drivers flock to the new capacity until it, too, becomes congested. The situation is aggravated even further when new highway capacity facilitates access to rural areas, which then become developed, generating still more traffic and still more congestion.[47]

Spreading Out Means Driving More to Do the Same

The evidence is substantial and growing to the effect that people in spread-out locations drive more, and people in compact locations drive less. This is due to a variety of reasons, but the associations are clear. For example, environmental researcher John Holtzclaw, working for the Natural Resources Defense Council and other organizations,[48] has been studying the relationships between vehicle use and neighborhood densities around the San Francisco Bay area for a decade. Recently, his research has extended to other regions in California, including Los Angeles, and to Chicago. Holtzclaw's work shows that vehicle use increases as neighborhoods become more spread out and, conversely, that use declines as neighborhoods become more compact and more typically urban. In particular, his analysis of travel data in a number of studies and communities indicates that, as residential density doubles, vehicle use declines some 20 to 40 percent. Vehicle trips per household, as well as vehicle mileage driven, decline with each incremental increase in density.[49] Strikingly similar results have been found in independent research in the San Francisco area by researchers from the University of California, and by research in Seattle.[50]

One such study of 20 California communities with varying characteristics found that, in general, suburbs with a "net" density (sometimes called "residential" density) from 2 to 15 households per acre had 75 percent more vehicle use per person than urban neighborhoods with a density range of 10 to 100 households per acre.[51] The least dense suburban community (Lafayette), at 2 households per acre, had four times more vehicle use per household than the most dense urban community (Northeast San Francisco), and twice the vehicle use of the city of San Francisco as a whole.[52]

Nationally, researchers at the Urban Land Institute have correlated household travel data from the NPTS with gross population density data, differentiated by zip

Figure 2-4
Relationship Between Annual Vehicle Miles Traveled Per Household and Household Density

Source: John Holtzclaw, "Using Residential Patterns and Transit to Decrease Auto Dependence and Costs," San Francisco: Natural Resources Defense Council, 1994, p. 18.

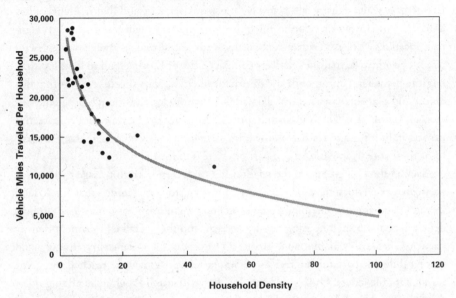

code in the 1990 census. (Gross population density, because it lumps widely varying amounts of nonresidential land with neighborhoods, may be a less accurate predictor of transportation behavior than net residential density; it nevertheless can serve as a rough proxy.) The correlations show that, as one moves from a gross density of 30,000 persons per square mile, corresponding roughly to a net residential density of garden apartments or condominiums at around 38 households per acre,[53] to 8,750 persons per square mile, corresponding roughly with townhouses at 11 households per acre, vehicle travel per person increases 62 percent. A further reduction in density to 4,500 persons per square mile, roughly equivalent to 5.6 households per acre, increases vehicle travel another 22 percent; a reduction to 1,500 persons per square mile, the average density of American development built since 1960, produces another 8 percent increase in driving.[54]

The research also suggests that, as neighborhoods become more compact, more trips are made by walking, bicycle, and public transit. And, as the Brookings Institution's Anthony Downs points out, even those trips that are made by car are shortened in more compact environments, because density shrinks the overall area occupied by a community or region.[55]

International research is consistent with that in America. Newman and Kenworthy cite findings from the United Kingdom indicating that automobile use per person rises sharply when density falls below eight persons per acre, and that residents of low density communities drive up to three times as much as their counterparts in compact locations.[56] The Newman-Kenworthy team also found in their own review of 37 cities worldwide that the relatively compact cities of Europe tend to have less than half the per-person automobile use of American cities, with shorter commuting distances and a larger share of travel claimed by other modes.[57] Although different policies, including much higher gasoline prices, also constitute a deterrent to excessive driving in Europe, and traffic volume is increasing there as well as here, land use patterns undoubtedly are also a large part of the reason for the difference.

Back in the United States, the relationship of declining transit usage to sprawl is particularly well documented. A Portland, Oregon, study concluded that "of 40 land use and demographic variables studied, the most significant for determining transit demand are the overall housing density per acre and the overall employment density per acre. These two variables alone predict 93 percent of the variance in transit demand among different parts of the region."[58] Similar conclusions were reached by recent research for the federal DOT's Transit Cooperative Research Program, analyzing ridership on 19 light rail lines in 11 U.S. cities and 47 commuter-rail lines in six cities. The researchers found that rail systems are more heavily used as the number of people living within two miles of the stations and the number of workers per acre in the central business district (CBD) increase.[59]

For bus transit, longstanding research holds that a minimum of 4 to 5 households per residential acre is necessary to support even hourly service, while 7 to 8 households per acre are necessary to support service at half-hour intervals and 15 households per acre are necessary to support service every 10 minutes.[60] Looking at San Francisco data for all forms of transit, Holtzclaw concludes that usage begins to rise at about six or seven households per residential acre and rises sharply above 10 households per acre; work-related transit trips increase in the same way.[61] Other researchers set the threshold above which transit usage rises significantly at various points between 7 and 13 households per residential acre.[62] While the threshold is imprecise, the general association between residential density and transit usage is clear.

Several researchers agree, also, on the importance of employment density.[63] Nonetheless, Robert Cervero observes that most new suburban workplaces in the United States are being built at floor-to-area ratios of only 0.2–0.3, about one-fifth the minimum Cervero says is required to support viable transit service; although the resulting densities are too low for transit, they are nevertheless high enough to cause traffic congestion.[64] ("Floor-to-area ratio" is the gross floor area of all buildings or structures on a lot divided by total lot area.)

Examining data at the regional level, Newman and Kenworthy have observed that the U.S. cities with the lowest overall densities are notable also for "extremely poor public transport" service.[65] The research team also notes, however, that even in Los Angeles, where transit usage is generally low, high-density neighborhoods exhibit nearly twenty times the per capita ridership of very low-density areas.[66]

Some critics of this growing body of research have questioned whether the differences in travel behavior associated with density are in reality due to other factors, such as income and life-style characteristics, for which density may only be a proxy.[67] Although these other factors undoubtedly are significant, nothing in the research so far suggests that land use is not also important.

In fact, Holztclaw's analysis of the San Francisco regional data reveals that, although there are expected differences in travel behavior among households with different income and lifestyle characteristics, the amount of driving per household increases in all income and lifestyle categories as density declines. For example, wealthy households drive more than the middle class, who drive more than the poor, at all levels of residential density; but the wealthy, middle class, and poor all drive more and use transit less as density declines. Moreover, the relative variations in travel behavior due to neighborhood density remain strong across all household types, including single adults, families with young children, families with driving-age children, and retired adults.[68]

Similarly, the Newman and Kenworthy team has observed that, on average, residents of the 10 large U.S. metropolitan areas in their study drive 2.17 times more than residents of metropolitan Toronto. This difference cannot be explained by a difference in wealth, since the average U.S. resident in the study is less than 20 percent more wealthy than the average resident of Toronto. The correlation is stronger with density, given that Toronto is 2.82 times more dense than the average of the U.S. cities.[69]

Most reviewers agree that the body of research on density and travel, notwithstanding some differences in methodologies and variations in the details among the findings, is generally consistent in its overall conclusions: as population and employment density decline, travel distances lengthen, vehicle trips and usage increase, and transit usage and walking decline. Indeed, Professor Susan Handy of the University of Texas points out that these associations have been demonstrated in research dating as far back as 1963.[70] Robert Cervero and his partner at the University of California,

Michael Bernick, conclude succinctly that many new suburban developments are being "built at densities that are intrinsically dysfunctional from a transportation standpoint."[71]

The Effects of Related Neighborhood Characteristics

While spread-out development generates substantially more automobile and truck traffic than compact communities, this seems especially the case when low-density development is coupled with other neighborhood characteristics that also are frequently associated with sprawl. These include the isolation of the various functions of community—housing, work, shopping, recreation—in single-use tracts, a lack of pedestrian amenities, and neighborhood location that fails to coordinate well with the rest of a metropolitan region. Unfortunately, the evidence suggests that we are not only sprawling out; we are doing so in a way that guarantees increased automobile dependence.

Separation of jobs, housing, and other activities   Robert Cervero, who has been studying America's suburban workplaces since the 1980s, is particularly concerned about the impacts of prescriptive zoning and high suburban housing costs that prevent employees, especially service workers, from living near their jobs. Inevitably, the result is longer and longer commute distances by most of the workforce. According to Cervero, a reasonable ratio of jobs to housing in a given suburban employment location, in order to control otherwise rapidly escalating commute distances, would be 1.5 jobs per resident. While not all residents would be likely to work within the community, some would. But the reality of edge-city business districts is nowhere near the target: in Silicon Valley, the jobs to housing ratio is 2.5 to 1;

Regional shopping malls, which are frequently difficult to access by transit or walking, generate tens of thousands of automobile trips per day.

RICHARD HOPPE

in the Route One corridor in central New Jersey, the ratio is 3.5 to 1; in the newest office markets outside of Atlanta, the ratio is 5 to 1.[72] (Jobs to housing ratios are also high in many urban downtowns, but their characteristics as regional centers and walkable transit hubs make the imbalance far less of a factor there in lengthening automobile commute trips.)

Equally troubling is the traffic generated by isolated suburban shopping locations. A large regional mall the size of northern Virginia's Tyson's Corner Center generates over 50,000 automobile trips per day.[73] The four big-box retail projects planned for Lancaster County, Pennsylvania, described above in chapter one, were similarly projected to generate as many as 60,000 additional automobile trips per day in that rural location.[74]

Cervero argues persuasively that, given the shift in job growth away from polluting industry and toward cleaner, office-oriented workplaces that make better neighbors, there is no longer a strong planning rationale for segregating employment from housing, shopping, and other community functions. Among the potential benefits of building more diverse communities that integrate their places of activity would be the following: an increase in ride-sharing and transit usage, since workers in neighborhoods with shopping and amenities are less likely to feel anxious about not having a car at work; a greater share of walking and bicycling trips, since a diversity of destinations would be proximate; and less need for allocating land to parking, particularly since activities that peak at different times during the day, such as offices and movie theaters, could share spaces.[75] Architect and planner Peter Calthorpe echoes the importance of mixed-use job destinations that are varied and walkable, so that transit riders are not functionally stranded once they arrive.[76] And both Cervero and Anthony Downs caution that it is desirable not just to mix jobs and housing in the abstract but to match the prices and styles of housing units to the economic capabilities of workers employed there.[77]

There is growing evidence that diverse, integrated communities do, in fact, reduce driving. Researchers in San Diego, for example, found that workers living in communities with a good mix of housing and jobs had average commute lengths almost a third less (8.8 versus 12.8 miles) than workers living in areas with an excess of housing in relationship to jobs. In Seattle, transit and walking were found to claim larger shares in mixed-use areas, even when densities and demographic factors were similar.[78] Research from San Francisco and Florida also has shown improved commuting patterns when communities exhibit a relative balance between housing and jobs.[79]

It is important to recognize that even incremental changes in neighborhood characteristics can produce significant results. Cervero found that a 20-percent increase in the share of retail and commercial floorspace in an employment center was correlated with a 4.5 percent increase in the share of commute trips claimed by ride-sharing and transit.[80] The Southern California Association of Governments concluded that directing 12 percent of regional job growth to areas of housing surplus, while directing 6 percent of new housing to areas of job surplus, might reduce traffic congestion by as much as 35 percent compared to current projections.[81] A comparative review of similar modeling exercises performed by regional governmental associations in six U.S. metropolitan areas (Baltimore; Dallas-Fort Worth; Middlesex, NJ; San Diego;

Seattle; and Washington, DC) reported that a stronger mix of housing and jobs could reduce automobile use compared to other scenarios in all six locations.[82]

Notwithstanding this evidence, some observers doubt a strong relationship between suburban jobs/housing imbalance and the continued growth of traffic. The California Air Resources Board (CARB), for example, cited studies in its literature review discounting the relationship and conceded that some of the jobs/housing research was "inconclusive."[83] Professor Handy's bibliography notes that the relationship has been "less extensively and less consistently explored" than that between density and automobile use.[84] CARB, nevertheless, found sufficient consistency among the entire body of research to allow a conservative planning conclusion that, overall, mixing uses within a neighborhood could reduce driving by around 8 percent.[85]

Lack of pedestrian amenities   In addition to isolation of uses, another common characteristic of fringe development is a striking lack of sidewalks, connectivity, safe crossings, and other amenities that can encourage pedestrian travel. This potentially has great significance, given that over 25 percent of all automobile trips are less than one mile in length.[86] This is true even in relatively higher-density edge city employment districts, such as Tyson's Corner in Virginia or Atlanta's Perimeter Center, where workers are well acquainted with the "drive-to-lunch" syndrome.[87]

Lack of pedestrian amenities can certainly hinder the usefulness of transit, especially in many newer residential or office neighborhoods that offer no natural and safe walkways to transit stops. As the authors of *Emerging Trends In Real Estate 1997* put it:

> In Atlanta, many [transit] riders not only face driving to the new suburban MARTA stations from home, but also encounter difficult walks to and from work. It's just not worth the effort navigating six-lane intersections and stepping through lawns soggy from overnight sprinkling. But the plaintive wail of the suburban commuter gets louder: "Traffic's getting worse. I may have to move."[88]

This is a shame, because CARB reports empirical research indicating that a pleasant and interesting environment can double the distance that people are willing to walk.[89]

Distance from downtown and transit   While a neighborhood's internal characteristics can have a significant impact on travel behavior, so, too, can its location. And, unfortunately for today's typical regions, whose new developments bypass centrally located sites for ever-outward sprawl, the amount of traffic is directly related to distance from the central business district. Indeed, in a study described by Professor Handy as "among the most methodologically sound," researchers found that neighborhood proximity to downtown had a strong effect on reducing automobile usage, enough to reduce driving by one-third when proximity was coupled with density.[90] Downs notes that residential areas near large downtowns yield much higher shares of transit trips than those with the same density but farther out.[91]

Wide streets, a lack of sidewalks, and few crosswalks discourage pedestrian travel and transit use.

The impacts of business and retail location on driving may be even greater than that associated with residential location. Cervero reports that, when a California company relocated from downtown San Francisco to the Bishop Ranch development 30 miles east, the share of the company's commute trips on mass transit plummeted from 58 to 3 percent, while vehicle miles traveled to and from work by employees tripled.[92] CARB notes that Horton Plaza, a major downtown shopping center in San Diego, attracts 60 percent of its customers from transit and walking, while a comparable suburban center attracts only 5 percent from non-driving modes.[93]

Regions also forego great potential benefits when they fail to coordinate development with planning for mass transit. As noted above, commuters living near rail transit stations, in particular, are much more likely than the average worker to use transit. CARB notes that residents living more than two miles away from a station are only one-tenth as likely to use transit as those who live within walking distance.[94]

The significance of proximity, mixed uses, and density to travel reduction does not necessarily mean that, in order to address escalating traffic problems, regions must return to the traditional, monocentric urban model of concentrating jobs in a single central business district. Indeed, some researchers are passionate in their belief that decentralization of jobs and housing reduces pressure on downtowns, relieving congestion and reducing commute times.[95] While the relationships are complex, and the studies on the subject do not all agree, there is at least a weak consensus to the effect that a polycentric regional form, with a number of "satellite" downtowns complementing a strong central business district, may in fact produce fewer and shorter automobile trips than either a monocentric form or a dispersed form with no strong centers.[96] Newman and Kenworthy observe that a region with such "subcenters" is most likely to be successful in containing travel only if there are the requisite densities and transit links in the subcenters. The Australian scholars note also that today's U.S. metro regions are more accurately described as "dispersed" rather than "multicentered".[97]

Building communities to reduce traffic   The potential advantages of polycentric urban form are entirely consistent with what has come to be known as "transit-oriented development" (TOD). TOD proponents, led by architect and urban planner Peter Calthorpe, hold that environmental benefits, including automobile traffic reduction, are maximized when a substantial share of regional growth is clustered around transit stops. Characteristically, TODs place the highest housing, job, and shopping concentrations, along with the most diverse and pedestrian- and amenity-rich neighborhood features, closest to the stops.[98] (Essentially the same concept is championed by Michael Bernick and Robert Cervero, who favor the term "transit villages."[99]) Such neighborhoods combine several of the features—density, diversity of uses, pedestrian amenities, proximity to transit—indicated by the research to hold the most promise for limiting growth in traffic. Ironically, TODs also mimic many features found in traditional urban and suburban neighborhoods built prior to the 1950s.

CALTHORPE ASSOCIATES

This drawing of a planned transit-oriented development shows that retail and commercial uses and high density housing should be placed near the transit stop.

We discuss the promise of TODs in more depth later, in chapter five, but pause here to note a number of studies relevant to traffic characteristics of neighborhoods that combine several of the principal characteristics thought to help reduce traffic. The conclusions, for the most part, are encouraging.

For example, Calthorpe cites California research indicating that, even in the suburbs, older neighborhoods with "traditional" characteristics of density and diverse uses exhibit lower vehicle use per capita than newer, single-use, sprawl-type neighborhoods.[100] Other California research demonstrates that a "traditional" suburb (with a pre-World War Two street grid and mixed uses) has fewer automobile trips per day, a smaller share of solo driving, and greater use of transit, walking, and bicycling compared to what has now become the standard, dispersed suburban neighborhood (with segregated land uses, limited street access, and little transit service).[101] Another study, comparing two Bay Area communities, shows that the one with higher density, mixed uses, and better walking proximity to the rapid transit system has 20 percent fewer people driving alone to work, as well as fewer commuters driving to the transit station. This was the case even though both communities have similar incomes and significant overall transit ridership.[102]

Even when transit amenities are not strong, neighborhood features can make a difference. A study of six communities in Palm Beach County, Florida, involving analysis of some 16,000 travel records, discovered that residents of a sprawling suburb spend almost two-thirds more time driving than residents of comparable households in a more traditional neighborhood with better access to a diversity of land uses. All six of the communities in the Palm Beach study region exhibited a high degree of automobile use, but there was a marked difference among them in the length of driving trips.[103]

Another careful analysis of travel, census, demographic, and land use data, this time in Washington state, showed that transit use and walking increased, and solo driving decreased, as neighborhood density and mixing of land uses increased, even when the data were controlled for income and other factors unrelated to neighborhood design. The findings were consistent for both work and shopping trips, and were most striking when density and mix of uses were considered in both residential and employment neighborhoods.[104]

Findings from predictive modeling exercises are supportive of this body of research. CARB reports an analysis of proposed development in California's San Joaquin Valley that suggests that directing growth to mixed-use village centers may reduce automobile trips per household by 13 percent, and reduce vehicle miles driven per household by one-third, over a typical single-use, low-density development.[105] The agency also cites analysis of alternative growth models in three New Jersey counties indicating that concentrating new suburban development into higher density, mixed-use centers may reduce vehicle trips by 18 percent and vehicle miles traveled by 12 percent compared to more conventional development.[106]

Lessons from LUTRAQ

By far the most ambitious study so far comparing the effects of conventional, dispersed, single-use development to those of more compact, diverse, pedestrian- and transit-oriented design is the LUTRAQ ("Land Use, Transportation, Air Quality") project in Portland, Oregon. LUTRAQ grew out of citizen opposition to a proposed suburban freeway and evolved into a sophisticated study of the effects of alternative growth scenarios, producing 11 detailed technical reports between 1991 and 1997.

The project has been led by 1000 Friends of Oregon, a conservation organization, and a host of highly respected technical analysts and advisors. LUTRAQ has enjoyed not only the full cooperation and support of local officials, but also that of the Federal Highway Administration, the U.S. Environmental Protection Agency, the Home Builders Association of Metropolitan Portland, and some 15 public and private funding institutions.[107]

The LUTRAQ researchers began with an extensive inventory of land available for development within a 100-square mile study area in Washington County, Oregon, west of Portland. They projected market conditions through 2010 for residential, commercial, and industrial uses, along with an expected dramatic regional growth of 53 percent in residents and 70 percent in employment over the planning horizon. The researchers also undertook an extensive survey of actual travel behavior within various neighborhoods in the Portland region, in order to produce an accurate predictive model of travel demand among the region's residents.

As an alternative to conventional sprawl-type development in the study area, the LUTRAQ team then constructed a vision of growth for some 22,000 acres of vacant and underutilized land roughly within the boundaries of the existing developed region in the county. The scenario proposed to direct new development into three categories of TODs: "mixed-use" centers, served by light-rail transit, including shopping and offices, as well as moderately high-density housing at 12 to 50 units per net acre; "urban" TODs, primarily residential neighborhoods situated around light-rail stations and express-bus stops, with a variety of housing types ranging from three-story apartment buildings (30 units per net acre) to small-lot, single-family houses (seven units per net acre); and "neighborhood" TODs, situated on feeder bus lines within 10 minutes of light-rail or express-bus stops, with housing types ranging from townhouses (20 units per net acre) to standard single-family homes (five units per net acre). The planners also integrated a number of design amenities, including bikeways, parks, and pedestrian-friendly streets, shops, and offices. All told, the planners were able to accommodate 65 percent of expected new residential units and 78 percent of expected new jobs into the three types of TODs.[108]

Attractive transit-oriented development and urban infill have helped reduce sprawl and encourage transit use in Portland, Oregon.

The study's findings, which have been thoroughly researched and documented, were dramatic. For commuting trips, TOD areas within the LUTRAQ study region are projected to have one-third less solo driving, triple the transit usage, double the share of walking and bicycling, and a greater share of carpooling than the more conventional "freeway" alternative. When TOD areas are combined with more conventional neighborhoods in a broad planning scenario, the results are only slightly less striking. LUTRAQ also is projected to produce less highway congestion and fewer overall miles of vehicle travel than the freeway alternative.[109]

Most significant for the environment, the LUTRAQ project also demonstrated that TODs have the potential to reduce energy consumption, greenhouse gas emissions, and unhealthful air pollution, as compared to conventional sprawl-type development.[110] These issues are discussed immediately below.

Gray Skies and Greenhouses

Unfortunately, the LUTRAQ project in Portland—a region we shall revisit in our final chapter—represents a rather striking departure from prevalent development and traffic patterns. The fact is that, almost everywhere, we are still spreading out and driving more. Beyond the personal inconvenience and economic costs associated with congestion, does all this traffic—twice the volume we experienced only two decades ago—matter to ecosystems or public health? As a society, haven't we been making good progress in energy efficiency and clean air? Is it time to stop worrying about this problem and move on to other issues? The answers are yes, yes, and no.

The Good News about Energy Consumption and Air Pollution

Achieving a sustainable level of energy consumption is critical to reducing our dependence on uncertain supplies of imported oil, limiting the accumulation of greenhouse gases in the atmosphere, and relieving the pressure to open the planet's remaining pristine ecosystems to exploration and development for fossil fuel production. The good news is that, at least by some measures, we are moving in that direction: the U.S. now uses about 28 percent less energy per dollar of economic output than it did two decades ago; we also have reduced the portion of the typical household budget claimed for energy use, from 3.2 percent in 1976 to 2.6 percent in 1993. Our cars are more efficient, too, with the best-selling Ford Taurus of the 1990s getting

29 miles per gallon on average, a marked improvement from the best-selling, 16-mile-per-gallon Chevy Caprice of 1976.[111]

We also have reduced levels of air pollution. National inventories of airborne lead pollution have been reduced 97 percent since 1977; carbon monoxide pollution is down 61 percent; ground-level ozone, or urban smog, is down some 30 percent.[112] The federal EPA reports that "the air in our cities is significantly cleaner than it was 25 or even 10 years ago."[113] Even in America's most notoriously polluted and automobile-dependent city, Los Angeles, so-called "stage one" smog alerts (when pollution is so severe that vulnerable people must stay indoors) have declined from 121 days in 1977 to 66 days in 1987 to only seven such days in 1996 and only one in 1997. Although the weather plays a role in how many such days occur in a given year, authorities agree that LA's air is, in fact, improving.[114]

A good deal of the credit for this achievement must go to advances in clean-vehicle technology. Today's cars typically emit 70 percent less nitrogen oxides and 80 to 90 percent less hydrocarbons over their lifetimes than their uncontrolled counterparts of the 1960s.[115] Altogether, the California Air Resources Board concludes that today's new cars in that state (which has stricter vehicle performance standards than the rest of the country) pollute only one-tenth as much as the cars of 25 years ago.[116] Indeed, in response to regulatory and competitive pressure, automobile manufacturers have begun to test the market with next-generation, advanced-technology models that are said to cut pollution even more, reducing the components of smog by 50 to 70 percent over today's models.[117]

Energy Trends and the Greenhouse

Unfortunately, even the cleanest available technologies address only part of the emissions problems that accompany sprawl-related traffic. In particular, they have done little to contain overall emissions of carbon dioxide, a potent greenhouse gas whose concentrations rise as a direct consequence of the combustion of fossil fuels, including gasoline, for energy. Although we Americans have been lured into complacency by continuing low gasoline prices and a laissez-faire government posture with respect to rates of fuel consumption and CO_2 emissions, the numbers show that our sense of security with regard to the issue is decidedly misplaced.

Transportation energy consumption   The bad news is that even today's relatively efficient passenger car requires some 550 gallons of gasoline per year, on average, to maintain our current driving habits. As an inevitable by-product of this rate of fuel combustion—carbon is always released when organic fuels are burned—today's car also releases some 8,800 pounds of CO_2 into the atmosphere. Moreover, typical consumption and CO_2 emission rates are roughly twice as high for today's average "light truck," a booming category of sales that includes such popular models as minivans, pickups, and sport-utility vehicles (SUVs).[118]

Indeed, sprawl-induced traffic and other transportation constitutes by far the largest consumer of petroleum products in the United States, accounting for some two-thirds of our overall oil consumption.[119] As of 1994, the U.S. was using around eleven million barrels of oil each day to support our transportation habits.[120] Slightly more than half of U.S. transportation energy is consumed by cars and light trucks, with heavier freight trucks accounting for another 23 percent.[121] Transportation alone consumes more oil than the United States produces, and also more oil than we import, each year.[122]

Our gluttonous appetite for oil is uniquely American, at least as a matter of degree. The average American citizen uses five times as much energy for transportation as the average Japanese and nearly three times as much as the average citizen of

---

Figure 2-5
Total Transportation Energy Demand in the United States and Selected Countries, 1992

Source: Bureau of Transportation Statistics, U.S. Department of Transportation, *Transportation Statistics Annual Report 1995*, Washington, DC: 1995, p. 75

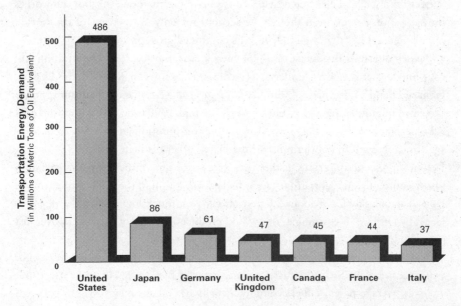

Figure 2-6
Fuel Consumption by All Motor Vehicles in the United States: Total and Per Vehicle Consumption, 1960–1995

Source: Bureau of Transportation Statistics, U.S. Department of Transportation, *Transportation Statistics Annual Report 1998,* Washington, DC: 1998, Table 4-12.

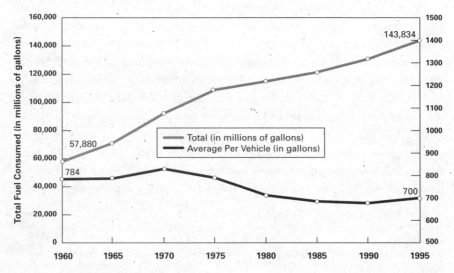

Western Europe.[123] The United States consumes more than one third of the world's transportation energy, even though we account for only 4.7 percent of the world's population and less than one fourth of its combined gross product.[124]

Under all foreseeable scenarios, U.S. energy consumption for transportation will continue to increase. Even under a very conservative forecast made by the Department of Energy's Information Administration, transportation energy consumption is projected to grow some 30 percent between the mid-1990s and 2015. This includes a 0.6 percent average annual growth in gasoline consumption and a 1.6 percent average annual growth in consumption of diesel and other distillate fuels.[125]

These projections, serious as they are, were based on a rather rosy interpretation of current trends. Actual transportation fuel consumption in the 1980s, for example, grew at an annual rate of about 2.6 percent per year, much higher than the rate projected by DOE.[126] If continued, this would produce a growth of 67 percent over just two decades.

Something approaching this more consumptive scenario is likely to be the case for two major reasons: First, the fuel economy gains of the late 1970s and early 1980s are over; average new-car fuel economy actually has fallen since 1987, in part as a

---

The Impact of Minivans and SUVs

A clean-transportation strategy that relies solely on improvements to vehicles is unlikely to succeed. Notwithstanding the efforts of regulators and a few car manufacturers to introduce some super-efficient, advanced-technology vehicles, the bulk of the industry's marketing is placed elsewhere, and consumers appear uninterested in efficiency.

In particular, the 10 most fuel-efficient vehicles in the country today account for only 0.7 percent of all vehicle sales.[127] Sales of traditional passenger cars of all types are declining, prompting manufacturers to discontinue once-popular models.[128] Instead, so-called "light trucks," including pickup trucks, minivans, and sport-utility vehicles (SUVs), now account for nearly one of every two family vehicles sold in America. And they are heavier, less aerodynamic, far less fuel efficient, and dramatically more polluting than regular passenger cars.

Indeed, benefiting from a regulatory system left over from the 1970s when vans and four-wheel drive vehicles were largely restricted to commercial, farm, and specialized recreational uses, manufacturers of today's family-oriented minivans and SUVs are allowed to sell a fleet average with only three-fourths the fuel efficiency required of cars. The largest models, including some in the popular Chevrolet Suburban line, are so heavy that they are exempt altogether from rules designed to regulate only cars and other light vehicles. Apart from greenhouse gas emissions (which rise proportionately as fuel efficiency declines), pickup trucks, minivans, and SUVs also emit as much as twice the per-vehicle nitrogen oxide, which causes smog, as do cars. The combined greenhouse gas emissions of cars, minivans, pickup trucks, and SUVs are projected to rise as much as 55 percent by 2010 if current trends in traffic and vehicle sales continue.[129]

---

result of the growing popularity of larger, less efficient vehicles (see box).[130] Second, as noted above, sprawl and other factors are causing miles of vehicle travel to grow at much higher rates than the 1.4 percent annual growth for cars and 1.6 percent annual growth for truck freight assumed by DOE.[131] Most observers predict that the growth rate will continue to be well above 2 percent per year.[132]

Carbon dioxide and global warming These consumption trends do not bode well for long-term planetary health. In particular, sprawl-induced automobile traffic and other forms of transportation contribute some 446.8 million metric tons of carbon emissions each year; this constitutes 32 percent of all U.S. carbon emissions. DOE projects that total U.S. carbon emissions will continue to grow at an average rate of 1.0 percent per year, with transportation sources growing 20 percent faster

Figure 2-7
Mobile Source CO$_2$ Emissions, Percent of World Total, 1993

Source: Bureau of Transportation Statistics, U.S. Department of Transportation, *Transportation Statistics Annual Report 1996*, Washington, DC: 1996, p. 224.

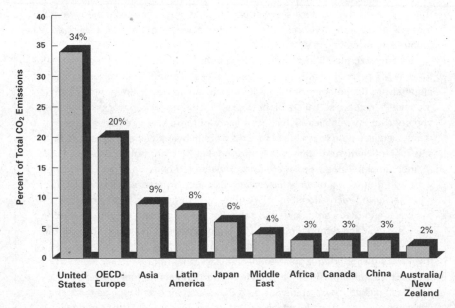

than the average.[133] For the reasons discussed above, DOE's projections may well understate the likely contribution of automobile traffic to the accumulation of greenhouse gases. In any event, continued growth in traffic-related carbon emissions will make it extremely difficult to meet American obligations to reduce greenhouse gases, as agreed at recent international meetings in Rio de Janiero, Brazil, and Kyoto, Japan.

All observers acknowledge, of course, that charting the past and likely future courses of global climate change involves scientific uncertainties. Still, instrumental data, paleodata, simple and complex climate models, and statistical models have combined to create a strong scientific consensus: there is indeed a significant global warming trend, and the trend is man-made, largely due to fossil fuel combustion from transportation and other sources. Indeed, these findings have been reached emphatically by the Intergovernmental Panel on Climate Change (IPCC), an organization involving thousands of scientists from 120 nations that assesses the peer-reviewed scientific literature and advises the world's governments on climate change.[134]

The IPCC reports that the mean surface air temperature of the earth already has increased 0.3–0.6°C (0.5–1.1° Fahrenheit) since the late nineteenth century, and the

20th century mean global temperature is at least as warm as any since about 1400 A.D. The last two decades have been among the warmest on record, despite the cooling effects of a major volcanic eruption at Mount Pinatubo in the Philippines in 1991. Global sea level has already risen 10.25 centimeters (about four inches) over the past 100 years, largely because of the rise in global mean temperature.[135] Beyond the findings of the IPCC, new research reported by the U.S. National Oceanic and Atmospheric Administration suggests that not only has the 20th century been the warmest in history, but the magnitude of the experienced warming is the greatest since at least 800 A.D.[136]

So far, the effects on our quality of life have not been dramatic. But they could become so. In 1995, the IPCC developed a range of projections of future climate trends, all of them indicating that average rates of warming probably will be greater than any seen in the last 10,000 years. The IPCC's mid-range, "best estimate" forecast is for an additional 2°C (3.6° Fahrenheit) warming in the 21st century. The "best estimate" scenario also forecasts an additional sea level rise of about 50 centimeters (20 inches) during the same time period.[137]

The potential consequences of these changes are not pretty. Health impacts, for example, could include an increase in cardiorespiratory deaths and illnesses as the result of an increase in the frequency, intensity, and duration of heat waves, such as the one that killed more than 500 people in the American Midwest in the summer of 1995. The IPCC working group charged with evaluating the impacts and mitigation options associated with likely rates of warming also predicts an increase in the risk of vector-borne tropical diseases, including malaria, dengue, yellow fever, and viral encephalitis.[138]

In addition, a rise in sea level and coastal water tables could cause contaminants from low-lying dump sites and septic systems to enter waterways and food chains.[139] Sea-level rise could wreak havoc in coastal areas, with negative impacts on tourism, fresh water supplies, fisheries, and biodiversity; high tides will be higher and flooding and storm surges will cover more area.[140] A 50-centimeter sea level rise, as predicted in IPCC's "best estimate," could damage or destroy up to 43 percent of the remaining coastal wetlands in the United States.[141]

Continued global warming also will bring risk to the earth's ecological equilibrium. A substantial fraction of the world's forested area could undergo major vegetation changes, with more frequent outbreaks of forest pests, diseases, and fires. Desert conditions could become more extreme. And much of the planet's existing mountain glacier mass could disappear, with significant downstream effects on river flows and water supplies, including water used for agriculture and hydroelectric generation.[142]

Many animal species could be put at risk, especially polar bears, marine seals, great whales, seabirds, and others that thrive in or migrate to cold climates.[143]

The role of greenhouse gases in this bleak picture is now well-documented. Perhaps the most prevalent and damaging of mankind's contributions to global warming is excess carbon dioxide. Atmospheric concentrations of the gas, which remains in the atmosphere for many decades, have grown 30 percent since pre-industrial times, and are projected to increase. The IPCC reports that, if carbon dioxide emission levels are maintained, concentrations will approach twice the preindustrial level by the end of the 21st century.[144]

Rising imports and energy security   Moreover, there is growing concern that present oil consumption trends in the U.S. risk an international crisis of considerable magnitude.

In particular, as of 1994, America was importing 45 percent of its annual oil consumption, already perilously close to the record high of 46 percent reached in 1977.[145] Even the conservative projections of DOE indicate that oil imports are likely to climb at an average rate of 1.9 percent per year through 2015, with driving and other transportation accounting for a whopping 71 percent of the increase.[146] By that time, the United States is expected to import nearly 60 percent of our oil, doubling our trade deficit in oil to some $100 billion per year.[147]

To make matters worse, the current glut of oil on world markets is likely to be transitory. The world's population is expected to increase by 50 percent between the 1990s and 2020. Much of the increase will occur in the developing world, which is undergoing an energy-intensive transformation to an urban and mechanized economy.

Increased demand for oil is expected to be supplied largely by the nations of the Persian Gulf region.[148] The U.S. already is importing more than twice as much oil from the Persian Gulf as at the time of the 1973 oil embargo.[149] This will continue to be a necessity, because the rest of the world is drawing down its oil reserves at double the rate at which the OPEC (Organization of Petroleum Exporting Countries) members are drawing down theirs.[150] Despite recent increases in production by non-OPEC nations, the U.S. and our non-OPEC allies have enough reserves to last only 17 years under current projections.[151] DOE projects that OPEC's share of U.S. imports will climb to 57 percent, with the Persian Gulf share of all imports at 50 percent, by 2015.[152]

DOE officials further report that, under present assumptions, the oil revenues of the Persian Gulf states will almost triple, from $90 to $250 billion per year in 2010, constituting a $1.5 trillion transfer in wealth to that "chronically unstable" region. The DOE officials note with concern that such resources could buy all sorts of.

weapons, influence, and mischief, seriously weakening American hopes for peace among countries increasingly hostile to our interests.[153] While sprawl-related oil consumption is hardly our nation's only concern—or even its main one—involving the Middle East, legitimate worries about international security form an additional strong rationale for embarking on a more sustainable path of consumption.

Traffic and Air Pollution

The news on unhealthful air pollution from our inefficient driving patterns is only slightly more encouraging. A recent government publication summarizes the situation:

> Despite considerable progress, the overall goal of clean and healthy air continues to elude much of the country. Unhealthy air pollution levels still plague virtually every major city in the United States. This is largely because development and urban sprawl have created new pollution sources and have contributed to a doubling of vehicle travel since 1970.[154]

In particular, cars and other highway vehicles continue to emit some 60 million tons of carbon monoxide per year, about 62 percent of our national inventory of that pollutant; cars and other highway vehicles continue to emit some seven million tons per year, almost 26 percent, of our volatile organic compounds (VOCs), which constitute a major precursor to ozone smog; and they emit around eight million tons per year, about 32 percent, of our nitrogen oxides, another ozone precursor.[155] Despite the improvements in clean vehicle technology noted above, today's average passenger car continues to emit 557 pounds of carbon monoxide, 75 pounds of VOCs, and 39 pounds of

Despite improvements in clean vehicle technology, automobiles are still major contributors to metropolitan air pollution.

nitrogen oxides each year.[156] Motor vehicles also emit as much as 50 percent of our carcinogenic and toxic air pollutants, such as benzene and formaldehyde.[157] In addition, motor vehicles, particularly diesel-powered buses and freight trucks, constitute a significant source of soot and other unhealthful fine particles that, when inhaled, lodge in and damage human tissue.[158]

Significant as they are, the national numbers may understate the contribution of sprawl-related traffic to air pollution in our cities and metropolitan regions. The federal

EPA attributes up to 90 percent of *urban* carbon monoxide, and up to 50 percent of urban smog precursors, to motor vehicles; the California Air Resources Board has reached the same conclusions for the entire state of California.[159] Vehicles are also the predominant source of particulate pollution in some urban areas.[160]

These ingredients make for a nasty soup. Exposure to carbon monoxide is associated with visual impairment, reduced work capacity, reduced manual dexterity, poor learning ability, and difficulty in performing complex tasks.[161] At sustained high levels, it can be fatal. Ozone, the principal component of smog, damages lung tissue, aggravates asthma and other respiratory disease, and leads to choking, coughing, and stinging eyes. It also inhibits plant growth and can cause widespread forest and crop damage, around $40 million worth each year in Maryland alone.[162]

Ozone smog, which has been described by the federal EPA as "this country's most intractable urban air-quality problem,"[163] has been the subject of substantial recent research by the nation's public health community. Indeed, an exhaustive three-year review of hundreds of studies on the health impacts of ozone smog led EPA to conclude in late 1996 that its national ambient air-quality standards, which establish allowable levels of ozone exposure, were too permissive. The agency is now phasing in a new standard, which changes the maximum allowable concentration from 0.12 to 0.08 parts per million.[164] A 1998 EPA study estimates that economic losses due

---

Figure 2-8
Contribution of Highway Vehicles to Total U.S. Emissions of CO, NO$_x$, and VOC, 1996
Source: Bureau of Transportation Statistics, U.S. Department of Transportation, *National Transportation Statistics 1998*, Washington, DC: 1998, Tables 4-35, 4-36, and 4-37.

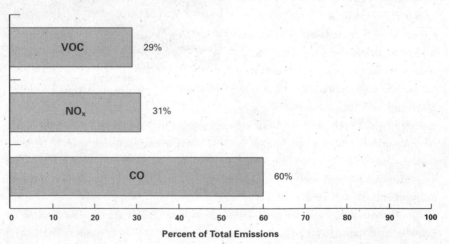

Percent of Total Emissions

Downtown Los Angeles on a clear day compared to a smoggy day.

to the health effects of traffic-related ozone pollution amount to between one and two billion dollars annually, depending on the value assigned to human life.[165]

These impacts are not isolated. In the early 1990s, over 90 U. S. metropolitan areas regularly exceeded the air quality standards for ozone. Nine areas, containing some 57 million residents, are considered "severely" polluted, meaning that they experience peak ozone levels that exceed the standard by 50 percent or more.[166] Las Vegas and Phoenix, two of our most rapidly sprawling cities, are now among the regions with the country's dirtiest air.[167] Despite the improvements noted above, Los Angeles, the nation's most severely polluted region, had 91 days in 1996 in which the 0.12 parts-per-million ozone standard was violated.[168] Even in 1997, a year in which mild weather helped reduce the number of violations, Los Angeles reported 67 days in which federal clean air standards were violated, and 135 days in which stricter state standards were violated.[169]

And the problems are not confined to metropolitan areas with large populations. Western North Carolina, for example, experienced a record number of 43 days in violation in 1998.[170] Wherever they occur, each day in violation poses a particular health risk to sensitive populations, including the elderly, the young, and persons with heart or lung disease.

All researchers agree that vehicle traffic contributes a major part of the country's inventory of ozone smog. Assessing the impact of traffic on the health risks related to

---

We Pollute with Trips, Not Just Miles

As we use our cars for routine trips in a spread-out lifestyle, we can increase emissions of air pollutants, particularly carbon monoxide and volatile organics, just by starting a car more often, even if we do not increase the mileage driven. This is because, for short trips, most emissions occur during the vehicle start, before the engine warms up; another set of emissions takes place by evaporation, each time the car is parked.[171]

---

particulate pollution presents a greater challenge because, in most areas with serious problems of particulate pollution, industrial and other non-vehicle sources overwhelm traffic sources.[172] Unfortunately, this says more about the sorry state of industrial emissions control than it does about the contribution of traffic.

In any event, there is no question that the threats presented by diesel soot and other particulate pollution can be extremely serious, and they have prompted EPA to tighten its standards for this category of pollutants, as well as for ozone. Specifically, health threats from particulate pollution include a variety of cardiac and respiratory symptoms, such as impaired breathing, damage to lung tissue, increased asthma attacks and emergency room visits, cancer, and premature death, particularly among the elderly and children.[173] The 1998 EPA study estimates the monetary cost of the health effects of *traffic-related* particulate pollution as between 20 and 64 billion dollars annually, again depending on the assumptions used.[174] As many as 16,000 premature deaths may be caused each year by exposure to particulate and ozone pollution combined from motor vehicle traffic.[175]

The number of air-quality violations will climb in future years, in part because of the more restrictive standards being phased in by EPA. But violations may rise also because of sprawl and related increases in traffic: EPA research indicates that, notwithstanding continuing improvements in emission control systems, the total national inventory of hydrocarbon emissions from gasoline vehicles could reverse direction and begin to increase again in the early part of the 21st century, because of increased driving.[176] Total nitrogen oxide emissions from motor vehicles already are at a higher level than they were two decades ago, despite improvements in the emissions performance of individual vehicles.[177] Ozone and particulate pollution are both projected to rise, and some observers believe that, by 2015, carbon monoxide will also be on a rising trend.[178]

EPA concludes that the persistence of mobile (as opposed to stationary, e.g., a power plant) source pollution in the United States is due to four factors:

• Increased vehicle miles driven.
• Longer commuting distances and more solo commuting.
• Buses and trucks that have not been cleaned up as much as cars.
• Automobile fuel that has become more polluting with respect to organic compounds, since the elimination of lead.[179]

The first two of these, as we have discussed, are directly related to sprawling development.

Research Linking Sprawl to Air and Energy Impacts

It goes without elaboration that, the more we have to drive a given car, the more fuel we consume, and the more greenhouse gases and unhealthy pollutants our vehicles emit. As a result, all of the research that shows a connection between sprawling land use and increased driving, as discussed above, also means that sprawling land use contributes to increased energy use and air pollution. Unfortunately, not many of the reported studies on traffic go further and reach direct conclusions with regard to

---

Figure 2-9
Summary of National Travel Trends, 1969–1990
Source: William L. Ball, *Commuting Alternatives in the United States: Recent Trends and a Look to the Future*, Washington, DC: U.S. Department of Transportation, DOT-T-95-11, 1994, p. 15.

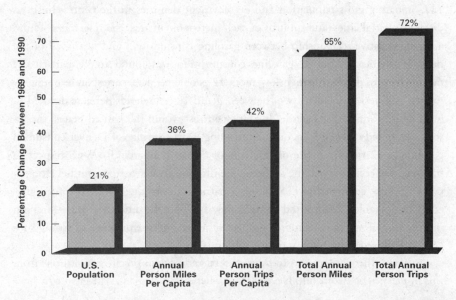

emissions. Those studies that do attempt explicitly to measure energy and air impacts, however, confirm the relationships between sprawl, consumption, and pollution.

The most expansive and ambitious of this research is undoubtedly that of the Newman-Kenworthy team, based in Australia's Murdoch University. Working for the World Bank and other institutions, these researchers have been tracking and conducting land, travel, and consumption data in some 32 cities worldwide, including 10 in the United States, for many years.[180] The sheer scope of the Newman-Kenworthy research—pulling together data from widely varying international locations and record-keeping systems—raises inevitable questions of data reliability and comparability, so some caution is appropriate in using it to draw precise conclusions. Nevertheless, the overall direction and trends of the research paint a compelling picture.

As discussed above, Newman and Kenworthy found that metropolitan areas in Europe typically have three to four times the population density, even in their suburbs, of American areas. What is significant for the current discussion is that the researchers also found that American cities had four times the per-person gasoline use of European cities, and substantially higher emissions of carbon dioxide, nitrogen oxides, carbon monoxide, and organic compounds per passenger mile of total travel (including travel by public transit and other alternative modes). Taking the comparison beyond Europe, American cities on average had a little less than twice the per-person gasoline use of Toronto and Australian cities, and many times the usage of three "westernized" cities in Asia.[181]

Comparing gross population and employment densities in the central business districts, central cities, and suburbs of each metropolitan area, the researchers found a strong negative relationship between gasoline consumption and nearly all of the density variables. Increased gasoline consumption was found to be particularly notable as gross density moves below about 12 people per acre, corresponding roughly with a "net" residential density of between 9 and 10 households per acre devoted to housing.[182] Citing a particularly dramatic contrast within the United States, the researchers noted that residents on the sprawling exurban fringe of Denver consumed gasoline at 12 times the rate of residents of dense Manhattan.[183] With respect to international comparisons, the authors note that the greater per-person fuel efficiency in Toronto, compared to U.S. cities, is particularly striking, given Toronto's generally comparable economy and lifestyle; they attribute the difference to the strength of Toronto's urban core, its more compact suburbs, and the presence of strong subcenters built around suburban transit stations.[184]

As noted, there are reasons to draw general rather than precise conclusions from this impressive body of work. Nevertheless, whenever Newman and Kenworthy have tested other variables in their research, they have found them not to undermine the central correlations between sprawl and fuel consumption. Variations in gasoline prices, income levels, and average vehicle efficiency, for example, have been analyzed and found to explain no more than half the differences in fuel consumption among the cities studied.[185] With respect to income variation in particular, outer residents have been found to travel more and use more energy regardless of income.[186] And, even though vehicles can become more efficient per mile in outer areas as congestion decreases and speed increases, the potential savings are overwhelmed by the longer distances traveled and the increased reliance on driving rather than alternative modes.[187]

Newman and Kenworthy conclude that previous research on the impact of land use underestimates the fuel savings potential of more efficient development, because traditional travel behavior models do not capture the fundamental changes in travel behavior that a more efficient pattern would support.[188] They cite a "theoretical potential" for fuel savings of 20 to 30 percent in now-sprawling cities that could take steps to accomplish the following: prevent leapfrogging of new development; increase housing densities near transit and in central areas; maintain a strong city center with well-defined subcenters; employ mixed land uses; and provide advanced transit systems through high-density areas.[189]

Beyond the Newman-Kenworthy research, a number of U.S. studies also have attempted to quantify the energy and pollution impacts of various types of cities and suburbs. A typical new household in the suburbs has been found, for example, to consume more energy than a traditional household in the inner city, even if it is assumed that the new suburban home has been upgraded to best-practice, energy-efficient standards for insulation, heating, and appliances; the reason is increased auto usage.[190]

The air-pollution impacts (as distinguished from energy impacts and related greenhouse gas emissions) of land use are more difficult to quantify precisely, because of the complication of variance with vehicle trips and starts, as well as mileage driven. Nevertheless, a typical auto-dependent suburban shopping center has been found to cause the emission of over half the nitrogen oxides of a major power plant, five times the organic gases, and over 30 times the carbon monoxide, all because of related vehicle travel.[191]

After reviewing all of the relevant literature, the California Air Resources Board concluded that a package of land-use strategies, similar to those recommended by Newman and Kenworthy, could reduce vehicle emissions of carbon monoxide, nitrogen oxides, and organic compounds in suburban communities in that state by around 10 percent, and reduce emissions in urban communities by more than 20 percent.[192] The LUTRAQ researchers in Portland, for their part, concluded that implementing the study's proposals for compact, transit-oriented growth would reduce that city's region-wide vehicle emissions, including greenhouse gases, by between 6 and 7 percent over recently experienced sprawling trends,[193] and by an even greater amount over an alternate scenario involving construction of a proposed freeway.[194] Already, some writers attribute Portland's recent success in avoiding violations of the carbon-monoxide and ozone-smog standards partly to the innovative land use and transportation measures that region has been putting into place since the 1970s.[195] In San Diego, just providing a better balance of jobs and housing in communities where there is now a mismatch has been projected to reduce vehicle emissions significantly, if not dramatically.[196] And, in fact, the potential for reduction in traffic volume to reduce emissions may be understated not just in San Diego but by much of the research, because the predictive models employed by transportation analysts seldom account for the dramatically increasing market share now claimed by higher-polluting trucks, minivans, and SUVs.

Research within other countries is generally consistent with these findings. Studies in the United Kingdom, for example, confirm that fuel consumption rises as the density of settlements decreases; this was also the finding of a study of 97 towns in Sweden, which concluded that annual fuel consumption per person increases 25 percent as the amount of land developed per person doubles. Additional research in the U.K. indicates that substantial potential savings (10 to 16 percent) in energy consumption and greenhouse gas emissions over time could be realized from a combination of land use and public transportation measures.[197] Still another U.K. study, reported by the American Planning Association, examined six alternative settlement patterns for a population of 124,000 people. The study found the most energy-efficient pattern was a compact urban core, surrounded by concentrated "urban villages," which were connected by both public transit and highways.[198]

Landscapes Lost (from Old MacDonald to the New McDonald's)

Our roadways and atmosphere are hardly the only repositories of damage done by untamed urban and suburban development. Indeed, the most visible damage is that done to one of America's most beautiful and storied resources: our landscape itself. From the redwood forests to the New York islands, this landscape is changing character rapidly.

The phenomenon has been summarized emphatically by writer James Howard Kunstler:

We drive up and down the gruesome, tragic suburban boulevards of commerce, and we're overwhelmed at the fantastic, awesome, stupefying ugliness of absolutely everything in sight—the fry pits, the big-box stores, the office units, the lube joints, the carpet warehouses, the parking lagoons, the jive plastic townhouse clusters, the uproar of signs, the highway itself clogged with cars—as though the whole thing had been designed by some diabolical force bent on making human beings miserable. And naturally, this experience can make us feel glum about the nature and future of our civilization.[199]

The impacts go beyond the depression of visual clutter, of course, to our working farms, our ecosystems, and our ever-more-tenuous connection as human beings to the mysteries of the natural world.

The Good News About Land Conservation

Before we discuss some of the specific negative impacts of sprawl on our land resources, it is appropriate to pause again and reflect on the good news. With respect to farmland, for example, the United States is fortunate still to retain over 400 million acres—around 20 percent of our total land base—in production for agricultural crops.[200] The amount of harvested land was greater in 1992 than in 1970 (although not greater than in 1980), and overall agricultural productivity has increased substantially since the 1960s.[201] At the same time, we have adopted a wealth of programs designed to preserve rural economies and character, including the federal Farmland Protection Policy Act, state right-to-farm laws, preferential tax treatment, agricultural conservation easements, and land-evaluation and site-assessment systems.[202]

In addition, beyond farmland, we have implemented a range of legislation and programs designed to protect other aspects of the American landscape and the benefits it provides. These include, for example, the federal Endangered Species Act, the Wilderness Act, the National Historic Preservation Act, the Highway Beautification Act, and measures to protect scenic, cultural, and ecological values on our public lands. These initiatives have indeed helped retain some of the most precious of our scarce resources. Indeed, some endangered and threatened species are now recovering,

Sprawl has destroyed some of America's most beautiful landscapes, such as these mountains in California.

SURFACE TRANSPORTATION POLICY PROJECT

among them the bald eagle, the gray wolf, the peregrine falcon, the whooping crane, and the mountain lion.[203]

These considerable achievements in agriculture and resource conservation are themselves now endangered and undermined by the relentless appetite of our cities and suburbs for land.

Threats to Farmland

In particular, while the U.S. continues to enjoy the appearance of abundant farmland, the best of that land is being lost at an amazing rate. At the conclusion of exhaustive research on the subject, the American Farmland Trust reported that from 1982 to 1992 we lost to urban and suburban development an average of 400,000 acres per year of "prime" farmland, the land with the best soils and climate for growing crops. This translates to a loss of 45.7 acres per hour, every single day. During that same period, we lost an additional 26,600 acres per year—three more acres per hour, every single day—of "unique" farmland, used for growing rare and specialty crops.[204] Put another way, for each acre of prime or unique farmland that is being saved by various farmland protection programs across the county, three acres are lost to development.[205]

To make matters worse, there is an unfortunate congruence between that land most suited and productive for farming and that land most in danger of urban encroachment. As Professor Ewing has put it, the "lands most suitable for growing crops also tend to be most suitable for 'growing houses.'"[206] This is because inland urban settlements in the U.S. have tended to situate in river valleys and other fertile areas that are also highly productive for farming.[207]

CHESAPEAKE BAY FOUNDATION

Across the country, suburban development is rapidly encroaching on prime and unique farmland.

As a result, most of the country's prime farmland is located within the suburban and exurban counties of metropolitan areas.[208] Such "urban-influenced" counties currently produce more than half the total value of U.S. farm production; their average annual production value per acre is some 2.7 times that of other U.S. counties. Yet, ominously, their population growth is also disproportionately high, over twice the national average.[209]

Within 127 highly productive farming regions across the United States identified in 1997 by the Farmland Trust, urban development has already consumed 32 percent of the regions' prime and unique farmland.[210] Those counties with prime and unique farmland found to be threatened by particularly high rates of current development collectively produce some 79 percent of our nation's fruit, 69 percent of our vegetables, 52 percent of our dairy products, and over one-fourth of our meat and grains.[211]

The nation's most threatened agricultural region, according to the Trust, is also one of its most productive: California's Central Valley, currently supporting a massive

---

Figure 2-10
High Quality Farmland in the Path of Development in California

Source: A. Ann Sorensen, Richard P. Greene, and Karen Russ, *Farming on the Edge*, DeKalb, IL: American Farmland Trust, 1997. Map produced by Lenny Walther, Northern Illinois University.

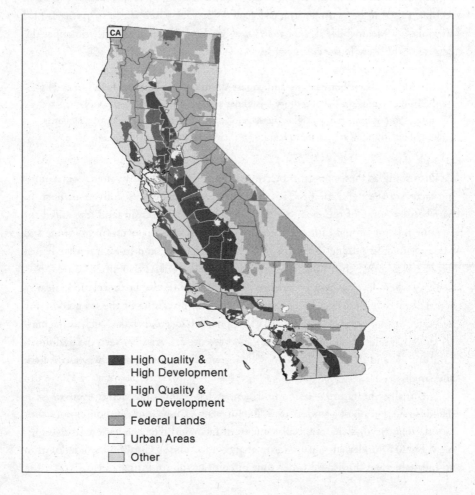

High Quality &
High Development

High Quality &
Low Development

Federal Lands

Urban Areas

Other

$13.3 billion farming industry.[212] The Valley contains six of the nation's 10 most productive farm counties, including Fresno, which alone outproduces 24 states.[213] And threatened it is: developed land in the region more than tripled in a single decade from 1981 to 1992, and the population is projected to grow more than three-fold between 1990 and 2040.[214] If today's development patterns continue, one million additional acres of farmland will be converted by then, potentially reducing the value of the Valley's agricultural production by a cumulative $49 billion, and taking a $76 billion chunk out of various agricultural support businesses.[215]

Other parts of the country are not faring much better.[216] In Loudoun County, Virginia, located within the Farmland Trust's second-most endangered farming region, a new development calling itself "Ashburn Farm" has sprouted up where a real farm used to be, with an ironic slogan: "The One Place Where Virginia Is Still Virginia."[217] Meanwhile, *Washington Post* writer Dan Eggen eloquently describes the demise of the New Jersey countryside:

> This lush, 150-acre horse farm—located just 40 miles from Manhattan and tended by the Palmer family for half a century—is under siege. A sea of cul-de-sacs and oversized trophy homes has risen nearly to the edge of the property from the north, while the neighbors to the west prepare to hand over their deserted cornfields to a developer.[218]

Disturbing as these trends, projections, and anecdotes are, there are compounding factors that extend the problem beyond the particular acres converted. First, in part because some of the most fertile soils are being paved over, land less suited for farming is being brought into production; this translates to conversion of forests and wetlands to crop production, more reliance on irrigation, and more intensive use of fertilizers and other chemicals.[219] Second, those farming acres that are converted, particularly when development occurs in a scattered or "leapfrog" pattern, affect nearby acreage still in production by reducing the scale and volume of the farm economy necessary to support an adequate level of support services and trades, such as machinery dealers and repair shops. In addition, lifestyle conflicts arise between the traditional rural culture and the new suburban residents, who may object to the way farms look and smell.

Eventually, the farming economy becomes less stable and viable, even when it retains some portion of a land base.[220] The Farmland Trust's study of the Central Valley reports that, beyond the one million acres of farmland likely to be lost to development by 2040 under current trends in that region, some 2.5 million will fall within an inevitable one-third-mile-wide "zone of conflict" around urban areas.[221]

Table 2-2
Farmland Conversion in the 20 Most Threatened Major Land Resource Areas (MLRAs), 1982–1992

MLRA	Acres of Prime or Unique Farm Land Converted to Urban (in thousands)	Total Acres of Land Developed (in thousands)	Percent of Developed Land That Was Prime or Unique
Sacramento and San Joaquin Valleys (CA)	62	159	39%
Northern Piedmont (MD, VA, PA, NJ)	115	333	34%
Southern Wisconsin and Northern Illinois Drift Plain (IL, WI)	81	136	59%
Texas Blackland Prarie (TX)	127	299	42%
Willamette and Puget Sound Valleys (WA, OR)	78	283	27%
Florida Everglades (FL)	57	141	40%
Eastern Ohio Till Plain (OH)	66	115	57%
Lower Rio Grande Plain (TX)	45	53	85%
Mid-Atlantic Coastal Plain (DE, MD)	16	37	43%
New England and Eastern New York Upland (CT, MA, NH, NY, RI)	61	435	14%
Ontario Plain and Finger Lakes Region (NY)	29	63	47%
Nashville Basin (TN)	47	120	39%
Central Snake River Plains (ID)	7	17	41%
Southwestern Michigan Fruit and Truck Belt (MI)	8	24	32%
Central California Coastal Valleys (CA)	18	82	22%
Columbia Basin (WA)	9	27	34%
Imperial Valley (CA)	8	19	42%
Long Island-Cape Cod Coastal Lowland (MA, NY, RI)	18	73	24%
Connecticut Valley (CT, MA)	18	62	29%
Western Michigan Fruit and Truck Belt (MI, WI)	9	32	27%

Source: A. Ann Sorensen, Richard P. Greene, and Karen Russ, *Farming on the Edge*, DeKalb, IL: American Farmland Trust, 1997, Table 10.

Figure 2-11
High Quality Farmland in the Path of Development in Illinois and Wisconsin
Source: A. Ann Sorensen, Richard P. Greene, and Karen Russ, *Farming on the Edge*, DeKalb, IL: American Farmland Trust, 1997. Map produced by Lenny Walther, Northern Illinois University.

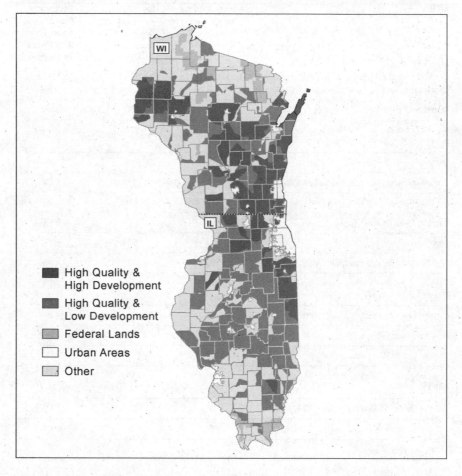

No wonder that the ironic declaration of many in the farm community is that the last crop that will be grown on America's farmland is not fruit, vegetables, or grain, but houses.

Sprawl and Wildlife Habitat

Beyond consequences for agriculture, loss of open space leads to fragmented ecosystems. They then can no longer support the most imperiled wildlife species, which

---

Farming Near Chicago

The Chicago metropolitan area touches and partially overlaps the Southern Wisconsin and Northern Illinois Drift Plain, identified by the American Farmland Trust as the nation's third-most-threatened agricultural resource. Today, more than 80 percent of the Plain is in farms, primarily for the production of feed grains and pasture; fully half the soils are classified as prime or unique. The Plain was responsible for two billion dollars worth of agricultural sales in 1992.[222] The state of Illinois ranks sixth among U.S. states by total agricultural market value, and first in the percentage of farmland that qualifies as prime or unique.[223]

Unfortunately, Illinois also ranks very high (third) among the 50 states in the proportion of land developed in the last decade that was prime or unique farmland (69 percent). It ranks seventh in the total amount of prime and unique farmland converted.[224]

The fastest-developing farm county in the Southern Wisconsin-Northern Illinois Drift Plain is Chicagoland's McHenry,[225] discussed in our first chapter as a focal point for real estate activity. Indeed, McHenry County lost over one-fourth of its farms between 1987 and 1995.[226] Kane and Will Counties, also in the Chicago region, have been identified by the Trust as additional sites with the troubling combination of both high quality farmland and rapid rates of development.[227]

---

require large, undisturbed areas. Instead, scattered development leaves only smaller, more isolated patches suited mainly for the generalist species that are already abundant. The effects are cumulative and worsen over time.[228] Thus, although we have enjoyed success through the Endangered Species Act and other efforts at meeting the needs of certain high-profile species, including those cited earlier in this chapter, we are witnessing a slow decline of others, including songbirds and amphibians.[229]

There is virtually no published literature that addresses directly the relationship between outward development and ecosystems, including wildlife habitat. Indeed, there is apparently no systematic, nationwide monitoring of ecosystems at all.[230]

The circumstantial evidence, however, indicates that there is great cause for concern. Research for the Biological Resources Division of the U.S. Geological Survey reports that 27 ecosystem types have declined by an alarming 98 percent or more since European settlement of North America.[231] Moreover, as of mid-1997 the U.S. Fish and Wildlife Service reported that 1,082 species of plants and animals were listed as threatened and endangered, with another 119 proposed to be listed.[232] The Nature Conservancy, in a comprehensive assessment of some 20,000 species of plants and animals native to the United States, reports that fully a third are "of conservation concern," believed to be extinct, imperiled, or vulnerable. According to the Conservancy, "current extinction rates are conservatively estimated to be at least 10,000 times greater than background levels."[233]

The Conservancy points directly to the culprit:

> The leading cause of imperilment is habitat degradation and destruction. While outright destruction is usually quite obvious, alteration and degradation of sensitive habitats can be subtle, often occurring over large periods of time and escaping notice.[234]

Not all damage to habitat occurs from urban and suburban development, of course. Large-scale, land- and water-intensive activities such as logging, mining, commercial fishing, and damming of rivers have taken a huge collective toll. But sprawl claims its share, both by paving over existing natural systems and by displacing other "rural" activities onto more sensitive lands. Moreover, sprawl causes habitat fragmentation, disrupting migration and breeding patterns even when it does not destroy habitat completely.[235]

Development certainly takes a toll on wetlands, our most biologically rich and ecologically productive forest, marsh, and prairie lands. Wetlands, which by definition are saturated by water or have their surface under water at least part of the year, have been called "the cradle of life" for waterfowl, fisheries, endangered species, countless small birds, mammals, and a wide variety of plant life. Wetlands also catch and hold floodwaters and snow melt, recharge groundwater, and act as natural filters to cleanse water of impurities.[236] About half of the animals and one-third of the plant species listed as endangered or threatened are dependent on wetlands.[237]

As a nation, we have not treated them well. The United States Geological Survey estimates that, on average, we have destroyed more than 60 acres of wetlands *every hour* over a 200-year period from the 1780s to the 1980s. Cumulatively, human activity has taken over 53 percent of the 221 million acres of wetlands that were once found in the lower 48 states. California is estimated to have lost 91 percent of its original wetland resource, and 6 other states—Illinois, Indiana, Iowa, Kentucky, Missouri, and Ohio—have also lost more than 80 percent of their original wetlands.[238] The Sierra Club concludes that it is hardly a coincidence that these states are among those that have suffered the heaviest losses of life and property to flooding in recent years.[239]

While cumulative national wetlands losses have slowed somewhat from the even higher rates of preceding decades, the Fish and Wildlife Service reports that there was a net loss of 117,000 acres per year from 1985 to 1995. The bulk of the loss was claimed by agriculture, but urban and other development accounted for 21 percent of the total loss.[240]

This leaves ample cause for concern, particularly in those states and regions where the wetlands resource has been depleted. Moreover, government ambitions to reverse the current net loss through a combination of restorations and avoidance of new conversions may be hard to realize if current regulatory trends are not reversed. In particular, recent court decisions have limited the federal government's authority to require permits in some areas defined as wetlands under current federal law, and the Army's Corps of Engineers, one of the agencies that oversees the regulatory process, is considering giving blanket authority for such wetland-wrecking activities as parking lots, shopping centers, and industrial parks, so long as each individual conversion is limited to three acres or less.[241] As of this writing, the regulatory environment for wetlands conservation appears unsettled, and new protective incentives and visions are very much needed.

Dryland habitat will need help, too. National overview statistics and trends are not readily attainable, but there are compelling regional stories. In fast-developing Florida, for example, 15 of the state's upland-community ecosystem types are said to be imperiled, some critically; Florida lost 88 percent of its longleaf pine ecosystems between 1936 and 1997.[242] In Pennsylvania, the Pocono till barrens and serpentine barrens, which hold that state's two largest concentrations of land-based endangered species, are now said to be under "severe threat" because they are being opened to suburban development.[243] In the state of Washington, researchers have documented that the amount of the Puget Sound region that is covered by trees has declined 37 percent in the last 24 years, causing billions of dollars' worth of losses in added stormwater runoff and air pollution.[244]

But undoubtedly the poster child for vanishing terrestrial habitat is found in Southern California, where sprawling development has wiped out over 90 percent of the coastal sage ecosystem, identified by the U.S. Fish and Wildlife Service as "one

---

Wildlife and Development Irony

It is ironic that native wildlife habitat should be so severely threatened near San Diego, whose world-class zoo displays and preserves exotic species far from their natural habitats. But worse may be the insult-to-injury situation in the new Highlands Ranch development south of Denver, where "streets are named for endangered species like the spotted owl."[245]

of the most depleted habitat types in the United States."[246] What is left of the coastal sage ecosystem is now badly fragmented and, as a result, the region—particularly around San Diego—has experienced a dramatic loss of native species of birds and small mammals. A rare bird with an unfortunately unheroic name, the coastal California gnatcatcher, is one of those that has suffered most. The gnatcatcher has now lost some three-fourths of its natural habitat, and its remaining population, now dwindled to perhaps 2,500 pairs, is hanging on in shrinking, isolated patches where it is more exposed to predators. It has recently been added to the U.S. Fish and Wildlife Service's list of threatened species.[247]

Indeed, sophisticated mappings of Orange, Riverside, and San Diego counties reveal that, in 1931, there were 180 distinct patches of coastal sage scrub within those counties' borders. By 1990, there were four times as many patches, each of them on average less than one-tenth the average size in 1931. In just a two-year period in the early 1990s, over 7,600 acres of undisturbed scrub were cleared in Orange and San Diego counties, with thousands more zoned and permitted for development.[248] A recent NRDC report describes the impact:

> What are the effects of urban sprawl on coastal sage scrub? If you imagine habitat to be like a living organism, with specialized features and functions that sustain life through constant change, suburbanization would be the equivalent to a shock to the system, exhausting it, lowering its resiliency. An organism whose resiliency falters cannot respond well to environmental stress—in just such a way coastal scrub has become dangerously vulnerable to erosion, fire, and the incursion of exotic plants.[249]

Noted wildlife ecologist Michael Soulé points out that, instead of this disheartening pattern, we should be doing just the opposite: "The best way to maintain wildlife and ecosystem values is to minimize habitat fragmentation." Natural elements of the landscape should be as large as possible and made contiguous. In urbanizing areas, natural corridors for species migration should be preserved.[250]

The Value of Landscape: Does Beauty Matter?
Beyond the farms, wetlands, and wildlife, there is an additional harm that we humans suffer when our countryside—our connection to nature and our sense of place—is gobbled up or cluttered by random development. Although the loss is sometimes hard to quantify, it is real. Writing in *The Washington Post* about a developing area in nearby Maryland, Todd Shields expresses something many of us have felt at one time or another:

The bulldozers came along and flattened a couple of acres of pine trees near Waldorf. As I drove home one evening, I was suddenly disoriented. Where did I miss a turn? Then the lack of trees registered. I realized that it was simply that the picture had been altered, as if someone had pulled down a new backdrop on a movie set.[251]

In fact, preservation of natural beauty and community character provides a range of tangible community benefits. Professor Ewing notes that "functional" open space, if permanent and public, can contain development, link neighborhoods, and buffer incompatible uses; if left natural, it can help control floods, purify runoff, recharge groundwater, support wildlife, and afford scenic views; where made into parks, it can provide gathering places for social interaction, recreation, and civic function. In the case of sprawling development, however, Ewing notes that such open space as there is tends to exist only between and among developments, no longer farmed but also inaccessible to the public, impermanent and without stable, useful public function.[252]

In visual surveys, citizens overwhelmingly prefer natural areas and open space to "cookie cutter" subdivisions.

There is plenty of evidence that we do value the benefits of a pleasant, visually intact landscape. Sixty-three percent of respondents in a recent public opinion poll cited "the beauty of nature" as a reason for wanting to protect the environment.[253] Similarly, a New Jersey survey reported that 78 percent of respondents supported changes in development patterns in order to preserve farmland.[254] In another study, citizens shown slide images gave the lowest rating to images of "cookie cutter" subdivisions and complexes, highway strip development, and shopping plazas with large front parking lots. They responded favorably, however, to pedestrian-oriented downtown areas and village-style housing on narrow lots with modest street setbacks. And they gave the highest visual rating to natural areas, farmland, woodlots, parks and streams.[255]

Aurora and Fort Collins, Colorado, are two cities that have undertaken sophisticated citizen surveys in recent years to assist local planning efforts. Working with visual images and questionnaires designed and administered by Rutgers University's Anton Nelessen, both cities found that the images most preferred by residents consisted largely of natural, open space. Sixty-seven percent of the Aurora respondents agreed that development should be restricted to preserve wetlands, stream corridors, natural vegetation, prairies, grasslands, and scenic vistas. Eighty percent of the Fort Collins respondents supported using public tax revenues to purchase and preserve open space.[256]

There is evidence that rural residents, too, support such measures. As this book goes to publication, emerging work by the American Farmland Trust in three farm counties in northeastern Illinois reveals that over 85 percent of survey respondents believe that saving farmland and open space is either "very" (over 50 percent) or "somewhat" important. Moreover, the preliminary findings suggest that households would be willing to spend hundreds of dollars per year each to fund a purchase of development

Greenfields Gone Around the Nation's Capital

The Washington, DC, metropolitan area, rich in deciduous forest land, is sometimes cited as the greenest in the United States. In the 1980s, however, the area surrounding the nation's capital lost to development some 211,000 acres—an area five times the size of the District of Columbia itself—of farmlands, forests, and wetlands. Between 1990 and 2020, the region is expected to lose an additional 309,000 acres of open space to residential, commercial, and industrial development. This projects to a loss of green land at the astonishing rate of 21 football fields per day.[257]

Much of the damage is being done in nearby Virginia, where Fairfax County, ranging from 5 to 20 miles from downtown Washington, has already lost 40 percent of its tree cover, most of that since 1976.[258] Loudoun County, still farther out than Fairfax and the heart of Virginia's famous "horse country," is projected to lose four football fields a day of pasture, forest, and other open space in the next three decades.[259] At least one study has projected that Fairfax and adjacent Prince William County, the next county out from Washington to the southwest, could be devoid of forest cover by 2020.[260]

The damage is also being done in nearby Maryland, which as a whole lost some 71,000 acres of forest land in just five years between 1985 and 1990.[261] Four "outer" Maryland counties near Washington that are still largely rural are projected to lose 144,000 acres of open space between 1990 and 2020.[262] Fully 84 percent of Maryland's residential development in the 1980s occurred outside of existing or planned water and sewer service areas.[263]

rights program to conserve farmland and open space in their home counties.[264]

Landscape writer Tony Hiss describes still other research documenting strong human preferences for green landscapes with water, winding paths, long and sweeping vistas, and hidden natural places.[265] When asked to describe a favorite childhood place, over 80 percent of University of California planning students cited wild or leftover, undeveloped places "that were never specifically designed."[266] A UNESCO study of children worldwide found that "the hunger for trees is outspoken and seemingly universal."[267]

Low density housing in Montgomery County, Maryland, just north of Washington, DC.

It is important to note that not everyone shares this hunger. Virginia developer Til Hazel, for example, was recently quoted in *The Washington Post*:

> You say 28 acres a day [is being lost], and my answer is: So what? The land is a resource for people to use. . . . Is the goal to save green space so the other guy can look at it?[268]

In addition to the findings with regard to preference, there is evidence that ugly development is not good for us. Research at Texas A & M and the University of Delaware indicates that humans' reactions to visual clutter may include elevated blood pressure, increased muscle tension, and impacts on mood and work performance. Recovery from stress has been measured as faster and more complete when we are exposed to natural outdoor environments. Indeed, research has demonstrated that hospital patients who could see clusters of trees instead of a brick wall outside their windows had shorter post-operative stays and needed fewer painkillers.[269]

Few would dispute that most of what has been plopped down where our greenfields once were is not pleasant to view. While urban and rural areas certainly have their share of ugly buildings and nondescript strip malls, landscape architects note that one is hard pressed to find anything else in many low-density suburban areas.[270] Landscapist Elizabeth Brabec writes:

> Very few communities have escaped the effects of strip development and large-lot subdivisions. It sometimes seems to occur overnight: where there was a farm field yesterday, today stands a Burger King, a 7-Eleven, or a Wal-Mart. The pace has been sometimes fast and sometimes slow, but relentless, to the point where it is often accepted as inevitable.[271]

Indeed, a study indicates that travel along unattractive suburban corridors may make people feel that they are driving for longer periods of time than they actually are. Traffic engineer Walter Kulash has found that individuals driving suburban arterial strips may perceive their driving times to be 23 percent longer than their actual time; in contrast, when driving down traditional neighborhood streets, drivers may perceive their times to be 16 percent *less* than their actual time.[272]

Landscape preservation has economic value as well. Over 130 million Americans enjoy observing, photographing, and feeding wildlife and fish, thus supporting a nature-oriented tourist industry in excess of $14 billion annually.[273] The National Survey of Fishing, Hunting, and Wildlife Associated Recreation found that 77 per-

cent of the U.S. population enjoys some form of wildlife-related recreation, and a 1987 poll sponsored by the President's Commission on Americans Outdoors found that "natural beauty was the single most important criterion for tourists selecting outdoor recreation sites." Travel ranks as the third-largest retail industry in terms of sales and the second-largest private employer.[274] Heritage tourism is one of the fastest-growing sectors. Independent of travel and tourism, proximity to open spaces has been found to raise the value of residential property by as much as a third in some cases, raising property tax revenues as well.[275]

Ugly, nondescript strip malls, large signs for fast food restaurants and gas stations, and stressful traffic have become a fact of life in most suburban communities.

Saving Open Space with Smart Growth

The prescription for saving farmland, wildlife habitat, open space, and the resources they harbor is largely the same as that for reducing traffic, saving energy, and reducing pollution from cars: channel growth more efficiently to be contiguous and occupy less land overall. Brookings economist Anthony Downs claims that shifting new growth from low-density to only moderately higher-density developments can cut open space losses by some 30 percent; where low-density growth can be shifted to high density, the savings can be 50 percent.[276]

Similarly, a comprehensive study for the state of New Jersey examined the likely impacts of a moderate planning scenario that favored channeling both job and housing growth to preferred locations but assumed that a majority of new homes would

The Importance of History

Americans for some time have had a sense that it is important to save pieces of our collective heritage for future generations. Until recently, however, we have focused almost exclusively on preserving specific historic buildings and sites. These are still important, of course, but increasingly we are learning that our heritage embraces much more than just rare, isolated relics: we suffer as a society also when we lose our sense of place—our main streets, neighborhoods, and landscapes—to haphazard development or to neglect because of the movement of investment to ever-new, ever-outward locations.

Take the celebrated example of the Virginia Piedmont, home to the Manassas National Battlefield and countless other Civil War sites, and once the land of Thomas Jefferson, James Monroe, John Marshall, James Madison, and Patrick Henry. Blessed with rolling hills, sweeping vistas, horse farms, and small towns, much of the Piedmont today remains similar in appearance to what it was 100 years ago. It was exactly here, however, beside the Little Bull Run creek and the town of Haymarket (population 483) that the Disney Company decided in 1993—in secret—to build its next large, recreational theme park. To be called Disney's America, the park would have carried a historic theme, in effect replacing a real historic site with a Disneyland facsimile. In the minds of many citizens, even worse than the park itself was the collateral sprawl development that Disney's America would inevitably have generated.[277]

Historians were outraged, and worked with nearby residents, the Piedmont Environmental Council, the National Trust for Historic Preservation, and others to campaign against the development, which the image-conscious company eventually withdrew. Still, because of its place in the path of development sprawling west from Washington, DC, the Piedmont regularly places one or more sites on the National Trust's annual "most endangered" list.[278] That list, unfortunately, also contains sites in many other locations around the country threatened by sprawl.

Even more poignant than the large, well-publicized conflicts, however, is the story of Minnie Johnson, 74, a resident of Howard County, Maryland, in the fast-developing corridor between Baltimore and Washington. As this book was being researched, Johnson was being forced to watch the rise of a $15 million warehouse that will isolate the small cemetery that for more than 100 years has been the resting place for her family, one of the largest African-American families in the county. Pursuant to state law, the cemetery itself will be preserved, but it will soon be surrounded by concrete, with an Interstate highway on one side and the new warehouse on the other. *The Washington Post* reports that hundreds of graves have been ruined or isolated by new development in Howard County alone in the last decade.[279]

remain single-family and detached. The study found that, compared to a "current trend" scenario, the plan would consume 28 percent less farmland, 43 percent less open space of all kinds, and an impressive 80 percent less environmentally fragile land, including valuable forests, steep slopes, and sensitive watersheds, all while accommodating a projected growth of 408,000 new households and 654,000 new jobs over 20 years. The planning scenario was able to do this without consuming any prime farmland whatever, in contrast to some 90,000 acres of prime and "marginal" farmland that would be lost under the current trend.[280]

In California's Central Valley, the American Farmland Trust found that doubling the average density of new growth from three to a moderate six households per acre could save some 561,000 acres of the nation's most productive and threatened farmland and shrink the "zone of conflict" between urban and rural areas from 2.5 to 1.6 million acres. It also could save some $26 billion dollars in direct sales of agricultural products, as well as an additional $41 billion in impacts to agricultural support businesses, by 2040.[281]

We discuss additional measures for saving prime farmland, natural habitat, and scenic beauty in Chapter 5.

Runoff Run Amok

Water has been called the essence of life. We cannot live without it, of course, and an astounding portion of our bodies—as well as our planet—consists of it. What is happening to our water can be a good indicator of what is happening to ourselves.

Although some of the news concerning the health of our nation's water is good, much of it is not. In the United States, we have persistent water-quality problems, many of them directly related to our sprawling late-20th-century development patterns.

The Persistent Challenge of Polluted Runoff

By and large, the enactment of the Clean Water Act, and that law's implementation over more than two decades, constitute an impressive environmental success story.[282] Science writer Robert Griffin, Jr., writing in *EPA Journal*, describes the accomplishment:

> Gross pollution of the nation's rivers, lakes, and coastal waters by sewage and industrial wastes is largely a thing of the past. Fish have returned to waters that were once depleted

of life-giving oxygen. Swimming and other water-contact sports are again permitted in rivers, in lakes, and at ocean beaches that once were closed by health officials.[283]

We would expect Gregg Easterbrook, the environmental optimist, to agree. In *A Moment on the Earth*, Easterbrook recounts a series of impressive stories involving the reduction of key pollutants from some of our nation's most storied waterways, among them the Chesapeake Bay (industrial pollution), Chicago River (sewage), and the Great Lakes (phosphorus).[284] The portion of U.S. river miles that meet Clean Water Act standards has approximately doubled (to 56 percent) since 1970, Easterbrook reports, and virtually all U.S. sewage is now treated before discharge.[285] These are indeed impressive achievements and, as a society, we can take great pride in them.

This does not mean, however, that all is well. Water pollution remains a serious problem in most parts of the country, including the places just mentioned. Various contaminants are still finding their way into the nation's waters, where they degrade ecosystems, pose health hazards, and impair our use of water resources.[286]

The principal obstacle to successful cleanup goes by the bureaucratic name of "nonpoint source" pollution. The phrase was coined to describe contaminated water that runs off from widespread surfaces, and to distinguish these from more specific and localized "point" sources, such as industrial drainage pipes and sewers. As an EPA publication puts it, nonpoint-source pollution occurs "when water runs over land or through the ground, picks up pollutants, and deposits them in surface waters or introduces them into groundwater."[287] Typical

MATTHEW RAIMI

Sedimentation from exposed soils at development sites contributes to water pollution.

nonpoint sources include agriculture, urban runoff, logging operations, large hydroengineering projects that alter water flow patterns, and construction sites.

By its very nature, runoff pollution is much harder to identify precisely and regulate than industrial discharges. Contaminants result not just from a concentrated single activity, such as a manufacturing process, but from a combination of varied activities that take place over wide landscapes as large as hundreds or even thousands of acres. Moreover, the reach of runoff pollution and the damage it causes are profoundly affected by rainfall and other natural precipitation. Therein lies the challenge for those of us who would like to bring it under control: we need management approaches that go beyond the inspection and regulation of individual discharges.

Runoff pollution is now the nation's leading threat to water quality, affecting about 40 percent of our nation's surveyed rivers, lakes, and estuaries.[288] Among the various pollution categories, urban runoff is the second-most prevalent source of impairments to our estuaries, affecting some 46 percent of the impaired estuaries in EPA's *National Water Quality Inventory*. It is tied for third-most-prevalent among sources of impairments to our lakes.[289] The damage is frequently incremental and cumulative, but it also can be acute and severe: the construction phase of new buildings and major land development projects, such as highways, can produce toxic materials and severe sediment loads up to 20 times greater than those experienced from agricultural lands.[290]

Meet the Culprit: Imperviousness

Development changes watersheds dramatically. Natural landscapes, such as forests, wetlands, and grasslands, are typically varied and porous. They trap rainwater and

CHESAPEAKE BAY FOUNDATION

Runoff from roads and other impervious surfaces pollutes streams and degrades watersheds.

snowmelt and filter it into the ground slowly. When there is runoff, it tends to reach receiving waterways gradually.

Cities and suburbs, by contrast, are characterized by large paved or covered surfaces that are impervious to rain. Instead of percolating slowly into the ground, storm water becomes trapped above these surfaces, accumulates, and runs off in large amounts into streams, lakes, and estuaries, picking up pollutants along the way. It is now thoroughly documented that, as the amount of impervious cover increases in a watershed, the velocity and volume of surface runoff increases; flooding, erosion and pollutant loads in receiving waters increase; groundwater recharge and water tables decline; stream beds and flows are altered; and aquatic habitat is impaired. As a result, there is a strong correlation between the amount of imperviousness in a drainage basin and the health of its receiving stream.[291]

The two primary components of urban/suburban impervious cover are rooftops on buildings and paved surfaces for motor vehicles, including roads, driveways, and parking lots. Sidewalks and patios also contribute to the problem. In addition, when soils are disturbed and compacted and especially when they abut roads, driveways, and parking lots, they too can contribute, exhibiting an "edge effect," whereby pollutants such as fertilizers and pesticides used in landscaping migrate to impervious surfaces and join the other forms of polluted runoff that are collected there.[292]

Frequently, we are completely unaware of these consequences. Urban watershed expert Tom Schueler of the Center for Watershed Protection warns that, because the damage done by development is gradual and incremental, involving many separate projects, the impacts of stream and watershed degradation may not manifest themselves fully for many years, after it is too late to reverse the process.[293]

But the consequences can indeed be dramatic. To grasp the impact of impervious surfaces on the volume of stormwater runoff, consider the effects of a one-inch rainstorm on a one-acre natural meadow: typically, much of the water from such a storm would infiltrate into the soil, causing only about 218 cubic feet of runoff, enough to fill a standard-size office to a depth of about two feet. On a one-acre paved parking lot, however, no water could settle into the soil and the storm would cause 3,450 cubic feet of runoff, nearly 16 times that from the natural meadow and enough to fill the standard-size office completely, as well as the two offices next to it.[294]

Along with increased water volume come changes in composition, as contaminants, including sediment, pathogens, nutrients (such as nitrogen and phosphorous), heavy metals, pesticides, and nondegradable debris, are picked up.[295] All told, some 67 toxic pollutants have been detected in runoff from urban areas.[296] Another consequence is "thermal pollution": impervious surfaces, in part because of the absence of trees for shade in paved areas, can reach temperatures in excess of 120 degrees Fahrenheit and raise the temperature of water flowing over them, causing temperatures to rise in receiving waters downstream.[297]

Stream degradation begins as impervious cover in a watershed exceeds 10 percent. This amount of imperviousness is typically achieved by the rooftops, streets, and driveways of even large-lot subdivisions whose density is one dwelling unit per acre or less. If one includes the arterial roadways and commercial parking lots and buildings typically surrounding such subdivisions, the threshold of 10 percent imperviousness in a watershed would be achieved even with much larger lots.[298]

Above 10 percent imperviousness, fish species begin to decline. Brown trout, for example, may disappear altogether at around 10 to 12 percent imperviousness. When the watershed reaches 25 percent imperviousness, as it might with half-acre residential lots coupled with modest convenience shopping and arterial roadways, additional species may disappear.[299] Indeed, at levels above 30 percent imperviousness, a watershed may be considered generally degraded.[300]

To put this in perspective, research indicates that residential subdivisions with one-acre lots may have from 10 to 20 percent impervious cover. Industrial, commercial and shopping center development brings 75 to 95 percent imperviousness. Smaller-lot subdivisions and multifamily housing are typically in between, at 40 to 60 percent imperviousness.[301]

Parking lots are one of the leading causes of runoff in urban and suburban areas.

The consequences of watershed degradation from development have been felt across the country. In the Puget Sound region of Washington state, for example, major floods that were 25-year events now occur annually; "the sponge is full," according to King County analyst Tom Kiney.[302] Similarly, in Akron, Ohio, runoff from residential areas has been estimated at up to 10 times that of pre-development conditions, and runoff from commercial development has been estimated at 18 times that before development.[303] In several Maryland, Pennsylvania, and Virginia watersheds that drain into the Chesapeake Bay, pollution from development has been found to exceed—in some cases dramatically—pollution from industry and agriculture. Even in counties that have enacted stormwater-management regulations, the pace of development is causing pollutant loads to increase.[304]

Indeed, in Fairfax County, Virginia, near Washington, DC, fecal coliform bacteria counts in local streams have tripled in the last two decades and are now three times greater than levels considered safe.[305] *Washington Post* writer Eric Lipton describes the degradation of the county's stream beds:

> Evidence of the damage is everywhere: fallen trees strewn randomly across the wooden lot, a five-foot-deep ditch cut into the stream bed and piles of silt muddying up the bottom of once-clear waters.[306]

Meanwhile, Fairfax County, with streams that drain into the Potomac River and ultimately into the Chesapeake Bay, lacks the financial resources (despite one of the highest per capita incomes in the country) to build flood-control projects necessary to prevent further damage from stormwater.[307] This is the plight of many local jurisdictions.

In addition to the permanent water flow changes inflicted by impervious cover, development sites can cause devastatingly acute consequences while they are under construction. In the new suburban boom town of Cary, North Carolina, for example, sedimentation and contaminants from some 190 active construction sites in 1997 produced a disturbing yellow slick on the Neuse River following a series of heavy rains.[308] Back in the Chesapeake Bay watershed, at least one study has reported that forest land stripped for construction produces 500 to 1,000 times more sediment (25 to 50,000 tons per square mile per year) than the forest that preceded it.[309]

The Pavement Associated with Sprawl

Between the two most important types of urban/suburban impervious cover—rooftops and transportation-related pavement—the latter is decisively more significant. In particular, roads, parking lots, driveways, and sidewalks typically constitute 60 to 70 percent of the total impervious surface in a watershed.[310] Moreover, concentrations of pollutants are higher in transportation runoff than in rooftop runoff, and pollutant loads in streams tend to increase with traffic volume in the watershed. The impacts may be particularly severe in such "hotspots" as vehicle-maintenance facilities and commercial parking lots, which collect both deposits from the atmosphere and high concentrations of pollutants that leak, drip, and wear off from cars and trucks.[311]

Another significant factor is that transportation surfaces, unlike rooftops, tend to be connected and continuous, with driveways leading to streets to roads to parking lots and so on. Such connected surfaces have been found to produce from two to four times the runoff volume of an equivalent amount of disconnected surface.[312]

Commercial parking lots are undoubtedly one of the biggest contributors to impervious surface in urban/suburban watersheds.[313] This is due in part to the common practice at many commercial locations of constructing lots with much more parking capacity than needed, even for peak hours. Vacancy rates in today's retail lots, using the standard practice of four spaces per thousand square feet of retail space, are frequently as high as 60 to 70 percent; some big-box retailers go further and supply five or more spaces per thousand square feet of retail space.[314] An extensive study of local impervious surfaces conducted by the City of Olympia, Washington, concluded that commercial establishments could easily provide adequate parking with a 20 percent or more reduction in lot capacity in most major categories, including retail, offices, restaurants, and multi-family residential units.[315] Even for single-family homes, developers typically provide excessive pavement for parking, with around six and one-half spaces (two in the garage, two in the driveway, and two and a half in the street) per residence.[316]

It is our sprawling growth patterns, of course, that are bringing more and ever-larger parking lots, roadways, and driveways to more and more watersheds. Indeed, in some locations we have been exacerbating the problem in the very name of water quality.

Expansive parking lots characterize most suburban shopping centers and office parks.

This is because well-intentioned planners and developers have essentially mandated sprawl and its adverse impacts by a misplaced reliance on what Schueler calls a "clumsy tool" for protecting watersheds: minimum lot sizes.[317]

Large lots are prescribed for many reasons, some of which go well beyond controlling runoff. In theory, however, they are also thought to reduce impervious cover by reducing the fraction of total surface occupied by a dwelling unit on each lot. In practice, this approach fails with regard to the impact on the watershed as a whole, because it largely ignores the more significant impact of the transportation sector. Because large-lot zoning requires a larger road network to serve a given number of houses, and spreads those houses over a greater number of subwatersheds, it not only usually fails to keep the total impervious cover below the 10 to 15 percent threshold necessary for watershed protection, but it actually increases total imperviousness both within a development and especially throughout a region.[318] Indeed, research shows that large-lot subdivisions increase imperviousness by 10 to 50 percent compared to cluster and traditional town developments with the same number of households, and that they deliver up to three times more sediment into waterways.[319] This is why, according to at least one ranking official of the U.S. Environmental Protection Agency, "managing growth remains the single greatest challenge to the [Chesapeake] Bay's health."[320]

Strategies for Improving Water Quality

Many of the same strategies for efficient growth that can reduce other adverse environmental impacts can also protect water quality. The highest-ranking substantive recommendation of the City of Olympia study was to "establish growth management

The Effect of Air Pollution on Water Quality

Beyond contaminants deposited directly on impervious surfaces, water quality is adversely affected by air pollution from traffic and industrial sources. Airborne nitrogen oxide emissions, derived substantially from vehicle exhaust, are responsible for somewhere between 10 and 40 percent of the Chesapeake Bay's nitrogen buildup, which enriches nutrients that choke out aquatic life.[321]

policies that encourage infill of urban areas and reduce urban sprawl." The authors point out that such policies would reduce the amount of impervious surface per capita, allow rural areas to remain in low-density or resource-based land uses, and require fewer roads and other impervious surfaces region-wide. Specific recommended measures include mixed-use zoning, cluster housing, increased building heights, and use of vacant or underused lots.[322]

Indeed, eight of the nineteen principal recommendations of the Olympia study for reducing imperviousness involve making more efficient use of land. In addition to regional growth management, the list includes the following:

• Providing public transit and other alternative modes of transportation that reduce the need for streets and parking.
• Using narrower residential streets, with reduced but adequate parking opportunities.
• Reducing the need for paved parking spaces by encouraging joint, shared, and co-ordinated parking among business and other parking-lot owners whose demand for spaces peaks at different times of the day or week (e.g., shared lots among churches and weekday workplaces or among nighttime theater operators and daytime offices).
• Using underground or under-the-building parking and multistory parking structures.
• Limiting land clearing on new residential and commercial sites, especially those with sensitive environmental features.
• Using cluster development that minimizes impervious surfaces and allows retention of large undisturbed areas.
• Using taller structures to reduce the size of building "footprints."[323]

Schueler elaborates that, to control imperviousness and promote regional water quality, jurisdictions should concentrate as much development as possible in high-density clusters in some subwatersheds, allowing them to be degraded at 25 to 100 percent imperviousness, in order to prevent other subwatersheds from exceeding the 10 percent maximum essential to protect water quality. In other words, once a watershed

The Water Supply Issue

In addition to its impacts on water quality, unmanaged growth can put a serious strain on water supplies, especially in arid regions like the American West. Private lawn and garden watering, for example, constitutes the largest component of water consumption in many cities. It is one reason why international research has shown that low-density suburbs use up to four to five times as much water as medium-density ones.[324] In Las Vegas, we are now building one of our country's largest and fastest-growing metropolitan areas in a region that receives only four inches of water per year; nevertheless, *The New York Times* reports that Las Vegas promises new water to virtually all new developments and, indeed, is moving aggressively to claim a larger share for itself from the federal government's allocation system for scarce water resources in the West.[325]

(or subwatershed, in Schueler's preferred distinction) has become biologically non-supporting, further development there should be encouraged rather than restricted. Schueler adds that development should not be extended beyond the reach of current water and sewer lines or beyond the capacity of existing wastewater treatment plants.[326]

In addition to changing the shape of development, it is also critical to delineate key natural areas—such as shorelines, wetlands, stream channels, steep slopes, flood-plains, and sensitive habitats—and use buffers and other measures to provide special protection for them. The goal is to take advantage of the natural drainage system as much as possible and to mimic the natural system even in highly developed areas with such measures as small green spaces, landscaping, and use of pervious pavement.[327]

Schueler emphasizes the importance of reducing the impact of parking lots, not only through the measures listed above, but also by making more frequent use of smaller parking stalls and angled stalls that reduce the space required for access lanes.[328] He also recommends a number of practical measures that would reduce the impact of streets, including reduced driveway lengths and smaller but still adequate turn-around areas for cul-de-sacs.[329] A strong advocate of watershed-based planning, Schueler believes we ultimately need "a fundamentally different approach toward development" in order to protect aquatic resources.[330]

Measures like those enumerated above can be expected to have a favorable impact. The introduction of shared parking alone, for example, can reduce the impervious "footprint" of suburban activity centers by as much as 25 percent.[331] On a larger scale, in the comprehensive New Jersey study of planned versus unplanned growth, the state's plan—which included modest increases in residential density in some areas, as well as directing where growth should occur—was predicted to lower pollutants in stormwater runoff by some 4,560 tons per year, a 40 percent reduction over that predicted for a more typical sprawling scenario. Much of the savings would be due to reduced impervious road surface, since road lane miles needed for new growth would be some 30 percent lower under the plan.[332] Similar savings were predicted by a South Carolina study that compared the runoff expected from sprawl development with that expected from a "town" scenario that employed higher residential densities, blended residential and commercial uses, and traditional street and parking configurations.[333]

From Green to Red
The Fiscal Impacts of Sprawl

When it comes to environmental policy, America has been a crisis-driven society. Many, if not all, of our prominent federal and state environmental regulations have been enacted as a result of crisis or disaster: the burning of the Cuyahoga River in Cleveland inspired the Clean Water Act; Love Canal in Niagara Falls, New York, prompted the enactment of the Superfund law governing the cleanup of sites contaminated with hazardous waste;[1] and the oil embargo by certain Middle Eastern countries in 1973 and 1974 resulted in regulations for more fuel-efficient cars, if only with limited results. In some respects, these national emergencies changed our societal perspective on the damaging effects people have on the natural environment.

However, notwithstanding the litany of environmental damage recounted in our previous chapter, there has been no single crisis or event on a national level demanding a change in how and where land development occurs. This is surprising, considering that people so often perceive direct connections between land-use patterns and the quality of life in their communities. For example, many citizens have fought the local siting of unwanted land uses such as landfills, major roadways, electric power lines, and airports, for fear that they will increase noise or pollution, result in public health impacts, or decrease property values. Others have opposed nearby development out of concern about the potential for increased traffic or the degradation of neighborhood amenities. As we have noted, in some cases this opposition has actually contributed to sprawl.

But public concern over land-use decisions has, for the most part, remained local. There has not been a national or, in many cases, even a regional dialogue on the issue of how to control where projects should be located or even what types of development

Land Use and Fiscal Stability

The following headlines are illustrative of the growing awareness that the fiscal stress is related to poor land-use decisions.
- "The Costs of Urban Sprawl Estimated in Billions"[2]
- "Budget Bust Follows Boom in Growth: '80s Suburban Sprawl is Drain on Schools, Services in 1990s"[3]
- "As Exurbs Grow, So Does Burden of Borrowing"[4]
- "Regional Sprawl Linked to Higher Property Taxes"[5]

and growth should occur and where. There has not yet been a collective recognition that a land-use crisis is at hand.[6]

Although few may recognize the land use crisis, many *are* aware that fiscal stress has been brewing in our cities and towns, especially in fast-growing jurisdictions on the fringe of metropolitan areas and in center cities. Every day, statements by public officials and local newspaper articles recount stories of the need to trim municipal budgets, cut services, and raise additional revenue (see box). And there is no question that our inefficient and costly growth patterns contribute to the fiscal stress. As it was put in a 1998 Environmental Protection Agency report, "Many of America's local governments are in the grip of a growing fiscal crisis. . . . Although the details of the story differ, they are linked by one recurring theme: much of the fiscal crisis stems from growth and development that could no longer be sustained."[7]

In this chapter, we discuss how land use affects the costs and fiscal burdens faced by local governments and their taxpayers. We discuss the leading research in the field, as well as several examples of complementary research. And we discuss several techniques being employed by governments to cope with the rising costs associated with sprawl, along with their advantages and shortcomings. We conclude the chapter with some recommended principles for improving communities' fiscal health through smart growth.

Fiscal Stress from Inefficient Growth

There is ample evidence that municipalities across the country are experiencing fiscal strain. Cities large and small, from the rapidly growing southeastern and Sun Belt states to aging industrial regions in the Northeast and Midwest, are all feeling the crunch of providing costly public services with limited fiscal resources. In many places this is occurring despite a booming national economy (such as in the late 1990s when some local governments have enjoyed budget surpluses). The strain is especially evident in fast-growing suburban jurisdictions where, according to Maryland Governor Parris Glendening, "Every new classroom costs $90,000. Every mile of new sewer line costs roughly $200,000. And every single-lane mile of new road costs at least $4 million."[8]

For example, one highly visible symptom may be found in increasing property tax rates being imposed around the country to pay for the rising costs of providing expanded public services. This trend is intensified in rapidly growing areas. For example, in the 10 fastest growing towns in southern Maine, property taxes increased by 43 percent between 1990 and 1995. During the same period, the 10 slowest-growing towns also increased taxes, but only by 27 percent.[9] In rapidly-growing Loudoun County, Virginia, close to Washington, DC, the annual tax rate increased from $0.99 to $1.06 per $100 of value in 1997, and to $1.11 in 1998 in order to pay for new schools and services.[10] Likewise, Prince William County, Virginia, another jurisdiction close to the nation's capital, has one of the highest growth rates and the highest real estate tax rate of any county in Virginia.[11] McHenry County, Illinois, outside of Chicago, increased its gasoline tax in 1998 from two to four cents in order to complete needed road projects caused by rapid growth and was scheduled in 1998 also to increase property taxes by an average of 3.3 percent, the maximum allowed by Illinois law.[12]

In response to the steady rise in property taxes that has accompanied sprawl—coincidentally or not—over the past several decades, many areas have experienced tax "revolts," with the electorate or the state legislature placing limits on the ability of municipal governments to increase property taxes. Following the example of California's Proposition 13 in 1978, which restricted the ability of all that state's local governments to raise taxes, many other states have adopted similar limitations.[13] For example, the Illinois counties around Chicago are now forbidden by state law to raise their tax levies by more than the rate of inflation or 5 percent, whichever is lower, without special voter approval. This cap was imposed in 1991 after several years of double-digit property-tax increases; DuPage increased its tax rates 20 percent in 1987, 15 percent in 1988, and 11 percent in both 1989 and 1990.[14] While citizens' concerns about rapidly escalating taxes are understandable, restrictions like these (and the sentiment behind them) have only compounded the challenges faced by municipal governments attempting to overcome the fiscal stress caused by growth.

A decline in the level of public services in many jurisdictions constitutes further evidence of fiscal stress. Perhaps the best example is the overcrowding of schools, especially in fast-growing areas on the urban fringe that cannot raise revenue fast enough to keep pace with the demand for classrooms. Although, as discussed in chapter one, parents often choose suburban locations precisely for the quality of their school systems, in reality many of them find the systems that they choose are over-crowded, with temporary classrooms, and lacking the financial resources to provide a wide array of extracurricular activities. For example, in Prince William County, Virginia, students cram into more than 100 temporary classroom trailers.[15] In Prince George's County, Maryland, about half the schools exceed capacity.[16] One high school in suburban Chicago has become so large and overcrowded that administrators have lengthened the time between classes to allow students to navigate crowded hallways; they also have transformed every vacant space into classrooms and have had to cut the 48-minute lunch period in half, while extending the time that students eat lunch from 10:30 AM until 2:30 PM.[17] Jurisdictions as geographically diverse as Tampa, New York City, Atlanta, and Denver have all reported overcrowding problems.

Other public services are also feeling the squeeze. The Mt. Prospect Public Library in the northwest suburbs of Chicago, which in the 1980s was the seventh-largest library in Illinois, was reported to be facing fiscal insolvency in 1999 and may face bankruptcy unless new sources of funding are found.[18] When Los Angeles County risked fiscal insolvency in 1995 as a result of a $1.2 billion budget shortfall, the county's chief administrative officer suggested a drastic reduction in services (by 20 percent), the elimination of 18,255 jobs, and the closing of 30 parks, 15 libraries, and one of the busiest hospitals in the nation, the County-USC Medical Center.[19]

The borrowing patterns of many jurisdictions may also provide evidence of fiscal strain. Although there are many reasons for increased borrowing by local governments, including the limits on raising taxes, discussed above, a trend of change in how long-term infrastructure is financed,[20] and a decrease in state and federal infrastructure subsidies, much of this debt is, in fact, incurred to pay for costly infrastructure improvements. The money has to come from somewhere.

There is little doubt that debt is increasing, sharply in some places. For example, in rapidly expanding Howard County, Maryland, in between Baltimore and Washington, DC, debt nearly tripled from $130 million to $384 million between 1987 and 1997; the debt is now $1,650 for each resident.[21] Loudoun County, on the Virginia side of Washington's Capital Beltway, is suffering a similar fate as a result of growth pressures. In 1990, debt payments consumed 3.3 percent of the budget. By 1995, debt payments consumed 6.5 percent and are expected to rise to 10.7 percent in 1999.[22] Further, in Johnson County, Missouri, outside of Kansas City, the combined debt of the county, school districts, cities, community college, and various special districts increased by over 25 percent in a five-year period prior to 1995.[23] In New York City, the government's $34.7 billion in debt amounted in 1998 to $4,400 per person, while the per capita debt in Chicago was around $2,200.[24]

The cost of building new infrastructure is only the beginning. The fiscal strain imposed by growth may only get worse for many jurisdictions due to the high costs of operation and maintenance. Across the country, we focused our resources for the last half-century (and continue to focus them) on constructing a vast network of roads, sewers, schools, power lines, and other facilities necessary to accommodate growth without sufficiently preparing for the time when that network would need to be repaired or replaced. As this infrastructure inevitably ages and deteriorates, we must now pay for maintaining it.

For example, the 1997 Draft Regional Transportation Plan (RTP) for the Los Angeles region states that $37 billion is needed for operation and maintenance of the area's road network between 1996 and 2020.[25] This amount

Maintaining existing infrastructure will reduce the funding available for new roads and transportation facilities.

necessarily will reduce the funding available for new roads and other transportation facilities. The RTP provides an excellent explanation of why this trend is occurring not only in Los Angeles but in many metropolitan areas across the country:

> Historically, the Southern California region has spent a much greater proportion of its revenue on capital—typically around 65 percent—than on operating and maintaining the transportation system. If the system were to be maintained consistent with best practices recommended in most transportation engineering handbooks, it is estimated that about two and a half times the amount currently spent on maintenance would be required. As both new transportation facilities are built and the vast amount of infrastructure put into place over the past several decades continues to age, a greater proportion of the finite amount of revenues will need to be expended on maintaining and operating the system. This, in turn, leaves far fewer dollars available to spend on capital projects from traditional funding sources.[26]

In Kansas City, where there are more freeway miles per person than any other major metropolitan area in the country, the Chamber of Commerce has estimated that repairing the neglected infrastructure will cost more than $2 billion. This is more than $1,250 for each person in the metropolitan area.[27]

To make matters worse, the costs of growth-related infrastructure are sometimes especially wasteful when viewed in the context of a region as a whole. This is because, as metropolitan areas expand, "new" suburban growth is not always new; substantial portions of it may instead be displaced from other parts of the metropolitan area. For example, in Montgomery County, Maryland, even though the county-wide school population *dropped* by 10,000 pupils between 1980 and 1990, 70 new schools were built. During the same period, 68 others were abandoned.[28] This has a damaging effect on a region's economy: cities and inner suburbs must repair and replace aging infrastructure with fewer taxpayers to cover the costs, while newer suburbs must find the resources to pay for costly new infrastructure to support growth. The result of displaced growth is a "lose-lose" combination for both types of jurisdictions.

Research on the Fiscal Costs of Sprawl

Anecdotal evidence that sprawl development imposes fiscal strain is backed strongly by structured research. Beginning in the mid-1950s, studies emerged examining how the costs of providing infrastructure and services varied according to the pattern and density of development. The premise of the argument is intuitively simple: lower-density development translates into more space between houses and businesses and thus requires more infrastructure and time to service each unit. Likewise, "leapfrog" development that skips over undeveloped land, regardless of its compactness, will require more miles of infrastructure and more travel time to provide services. This translates into higher construction and maintenance costs for a variety of services and infrastructure.

Overview of Costs-of-Sprawl Studies

Although there are gaps in the literature and some differences in the order of magnitude of the results, the studies are overwhelmingly consistent in their conclusion that sprawl is a more costly form of development than compact alternatives. Planning where, when, and in what fashion growth occurs can substantially reduce the costs of providing infrastructure and services, as well as reduce the fiscal burdens faced by governments.

According to Robert Burchell and David Listokin of Rutgers University, much of the literature on the topic historically was limited to the relationship between the density of development and the cost of required "on-site" capital improvements.[29] This on-site category includes such necessities as water and sewer pipe, sidewalks, curbs, and subdivision roadways, connecting each dwelling unit to various off-site public facilities. By and large, the studies found that the capital cost per dwelling decreases as the density of development increases, because per-mile or per-foot costs are spread over a larger number of units. [30] For example, Burchell and Listokin state that the cost for sidewalks per dwelling would be cut in half with 50-foot frontages, compared to 100-foot frontages.[31] Despite the fact that such "on-site" infrastructure and services are more costly per unit, they do not necessarily increase capital costs for taxpayers at large because they tend to be paid by the owners of each unit within a development.[32] (Maintenance costs are another matter, as additional research—discussed later in this chapter—has revealed.)

More recent studies have expanded the scope of analysis to include the interrelationships between the pattern and density of development, and to the costs of off-site as well as on-site capital facilities.[33] According to a report prepared by the Congressional Office of Technology Assessment, off-site capital facilities can be divided into three levels. *Neighborhood* costs include collector streets, water distribution lines, sewer collector lines, and recreational facilities. *Community* costs include roads, water and sewer trunk lines, electricity lines, telephone lines, education, emergency services (police, fire, and rescue) and libraries and parks. *Regional* costs include regional roads, central water and sewer treatment, solid waste disposal, and central electricity and telephone facilities.[34] Sprawl development costs more across all three categories because it requires more infrastructure and more travel for service per unit. With more compact, planned growth, on the other hand, the need for new infrastructure and services can be reduced, because growth can be directed to areas with existing service capacity, such as schools with additional classroom space. Where new infrastructure must be built, compact growth requires less of it to serve the same number of new units and also enables economies of scale for some services such as water and wastewater treatment.

Comprehensive Costs-of-Sprawl Studies

While there have been many studies on the costs of providing services to various densities and patterns of development, there are four that are considered landmarks in the field: *The Costs of Sprawl: Environmental and Economic Costs of Alternative Residential Development Patterns at the Urban Fringe,* by the Real Estate Research Corporation[35]; *The Costs of Alternative Development Patterns: A Review of the*

Literature, by James Frank;[36] *The Search for Efficient Growth Patterns,* by James Duncan and Associates;[37] and *Impact Assessment of the New Jersey Interim State Development and Redevelopment Plan,* by the Robert Burchell-led research team at Rutgers University.[38] These studies are complemented by numerous others that both reinforce the conclusions of prior research and add depth to the argument that sprawl is a costly and inefficient pattern of development.

When reviewing costs-of-sprawl studies, especially the four primary reports, it is important to understand that different methodologies have been used and that these differences have affected the results, sometimes dramatically. It is therefore difficult to compare the studies directly and reach a consensus on the exact cost savings that could result from altering our patterns and densities of development. However, the basic conclusions are consistent, as noted by the Office of Technology Assessment: "Though there is a good deal of disagreement on the assumptions and calculations for such estimations, there is general agreement that decreased density leads to increasing public and private development costs."[39]

Real Estate Research Corporation, *The Costs of Sprawl*[40]. One of the earliest and most widely cited studies on the costs of alternative development patterns is *The Costs of Sprawl,* conducted by the Real Estate Research Corporation and commissioned by three federal government agencies (the Council on Environmental Quality, the Department of Housing and Urban Development, and the Environmental Protection Agency) in the early 1970s. This landmark report examined how neighborhood and community costs[41] might be affected by hypothetical changes in development density (from 3 to 30 dwelling units per acre), housing type (ranging from single family homes to high rise apartments), and land-use pattern (i.e., sprawl versus planned growth).[42]

The report concluded that planned growth is less costly than sprawl and that per-unit costs are significantly less at higher densities than at lower densities. According to Frank's summary and critique of the RERC study in *The Costs of Alternative Development Patterns* (see below),[43] neighborhood capital costs, which are usually provided by the developer and paid by the homeowners, vary substantially with the density of development, with costs increasing as density decreases.[44] Publicly provided community infrastructure and services, such as arterial roads and sewer trunk lines, were found to be most affected by the pattern of development, with sprawl being more costly than planned growth.

The Costs of Sprawl has not been without criticism, however. Frank noted that the analysis did not include the cost of providing public or private services required to serve the hypothetical communities studied but located outside their boundaries.[45] If these facilities and services, which include regional roads and water and sewer transmission lines, were included in the analysis, the cost difference between high-density, planned growth and low-density sprawl would likely be much greater than that observed.

On the other hand, Duane Windsor, in a widely cited *Journal of the American Planning Association* article, argued that *The Costs of Sprawl* overstated the benefits of high-density planned growth.[46] Windsor observed, for example, that the study assumed that multi-family dwelling units housed fewer students and thus presented lower school costs than the single-family homes. Although this is typically the case, it skews the results in favor of higher-density developments by ignoring the fact that families with school-age children would have to be accommodated elsewhere. Another criticism is that the study assumed that bypassed (or leapfrogged) land would remain vacant, thereby increasing costs for all residents. In reality, Windsor argues, future developments would fill in some of the bypassed land and lower per-unit costs. Despite these limitations, *The Costs of Sprawl* remains influential and is largely credited with increasing national awareness that low-density sprawl is more costly than higher density patterns of development.

James Frank, ***The Costs of Alternative Development Patterns: A Review of the Literature***[47] This study synthesizes and critiques the major research conducted prior to 1989 (including the landmark *Costs of Sprawl* report by the Real Estate Research Corporation, discussed above). Frank translates the results of the studies and compiles a summary table in equivalent dollar terms comparing the costs of developments at different densities. For each density, costs are broken down into service category (i.e., streets, utilities, and schools), the pattern of development (i.e., contiguous or leapfrog), and the distance from central, or regional, facilities (i.e., employment centers, sewage and water plants, and receiving body of water) (see Table 3-1 for the results of the analysis). Frank's study does not include on-site costs because, as noted, these costs are usually borne by the homeowners in the sale price of the unit.

Frank concludes that the principal factors affecting the cost of providing infrastructure and services are density and lot size, municipal improvement standards, demographic characteristics of the population (i.e., number of school-age children), contiguity of development, distance to central facilities, and size of the urban area. Frank found that the highest capital costs of services per unit are found in the lowest-density areas, while the lowest costs are in the highest density areas:

When all capital costs are totaled... the total cost for low-density [three dwelling units per acre] sprawl [noncontiguous] growth is slightly more than $35,000 [all amounts are in 1987 dollars] per dwelling unit .... Further, if that development is located 10 miles from the sewage treatment plant, the central water source, the receiving body of water, and the major concentration of employment, almost $15,000 per dwelling unit is added to the cost for a total of $48,000 per dwelling.

Costs of infrastructure can be reduced to about $24,000 by locating developments close to central facilities and employment centers... and by including multifamily housing types....[48]

In 1998 dollars, these costs would translate to nearly $69,000 per dwelling for low-density, non-contiguous developments, compared to $34,500 per dwelling for the more contiguous and compact alternative. Thus, the potential savings from compact, contiguous growth are around $34,500 per dwelling unit.

As can be seen in Table 3-1, the relationship between the density and pattern of development and costs also holds true for individual service categories. For example, it cost $18,594 per dwelling unit (again, in 1987 dollars) to provide water and sewer infrastructure to low-density sprawl developments, while the contiguous, mixed housing alternative would cost $6,865—thus saving $11,729 per dwelling unit.[49] Frank's study also found that the capital costs of providing roads for low-density sprawl were $11,474 per dwelling unit (in 1987 dollars), whereas the higher-density alternative cost $6,229, or $5,245 less, per dwelling unit.[50] Updating these findings to 1998 dollars, the savings for compact, contiguous developments would be $16,850 for water and sewer infrastructure and $7,535 for roads.

James Duncan and Associates, *The Search for Efficient Urban Growth Patterns*[51]
Also in 1989, James Duncan and Associates completed a large-scale study for the state of Florida on the public costs of providing services to different development patterns. Duncan analyzed eight actual locations (as opposed to the hypothetical developments studied in previous literature), each larger in size than individual developments and containing a mixture of land uses—either a variety of housing types or, in some cases, a combination of residential and nonresidential land uses. These areas were refined for purposes of the study into five development patterns: scattered (low-density, leapfrog development), contiguous (moderate density and contiguous with existing developments), linear (low density extending out from urban areas along major transportation corridors), satellite (moderate density, mixed use but physically separated from an urban center), and compact (high-density development in a major urban area).

Table 3-1
Capital Costs Per Dwelling Unit
(in 1987 Dollars)

Density and Dwelling Type	Service Category	Neighborhood Costs	COMMUNITY COSTS Contiguous	Leapfrog	COSTS FOR DISTANCE TO REGIONAL SERVICES[a] 5 miles	10 miles
.1 d.u./4 acres (SF)	Streets	24,848	—	—	2,500	5,000
	Utilities	39,951	—	—	4,800	9,600
	Schools[b]	12,813	—	—	NA	NA
1 d.u./acre (SF)	Streets	12,308	—	—	2,500	5,000
	Utilities	19,789	—	—	4,800	9,600
	Schools	12,313	—	—	NA	NA
3 d.u./acre (SF Conventional)	Streets	7,083	—	1,891	2,500	5,000
	Utilities	11,388	—	2,406	4,800	9,600
	Schools	12,313	—	—	NA	NA
5 d.u./acre (SF Clustered)	Streets	6,121	1,405	—	2,500	5,000
	Utilities	7,574	1,279	—	4,800	9,600
	Schools	12,313	—	—	NA	NA
10 d.u./acre (Townhouses)	Streets	4,855	1,930	2,788	2,350	4,700
	Utilities	4,920	1,099	2,231	4,525	9,050
	Schools	10,438	—	—	NA	NA
15 d.u./acre (Garden Apartments)	Streets	3,367	1,930	2,788	2,350	4,700
	Utilities	3,285	1,099	2,231	4,525	9,050
	Schools	10,438	—	—	NA	NA
30 d.u./acre (High-rise Apartments)	Streets	1,843	1,930	2,788	2,000	4,000
	Utilities	1,997	1,099	2,231	3,840	7,680
	Schools	3,786	—	—	NA	NA
12 d.u./acre[c]	Streets	4,653	1,576	2,194	2,350	4,700
	Utilities	5,789	1,076	1,676	4,525	4,700
	Schools	9,860	—	—	NA	NA

d.u. = dwelling unit   SF = single family

[a] Regional services identified by Frank include employment, sewage plant, water plant, and receiving body of water.

[b] *Note:* Frank's calculations of the capital costs of schools were not included in the discussion in this chapter because they were based on the number of pupils, which are found to vary with dwelling unit type.

[c] Mixture of 20 percent each of single-family conventional units, single-family clustered, townhouses, garden apartments, and high-rise apartments.

Source: James E. Frank, *The Costs of Alternative Development Patterns*, Washington, DC: Urban Land Institute, 1989.

Table 3-2
The Relationship Between Development Patterns and Public Facility Costs

Study Area	Urban Form	Cost (in 1989 dollars)	Cost (in 1998 dollars)
Downtown	compact	$ 9,252	$12,177
Southpoint	contiguous	$ 9,767	$12,855
Countryside	contiguous	$12,693	$16,706
Cantonment	scattered	$15,316	$20,158
Tampa Palms	satellite	$15,447	$20,330
University	linear	$16,260	$21,400
Kendall	linear	$16,514	$21,735
Wellington	scattered	$23,960	$31,534
Average		**$14,901**	**$19,612**

(*Note:* Costs for the following services were calculated: roadways, education, wastewater, potable water, solid waste, law enforcement, fire and emergency protection, and parks.)

Source: James Duncan and Associates, *The Search for Efficient Urban Growth Patterns*, Tallahassee, FL: Florida Department of Community Affairs, July 1989.

For each study area, Duncan examined not only the actual capital costs but also the costs of annual operation and maintenance and the total revenues generated.[52]

Duncan found that the pattern of development had a significant impact on public capital and operating costs (see Table 3-2). Costs per dwelling unit varied widely, from $9,252 to $23,960 (in 1989 dollars), and the lowest costs were all found in the compact and contiguous urban forms.[53] Conversely, the highest costs per residential dwelling unit were found in the satellite, linear, and scattered urban forms. In fact, the compact and contiguous forms all had per-unit costs below the average cost of all sites, whereas the scattered, linear, and satellite areas all had costs above the average. The impact of the pattern of development on costs was so great that the cost of servicing Wellington, a scattered development, was more than twice as expensive as servicing the Downtown study area.

The Environmental Protection Agency's Chesapeake Bay Program has observed that the Duncan study was important because it confirmed the more theoretical research of studies like *The Costs of Sprawl*:

> The intuitive insights and theoretical studies on the public infrastructure costs of development [now] had a basis in reality: compact, infill, and higher-density land development was more efficient to serve than scattered, linear, and low-density sprawl development.[54]

Robert Burchell *et al., Impact Assessment of the New Jersey Interim State Development and Redevelopment Plan*[55]   The third major study on the costs of alternative development patterns compared the 20-year projected costs for the state of New Jersey for two alternative, comprehensive growth scenarios—one that would follow a plan to increase densities somewhat and concentrate development around population centers (called IPLAN), and one that would continue the trend of low-density, scattered development (called TREND). This study, which was conducted by a team of researches led by Robert Burchell of Rutgers University, used computer models to estimate the fiscal, economic, and environmental impacts of the two scenarios for the entire state.

One part of this large study calculated the total cost of providing major infrastructure (schools, roads, and water and sewer facilities) for new residential and nonresidential (commercial, industrial, and retail) growth under both the IPLAN and TREND scenarios. The study found that New Jersey could save $1.43 billion (in 1990 dollars) between 1990 and 2010 under the IPLAN scenario— i.e., by planning where, when, and at what density new growth occurs (see Table 3-3).[56] Updated to 1998 dollars, the projected 20-year savings would be an impressive $1.79 billion.

Specifically, the infrastructure analysis found that, over the 20-year planning period, compact development around existing centers (IPLAN) would save the state $699 million in road construction, $561 million in water and sewer utility construction, and $173 million in school construction (all in 1990 dollars)—a total of 9 percent compared to TREND.[57] These savings generally resulted from the inherent efficiencies

Table 3-3
Infrastructure Impacts of Sprawl Versus Planned Development
(in millions of 1990 dollars)

Growth/Development	TREND Development (dollars in millions)	IPLAN Development (dollars in millions)	IPLAN Savings (dollars in millions/pct)	Savings Updated to 1998 Dollars (in millions)
Roads	$ 2,924	$ 2,225	$699 / 23.9%	$ 873
Water/Sewer	$ 7,424	$ 6,863	$561 / 7.6%	$ 700
Schools	$ 5,296	$ 5,123	$173 / 3.3%	$ 216
Total	**$15,644**	**$14,211**	**$1,433 / 9.2%**	**$1,789**

Source: Robert Burchell et al., *Impact Assessment of the New Jersey Interim State Development and Redevelopment Plan. Report II: Research Findings*, Trenton, NJ: New Jersey Office of State Planning, February 20, 1992.

in more compact developments (as described above) and by channeling growth to areas with excess school, road, and water and sewer capacity.

Some Complementary Research

Besides the comprehensive undertakings on the costs of sprawl summarized above, there are numerous more limited reports and studies that address aspects of the relationship between service costs and the density and pattern of development. Because the range of this research—much of it done for individual communities and unpublished—is potentially quite extensive, we have not attempted to be exhaustive in our research or our presentation below. Instead, we summarize only a few that we have found to be particularly relevant to our discussion. These additional studies confirm and, in some cases, expand to new categories the findings of the comprehensive research with regard to the higher costs of sprawl and the potential savings of more compact and contiguous growth.

Studies by the American Farmland Trust The American Farmland Trust (AFT), whose work on farmland loss was cited in chapter two, has conducted numerous studies on the fiscal consequences of development as well. Here, we discuss three that have examined the costs of providing public services and infrastructure to different patterns and densities of development.

First, a 1995 AFT report examined the impact of potential development on local government costs in an 11-county region in California's Central Valley between 1992 and 2040.[58] The report contrasted two growth scenarios—low-density sprawl and a more compact, higher-density alternative—and found that changing the density of development even to only 6 dwelling units per acre and planning where growth occurs could reduce municipal service and infrastructure costs by more than 19 percent or $1.1 billion annually (in 1993 dollars).[59] These savings occur because building at moderately higher average densities would lower capital and operation and maintenance costs for a variety of public services, such as police, parks and recreation, planning and administration, fire protection, roads, and water and sewer service.

The Central Valley study is also noteworthy because it clearly outlines that public costs can be substantially reduced without infringing upon the preferences of many Americans to own a single-family home in the suburbs. As the report states:

> Though higher density may be wise from the standpoint of maintaining Central Valley agriculture, we used six dwelling units per acre because development at this density would not depart significantly from traditional California-style subdivision patterns. It

would consist mostly of single-family detached housing built somewhat closer together within currently designated urban growth areas, with superior urban and landscape design making up for smaller average lot size.[60]

An earlier AFT report focused almost exclusively on the relationship between community density and public costs. This study, which used data from Loudoun County, Virginia, near Washington, DC, compared the costs of public services for 1,000-household hypothetical developments at densities ranging from 1 dwelling unit per five acres to 4.5 dwelling units per acre.[61] This study found that public school transportation costs, public road maintenance costs, and water and sewer operating costs all varied with density.

Of particular interest is the finding that total school transportation costs for a 1,000-unit development at one dwelling unit per five acres would be over five and a half times greater than for the same number of units at 4.5 dwelling units per acre.[62] This large cost difference occurred in part because 93.5 percent of the students would need to be bused to school in the lowest-density development, whereas only 36.1 percent of the students would need to be bused in the 4.5 dwelling units per acre alternative.[63] (Although school transportation costs are generally not a large component of school district spending, these savings could help ease financial problems facing many school districts.) In addition, the study found that public road maintenance costs were more than four and a half times higher in the least dense development than in the most dense, and that water and sewer operating costs were almost three times higher.[64]

The finding on school transportation costs is supported by a third AFT study that examined actual development in three municipalities on the outer fringe of metropolitan Chicago.[65] This study found that annual busing costs for low-density, rural areas ranged from $278 to $405 per student compared to between $44 and $155 per student in the higher density townships.[66] Again, the differences result from the higher percentage of students who require busing and the greater distances that the buses must travel. In addition, this study found a corresponding social cost for students living in rural sprawl areas: time spent on buses. AFT researchers concluded that students in rural areas spend the equivalent of up to 24 school days (159 hours) every year on the bus.[67]

NRDC research on wastewater infrastructure   One cost category that is only now beginning to be examined in depth is that of infrastructure operation and maintenance (O&M). As discussed, most available data examine only initial, capital costs.

Additional Public Safety "Costs" of Low-Density Development

The AFT study in the Chicago region found that, besides the monetary costs of sprawl, low-density, dispersed developments bring other negative impacts, including response times for emergency services that are far longer in low-density rural areas than in higher-density townships.[68] Specifically, the study found:

- Police response times were as much as 600 percent longer.
- Ambulance response times were as much as 50 percent longer.
- Fire response times were as much as 33 percent longer.

Differences in O&M costs can be particularly significant, however, given that the category typically constitutes a majority of most municipalities' annual budgets. They also represent a category in which even "on-site" (within a development, as discussed above) costs are usually borne by the public at large, not just individual homeowners.

To begin to fill this gap in the data, NRDC commissioned research to address the relationship between the density of development and the operation and maintenance of wastewater pipes and related infrastructure. [69] Using data from 10 wastewater systems in the Chicago and Cleveland metropolitan areas, the study found that the density of service connections was the primary indicator of per-unit O&M costs for the systems examined.[70] The least costly land-use patterns were those that minimize the distance over which lines must run to reach the treatment plant and maximize the number of households and jobs served per mile of pipe. In some cases, unit O&M costs for conveyance in low-density service areas were more than twice as high as in the highest-density service areas.[71] Moreover, although this study concentrates on wastewater systems, similar results would be expected for water distribution systems and (as discussed below) perhaps even for the operation and maintenance of other linear infrastructure, such as that for transmission of natural gas and electricity.

Research on private costs   As with public infrastructure and services, the costs of providing private services[72]—such as telecommunications, electricity, natural gas, cable TV, and parcel delivery—should also vary with the pattern and density of development. There is little reported literature on the subject, but what has been published does support the hypothesis.

In particular, a study by R.W. Archer, which was reported in the early 1970s using 1962 data, examined the additional costs of providing services to a 200-acre leapfrog development.[73] The study found that the extra distance required to extend services beyond the pre-existing developed area increased the costs of all services (public and private), as a consequence of the additional infrastructure, travel time, and operation and maintenance required. Private services examined in the study included natural gas, electricity, telecommunications, and commercial delivery, while public services included sanitary sewage, waste collection, fire and police protection, mail delivery, school bus service, and road maintenance. Although the Archer study is dated, its findings remain instructive as general indicators of how sprawl affects the costs of a range of service types.

There are also references in the literature to density-related cost differentials for electric power and telephone service. In particular, a staff report by the California Public Utilities Commission found that the cost of constructing and operating electric utility infrastructure is more expensive per unit in low-density rural areas than in higher-density urban areas.[74] According to the report, despite the fact that the initial capital cost of providing infrastructure to urban areas can be more expensive per mile, the overall cost of serving rural areas is 10 to 25 percent higher because "the large distances between customers make rural distribution more expensive than urban distribution."[75] Likewise, "cost differences [of 10 to 25 percent] are suggested by the available data for operation and maintenance expenses, residential customer access equipment, and meter reading expenses."[76] Although the report does not differentiate between urban and suburban areas, the implication is clear that, in general, higher-density areas are less expensive to serve than lower-density ones. With respect to telephone service, a representative of a regional Bell operating company has said that, compared to the central business district, it costs twice as much to service households in the rest of the city and approximately ten times as much to service households on the fringe of metropolitan areas.[77]

Dissenting Opinions

Despite this body of work, the University of Southern California's Peter Gordon and Harry Richardson, who also dismiss the environmental research on the impacts of sprawl,[78] argue that the higher infrastructure and service costs of sprawl have "never been adequately demonstrated."[79] In particular, they cite research by Richard Peiser and Helen Ladd for the proposition that sprawl is not more costly than high-density development.

The works of Peiser and Ladd are, in fact, worth mentioning. In a 1984 study, Peiser estimated the infrastructure costs for two hypothetical developments in Houston, Texas—one "planned" and one "unplanned"—and found only a 1 to 3 percent difference in total costs in favor of planned growth.[80] In another study, Peiser found that, contrary to the common belief, leapfrog development actually promotes higher densities than if the land had not been skipped over.[81] Gordon and Richardson also discuss a 1992 study by Ladd and state that, "except within a range of very low densities, public service costs for traffic management, waste collection and disposal, and crime control increase with higher densities." [82] Ladd's study also reached another interesting conclusion, however: in support of our point that fast-growing areas experience fiscal stress, Ladd found that rapid population growth may place a "fiscal burden on established residents in the form of lower service levels."[83]

In response to Gordon and Richardson, Professor Reid Ewing concludes that "within a normal range of urban-suburban densities, per capita infrastructure costs almost certainly fall as densities rise. However, at the density extremes, there could be some surprises."[84] For example, at very low, rural densities, there are low costs because fewer public services are provided (e.g., costs decrease with the use of septic systems, wells, and open drainage). Conversely, costs at very high densities tend to be higher due to special needs (e.g., more traffic lights and sidewalks). Ewing likens the cost curve to an equivalence sign (~) that starts low, rises, dips, and then rises again. In other words, Ewing concludes that it is the typical densities of urban sprawl that are far more costly in terms of public services than the typical smart-growth alternatives and, by implication, that moving from sprawl to moderate densities produces the greatest incremental benefits.[85]

Paying for Sprawl: We All Bear the Burden

There is little question that, in the abstract, sprawl costs more. But the dynamic is far from abstract for local governments and their taxpaying constituents. We now turn to a second set of important—and far more concrete—questions: Who pays the increased costs of providing infrastructure and services to sprawling developments? Are those who benefit from costly development paying for the impact of their decisions? Or is inefficient growth subsidized from other revenue sources, including other geographic areas and other land-use types?

This section shows that sprawling developments rarely generate sufficient revenues from taxes and traditional fees to cover the costs of providing services. Impact fees help to some degree but not enough. In the end, new growth is subsidized by a variety of sources, including other users of public services and infrastructure and other taxpayers.

Farmland, Forests, and Open Space Reduce Fiscal Burdens

According to the American Farmland Trust, farmland and open space actually provide a fiscal surplus for municipal governments.[86] Although residential developments generate more total revenues than farmland, forests, and open space, residential land uses also require more in public services. The net result is that residential development produces a fiscal loss, while farmland, forest, and open space produce a fiscal benefit. This is a strong argument for managing growth and maintaining open spaces, including farmland.

Traditional Tax Revenues Often Fall Short

Very few residential developments "pay for themselves" through traditional sources of revenue (e.g., by generating sufficient funds from property taxes to meet the public costs required to serve them).[87] This is true for both sprawling and more efficient forms of development. And, in individual cases, the extent to which a development can pay for itself through traditional revenue mechanisms depends on a range of quirks and variables, including the local tax and rate structure, the value of housing, and the age and capacity of existing infrastructure.

It is still possible to make some generalizations, however. And the thrust of available evidence indicates that, even when revenues are factored into the equation, sprawl development fares more poorly than do compact and contiguous developments.

The American Farmland Trust, whose work was cited earlier, has conducted extensive research comparing the net fiscal impacts of different land uses (i.e., residential, commercial/industrial, and farmland/forests/open space) on the budgets of local governments. Specifically, AFT has analyzed data from at least 40 communities in the Northeast and Midwest during the last decade, using the information to create a ratio of annual revenues generated from property taxes to annual expenditures for each land-use type. In a summary of this work, AFT concludes that residential land uses generally cost more in services than they generate in property taxes, and that they are subsidized by commercial and industrial developments and by farmland, forests, and open space. [88] Specifically, AFT finds that the average revenue-to-cost ratio is 1:1.11 for residential development (for every $1 in revenue, the developments cost $1.11 in services). Meanwhile, the ratios are much more favorable for commercial and industrial land uses (1:0.29) and for farmland, forests, and open space (1:0.31).[89]

Consistent with the AFT research, Duncan's study of eight Florida communities also compared the revenues to the costs of providing public services in each community.[90] As Table 3-4 shows, the only development pattern with a revenue-to-cost ratio of greater than 1.00 (that is, the development generated more revenues than costs) was a contiguous one. The remainder of the developments in the sample all generated

more costs than revenues. However, the highest ratios within this category were urban forms that are more compact and more centrally located. All of the sprawl developments exhibited below-average revenue-to-cost ratios, while the compact, higher density forms exhibited higher-than-average ratios.

Finally, the Burchell-led study of New Jersey, which compared TREND (or sprawl) with IPLAN (or planned growth), calculated the net fiscal impacts (revenues compared with costs) on the budgets of municipalities and school districts for the entire state. For each scenario, the fiscal model calculated the total revenues expected from property taxes and other traditional revenue sources and compared the total to the capital and operating costs of municipalities and school districts.

Farmland and open space produce fiscal benefits for local governments.

The model predicted a surplus under both scenarios when school costs were excluded and a deficit for both when school budgets were considered. However, it found that IPLAN had a much better annual fiscal outcome than TREND for both municipalities and school districts. In particular, over the 20-year period, New Jersey municipal governments would receive a net fiscal surplus under IPLAN of $502 million per year (all figures are in 1990 dollars) compared with a net fiscal surplus of only $390 million under TREND—a difference of $112 million per year ($2.2 billion dollars over 20 years) in favor of more compact, planned growth.[91]

For school districts, the study found that the annual fiscal deficit under the TREND scenario would be $1.084 billion, compared to $798 million under the IPLAN scenario—a difference of $286 million per year.[92] Combining the budgets of municipal governments and school districts produces nearly a $400 million annual comparative benefit (eight billion dollars over 20 years) in favor of IPLAN over the study horizon.[93]

Before leaving this part of the discussion, we should also note briefly that, while new suburban residential growth almost always costs more than it pays back, there is some research concluding the opposite with respect to inner-city neighborhoods. In particular, University of Illinois at Chicago researchers Joseph Persky and Wim

Table 3-4
The Relationship Between Development Patterns and Revenue-to-Cost Ratios

Area	Urban Form	Revenue:Cost Ratio
Southpoint	contiguous	1.36
Downtown	compact	0.90
Countryside	contiguous	0.78
Kendall	linear	0.62
Tampa Palms	satellite	0.45
University	linear	0.43
Wellington	scattered	0.43
Cantonment	scattered	0.41
		Average: 0.68

Source: James Duncan and Associates, *The Search for Efficient Urban Growth Patterns*, Tallahassee, FL: Florida Department of Community Affairs, July 1989. (As found in Office of Technology Assessment, Congress of the United States, *The Technological Reshaping of Metropolitan America*, Publication No. OTA-ETI-643, Washington, DC: U.S. Government Printing Office, September 1995.)

Wiewel have estimated that each new middle-income household that moves to the outer suburbs creates a public cost of between $900 and $1,500 per year, while similar new households in the inner city actually contribute between $600 and $800 per year.[94] Persky and Wiewel conclude that "locating a household in the suburbs as opposed to the central city costs society on net between $1,500 and $2,300 per year."[95]

Impact Fees: A Step in the Right Direction

Based in part on the realization that most new residential developments place a strain on the fiscal capacity of local governments, many communities now impose one-time, lump-sum "impact fees" on developers to pay the costs of providing capital infrastructure. These fees are designed to cover or mitigate the initial costs of new or expanded public facilities required to serve a specific development. In this way, impact fees are directly tied to the impacts of growth and, as such, they do help defray some of the high public costs discussed above. However, as observed by the American Planning Association, impact fees are not a "panacea" to fund capital improvements and do not stop inefficient growth.[96]

The incidence of use of impact fees, as well as their structure, varies greatly among jurisdictions. The American Planning Association notes that their most widespread use is for water and sewer facilities, parks, and roads. Some jurisdictions, however, are also charging impact fees for schools, libraries, public safety, and other public facilities.[97]

In most jurisdictions, the fee structure varies according to the type of unit and the expected impact. For residential developments, single-family homes are usually charged the highest rate, followed by townhouses and then apartments. Some jurisdictions go even further by developing complex calculations that include the number of bedrooms or the square footage of the unit in order to better align the impact of each with the amount of the fee. For example, Dade County, Florida, created a sliding scale based on local, state, and national socioeconomic data that showed that larger housing units generally have a greater number of school-age children.[98] Nationally, the amount of the impact fee varies greatly by jurisdiction but, in some locations, it can reach as high as $20,000 to $30,000 per dwelling unit.[99]

Despite their obvious benefits as fiscal tools, impact fees do not (and perhaps cannot) cover many of the costs imposed by sprawl development. For example, the amount of the fee is usually derived from individual unit size and does not vary according to the location or pattern of development.[100] In a review of how impact fees are employed, James Frank and Paul Downing report that "less than 3 percent of sewer impact fees and 5 percent of fire impact fees vary by location,"[101] while Frank writes that "the costs associated with distance from central facilities... are almost completely ignored in pricing schemes like impact fees."[102] As a result, according to Frank and Downing, "the impact fee cannot operate to discourage development at locations that are expensive to serve."[103]

Another problem is that most impact fees do not even attempt to recover certain important cost categories. Most important, impact fees are generally designed to address only capital facilities and "cannot be used to cover the staggering costs of maintenance and repairing the existing infrastructure."[104] These costs, as discussed above, constitute the majority of most local governments' budgets and can increase dramatically as developments become more sprawling. Another problem is that impact fees are frequently not designed to meet the costs of arterial roads and trunk lines for infrastructure located outside a new development but necessary because of it. This is in part because courts have imposed strict legal criteria requiring that, in order for a fee to be upheld, the proponents must prove the need for new infrastructure, that the fee is proportional to the need, and that the new development will benefit from the use of the fee.[105] Out of fear of litigation by landowners over the assumptions and methods of fee calculations, some local governments dramatically reduce the amount; Anne Arundel County, Maryland, for example, reportedly halved the amount of an originally proposed fee to "insulate the bill from legal actions."[106]

User Fees

Many homeowners are familiar with the user fees charged for some types of public and private services and infrastructure. These fees, typically collected for specific services or activities such as water and sewer service, are helpful too in recovering public costs. They often contain hidden inequities, however, because they usually are based on average cost pricing. Under this system, each user pays the same per-unit cost (e.g., the same price per cubic foot of water or per kilowatt hour of electricity consumed) regardless of differences in the cost of providing service to different locations and forms of development.

On the surface, average cost pricing enjoys the advantage of simplicity and appears to be equitable because fees are spread evenly among all users. However, the method obscures dramatic differences in the cost of providing service that vary by the pattern and density of development, as discussed above. The result is a subsidy of households and businesses in costly-to-serve areas by those located in areas with below-average costs. Typically, the subsidy flows to lower-density, scattered developments from higher-density, urban, and contiguous developments and, in some cases, to the rich from the poor.

Some evidence of this phenomenon has been reported in an examination of the Twin Cities region of Minnesota by Thomas J. Luce, Barbara L. Lukermann, and Herbert Mohring of the Hubert H. Humphrey Institute of Public Affairs.[107] According to the researchers, average cost pricing causes customers in the central cities of that region to pay over $6 million more each year in sewage fees than they receive in sewage services. Put another way, each Minneapolis city household subsidizes the sewer system by $19 per year and each Saint Paul city household by $25 per year. Meanwhile, in the growing suburbs, households receive a subsidy of between $10 and $126 per household, with some of the highest subsidies going to the wealthier suburbs.[108] Although these figures are not high when viewed in isolation, they are compounded in context. Given the range of services whose costs vary with the form of development but whose rate structures are uniform—sewage, water, electricity, natural gas, telephone, cable television, postage, and parcel delivery, etc.—the cumulative, per-household subsidy is potentially quite substantial.

An examination of water rates in Cleveland, Ohio, by NRDC sheds additional light on the relationship between user fees and the cost of providing utility service.[109] In particular, the Cleveland Division of Water (CDOW), the regional water supplier for the Cleveland metropolitan area, is one of the few utility systems in the United States that has developed a system of geographic zone-based user rates. Outlying customers pay more under CDOW's rate structure, which is intended to take into account the higher costs of pumping water to customers located at higher elevations. (It is a bit of a coincidence that, in greater Cleveland, outlying customers also are at higher elevations.) In order to consider whether the zones are fairly based, a rough analysis (included alongside NRDC's more detailed evaluation of wastewater infrastructure, described above) compared in-city and out-of-city costs, along with in-city and out-of-city rate differentials. The analysis found that the rates generally do correspond to approximate differences between the costs of providing water to city customers and the higher costs of pumping water to suburban customers. In this sense, the CDOW's geographic, zone-based user rates represent a step in the right direction toward redressing inequities inherent in single-rate systems that serve areas with differing service costs.

The analysis also found, however, that CDOW's geographic, zone-based user rates do not attempt to recover—nor do they inadvertently recover—the differences in costs attributable to neighborhood density. Because these differences can be substantial, as the studies summarized above show, it is likely that customers in more compact neighborhoods (both city and suburban) within the Cleveland water service area are continuing to subsidize those customers living in more sprawling areas, even with the geographic, zone-based rates. The study notes that the rate structure, although better than most, may continue to harbor a subsidy of higher-income customers because lower-income households tend to live in older, higher-density areas.

Subsidy of Residential Development by Commercial Land Uses

There is a common belief among local governments that, contrary to the situation with respect to residential neighborhoods, the revenues generated from commercial land uses have only positive fiscal benefits and may be used to offset the high costs of providing public services to residential developments. This belief is reinforced by a widely accepted "fiscal hierarchy" that ranks various types of commercial and residential facilities based on a comparison of revenues versus costs. The hierarchy, perhaps most closely associated with the Rutgers University researchers Robert Burchell and David Listokin, who also conducted the New Jersey study discussed at length in this chapter, attempts to consider "the absolute level of revenues paired against the array of costs (public safety, public works, education, and the like) that are generated by the various [categories of] land uses."[110] The rankings (which do not consider the impact of location or neighborhood density) range from office parks and industrial development, said to generate the most favorable ratio of revenues to costs, to mobile homes, said to generate the least. In general, the fiscal hierarchy holds that nonresidential developments typically generate more revenue than they cost in services.

Most types of residential land uses are said to produce a fiscal deficit, either for municipal governments, school districts, or both.

However, in many ways the fiscal hierarchy is an insufficiently sophisticated—and perhaps overly optimistic—predictor of the revenue-generating potential of different land uses. By the mid-1990s, the traditional fiscal hierarchy had begun to fall out of favor because *most* land use types were increasingly found to be fiscally inefficient, and because of a greater understanding of the complex interrelationships among land use types. Although there still may be a hierarchy, it has shifted downward so that most development types may now require more in public costs than they generate in revenue.[111]

Unfortunately, these nuances are not well understood or appreciated by many local governments. As a result, many local governments still aggressively seek commercial and industrial developments to subsidize the negative fiscal impacts of residential developments. For example, the planning goals of Howard County, Maryland, state that commercial property should account for 25 percent of the county's tax base because these developments provide revenue without adding students to the school system.[112] The expected revenue gains have created a situation where jurisdictions entice these land uses with tax breaks and other incentives, as we discussed above in chapter one.

In fact, there are major problems with attracting nonresidential developments to subsidize residential growth. First, several studies have questioned the assumption that nonresidential development produces a fiscal boon for local governments. A 1991 study by the DuPage County, Illinois, Development Department found that, between 1986 and 1989, areas of the county with significant nonresidential development experienced a *greater* increase in taxes than did areas without nonresidential development.[113]

Although the increase could not be attributed directly to any one factor, part of the answer may lie in the complex interrelationships between residential and nonresidential land uses. In particular, commercial development may create a demand for additional nearby residential development which, as discussed earlier, brings a fiscal drain that offsets the benefits. In response, local governments may seek to attract still more commercial development to offset the costs of providing public services to the just-attracted residential developments. The result is a vicious cycle whereby many jurisdictions are constantly failing in their attempt to pay for residential growth with nonresidential development. It is not surprising that the Rocky Mountain Institute uses a quote from *Alice In Wonderland* to describe this fiscal tail-chasing: "The hurrier I go, the behinder I get."[114]

Similar conclusions were reached in a Montgomery County, Maryland, study that examined the fiscal impacts of both business developments and the employees' residences associated with them.[115] The study found that business activities alone did indeed produce positive net fiscal impacts. However, when employee residences were included in the calculation of fiscal impacts, the positive impacts were greatly reduced to the point where some land use types resulted in a net fiscal deficit.

A related problem is that, even if a business development does produce a positive fiscal benefit for one community, it may have the opposite effect on neighboring communities. Studies have shown that employment growth increases the population in both the host community and its neighbors. William Oakland of Tulane University and William Testa of the Federal Reserve Bank of Chicago examined the effect of business development on tax rates across jurisdictional lines and concluded the following:

> Economic development activities of one's neighbors can have significant implications for one's own residential development. And if it is the case that residential growth is accompanied by costly fiscal consequences, then business development in a neighboring community has been found to indirectly place added pressure on residential property tax rates.[116]

Any potential revenue gains from business development will be further reduced, of course, if the jurisdiction has attracted the development using tax breaks and other fiscal incentives. Examples from across the country are abundant. Princess Cruise Lines, for example, was offered an incentive package that would absolve the company of paying business taxes for at least 15 years if it moved its headquarters to the city of Santa Clarita, California.[117] Packard Bell was offered a $5 million tax break and a $26 million loan to relocate in Sacramento, California.[118] In 1995, Palm Beach County, Florida, planned to offer $7.8 million in cash and incentives for businesses that started up or expanded in the county.[119] And in Erie County, New York, a state tax exemption designed to keep or attract businesses has been said to cost county taxpayers $132.33 million; some observers have contended that, in Erie County, many of the businesses cashing in on the tax break—such as gas stations and fast food restaurants—might have stayed or located in the area even without the incentives.[120]

Finally, the competition for commercial and industrial developments may diminish collective fiscal resources attainable within a region as a whole, since luring businesses from central cities to suburbs or from one suburb to another may cause some jurisdictions to forgo revenues even while enriching others.[121] According to Deborah

Stone, executive director of the Metropolitan Planning Council in Chicago, the competition "can be a drain if scarce resources, through the granting of incentives, are used simply to compete for a piece of a regional economic development pie that does not actually grow larger."[122] The only true winners in these circumstances are the businesses that receive the tax breaks.

Reversing the Fiscal Drain with Smart Growth

So what can we do to reverse our fiscally detrimental land use habits?

First, we must recognize that the cost of providing public services to low-density, sprawl developments contributes to the growing fiscal stress among governments. Study after study has shown that increasing the distance over which service and infrastructure must travel increases costs. The greatest cost savings come from reducing the total amount of linear infrastructure, especially roads and water and sewer lines, required to serve a given number of households or businesses. One synthesis of several studies concluded that directing growth to areas with existing infrastructure and modestly increasing the density of development could reduce the total capital costs for roads by 25 percent and water and sewer infrastructure by 15 percent.[123] Other research has put the savings even higher—up to 60 percent for roads and 40 percent for water and sewer lines.[124] School capital costs can also be reduced by targeting growth to areas where schools have excess capacity. And the savings will only begin with capital costs, since operating and maintenance savings will continue to produce benefits over time from smart-growth communities.

Second, governments should conduct more sophisticated fiscal impact analyses of proposals for new development. All too often in current practice, the costs of different development patterns are calculated—if at all—without looking at a complete range of public and private service costs related to new developments. For example, the focus of fiscal impact inquiries usually does not fully account for the costs of operating and maintaining required services and infrastructure into the future, even though such costs constitute the majority of local governments' annual budgets. Such studies also universally ignore the effect on citizens of increased costs of providing private services, such as telecommunications, cable television, and electricity, even though the available evidence shows that these services also vary by the density and pattern of development and additional costs may ultimately be subsidized by existing citizens and businesses within a community. These constituents deserve to know that sprawl can lead to rate increases for them, not just those living on the fringe.

Third, where subsidies for sprawl are suspected, they should be identified and eliminated, perhaps through more sophisticated and equitable application of financing mechanisms, such as impact fees that vary by the cost of providing services and variable utility rate structures. This is true wherever subsidies exist, whether within public or private service systems. For subsidies that are hidden by average cost pricing systems, the argument is especially compelling because in many locations subsidies may be paid by inner-city, lower-income residents who can least afford them.

Fourth, state, county, and local governments must recognize that a strategy of attracting commercial developments to offset the high costs of providing services to residential developments does not always produce positive fiscal impacts.

Finally, we must recognize that "new" growth in suburban areas is particularly costly and inefficient when people and businesses move within a metropolitan region from built-up areas to previously undeveloped ones. These new areas require new buildings, infrastructure, and services, all at high costs to taxpayers; meanwhile, vacated buildings, infrastructure, and services are allowed to decay. From a regional standpoint, a more economically sound strategy is to fix what we already have and target development to already built-up areas or to locations adjacent to existing development. This will require a far greater level of regional cooperation for the collective benefit of all jurisdictions.

There Go the Neighborhoods
Sprawl and the Quality of Life

The preceding chapters describe how ever-outward, expanding development undermines the health of our ecosystems, the robustness of our economy, and the fiscal bottom line of our governments—information that typically dominates policy debates over "the impacts of sprawl." With this mountain of damning evidence, one might expect to see an all-out war on the forces that encourage sprawl development.

So why hasn't this happened? The stock explanation is disarmingly simple: "a lot of people like fringe development."[1] Among many local decision makers, there is a widespread perception that the construction of suburban housing—even in the most distant, sprawled-out areas—provides people with a decent place to live and work. Defenders of sprawl often invoke this argument, as some developers did in criticizing a recent analysis of current trends in land use by the Sierra Club: "[It] panders to a constituency more interested in stopping growth than improving the quality of urban life."[2]

Of course, the debate over sprawl is fraught with complexities and nuances, but this rather simple assumption lies at the heart of the battle. For example, in a recent "Special Issue on Sprawl," *Builder* magazine editorializes that, "Granted, we're developing land faster than the population is growing....Granted, new development puts pressure on communities to provide schools, roads, sewers, and other services. Granted, certain land in this country needs to be preserved....But the nation still needs housing, especially affordable housing....And the most affordable place to build homes is often on the suburban fringe, where land is cheapest."[3] In other words, despite the environmental and fiscal consequences, some people are convinced that the socioeconomic benefits associated with inexpensive housing justify sprawl development.

117

But is this type of growth in fact synonymous with a good "quality of life"? This chapter assesses how living in low-density sprawl affects the day-to-day lives of people, the well-being of households, and the social fabric within neighborhoods. The discussion is divided into four parts. First, we recount some of the social forces that have led to sprawl. Second, we examine how sprawl development has affected the viability of existing communities, such as nearby urban centers. Next, we examine the social problems associated with living in sprawl. Finally, we summarize the social rationale for replacing sprawl with smart growth. In short, this chapter explores the human dimensions of the land transformation, suburban migration, and economic shifts, to determine whether the benefits of sprawl are worth it and whether there are smarter ways to grow.

Is Sprawl a Social Imperative?

As we have noted before, this book is much more about the consequences of inefficient growth patterns than it is about their causes. Nonetheless, we believe it useful to supplement chapter one's brief review of the reasons why with an observation here that, historically, many of the reasons have been social in nature.

In particular, social concerns explicitly drove many of the original calls for suburban development, partly through theories of city planning championed by landscape architects like Frederick Law Olmsted, Ebenezer Howard, and A. R. Sennett.[4] Their visions of integrated neighborhood parks, lower residential densities, and tree-lined streets were largely responses to overcrowding, pollution, and other social problems associated with the cities of their day.

By the 1920s, suburban development was already well under way in the United States, fueled by rising automobile ownership and decreasing home construction costs.[5] Generous federal subsidies, for mortgages, transportation infrastructure, and the extension of public services, were designed to aid this trend. Historical accounts demonstrate that the push for suburbanization was an open, almost universally applauded effort that gained unstoppable momentum. As Jane Jacobs writes in her landmark book, *The Death and Life of Great American Cities*:

> The idea of diverting huge sums of money to thin suburban growth *at the expense of starving city districts* was no invention of the mortgage lenders. . . . It originated with high-minded social thinkers. By the 1930's, when the [Federal Housing Admin-

istration's] methods for stimulating suburban growth were worked out, virtually every wise man of government—from right to left—was in favor of the objectives....A few years previously, Herbert Hoover had opened the first White House Conference on Housing with a polemic against the moral inferiority of cities and a panegyric on the moral virtues of simple cottages, small towns and grass. At an opposite political pole, Rexford G. Tugwell, the federal administrator responsible for the New Deal's Green Belt demonstration suburbs, explained, "My idea is to go just outside centers of population, pick up cheap land, build a whole community and entice people into it. Then go back into the cities and tear down whole slums and make parks of them."[6] (author's emphasis)

These sentiments were held not only by august men in Washington, but also by local authorities. In *The Power Broker*, Robert Caro recounts how Robert Moses, who aggressively created a public works empire and built much of New York City's infrastructure, started off as a youthful idealist, hell-bent on improving living conditions in communities through massive public works projects.[7] According to historian Jon Teaford, a variety of factors contributed to this collective mission, not the least of which was a period of "arrested urban development" that had gripped American cities throughout the Great Depression and the Second World War.[8] During this time, Teaford argues, "A tourist visiting New York City, Chicago, Philadelphia or Boston in 1931 who returned fourteen years later would find few changes in the cityscape." Following this period of low investment, the combination of awful urban living conditions, substandard housing (often in the form of makeshift tenements), and demand for housing for returning soldiers drove the social urgency to find a way to provide people with better places to live.

On the Road

Advertisements often promoted suburban life and the car culture.

Of course, there were a few dissenters. As Witold Rybczynski argues in *City Life*, numerous civic-minded groups attempted to preserve urban neighborhoods, stanch the flow of people migrating to the suburbs, and protect residential areas from the wrecking ball.[9] But such organizing efforts were often met with indifference, even scorn, as illustrated in Charles Bowden and Lew Kreinberg's neighborhood history of Chicago, *Street Signs Chicago: Neighborhood and Other Illusions of Big-City Life*:

> Some looked at the slums, at the filth, at the babble of tongues, the madness of the street alive with burning fires of Europe, and imagined neighborhoods, settlement houses, communities waiting, yearning to be born. They thought a dash of education, or a new ordinance, or a new alderman, or prayer would unite the masses and end the horror. Their dream was crushed by out-migration of the district's inhabitants and the constant replenishment of poor people with yet new, poorer people, the replacement of one strange tongue with another and another.[10]

Instead, many planners promoted visions of suburban development inspired primarily by the "garden city" models popularized through Sennett's work. These plans, first featured in advertisements for "streetcar suburbs," typically included main street commercial districts, parks, good transportation access, and single-family homes. To this day, many Americans long for this mix of attributes. In this light, the initial motivations behind mortgage incentives, highway funding, and other subsidies for suburban development appear to be well-intentioned. However, as the development of housing stock in the suburbs unfolded, many merely found vast tracts of cheap housing without the parks, downtowns, and inviting streetscapes that were so treasured. But they came anyway. In droves.

What Got Left Behind in the Suburban Exodus

Within a few decades, the United States had been transformed from a nation of city dwellers to one of suburbanites. Census figures show that at the end of World War II, roughly 70 percent of the U.S. population lived in central cities. As noted in chapter one, within four decades that figure had dropped to less than 40 percent.[11]

Some attribute the rate of American suburbanization to the affordability of the automobile, the low costs of construction, and post-war housing needs. However, this demographic shift was not just a result of market forces. Households were also encouraged to move to the suburbs by a variety of public programs, as noted above. Meanwhile, in the private sector, automobile manufacturers and real estate developers were quick to capitalize on these factors in their advertising, which typically portrayed dreamy images of suburban life and car culture.[12] What was not portrayed, however, was the effect that mass suburbanization had on the people who were left behind or, for that matter, its effect on the loss of community for those making the move.

Communities Crippled by Road Construction

In older urban areas, neighborhoods were carved up and plowed through to make room for the new roadways built to provide access to suburban locations. Numerous accounts document the way these corridors of pavement displaced families, divided communities, and created physical barriers between neighborhoods, commercial areas, and other activity centers.

Indeed, many urban freeways were deliberately planned to run through low-income neighborhoods. Their construction was viewed as a win-win-win strategy of employing demolition and highway construction workers, providing access to growing suburban areas, and eliminating "urban blight."[13] In effect, highway agencies were practicing their own program of urban renewal.

During the first decade of Interstate highway construction, 335,000 homes were razed, forcing families to look elsewhere for housing. As sociologist David Hodge notes, these households rarely received any compensation

Urban highways, such as this one in Boston, cut through existing neighborhoods and displaced families and businesses.

from highway agencies. During this period, "relocation assistance was negligible; displaced households were simply forced to absorb fiscal and psychic costs."[14] Only after the 1970 Relocation Assistance Program was initiated was there any degree of standardization for compensating displaced households and businesses. Even so, numerous studies indicate that money for destroyed homes often did not enable households to attain the same level of housing satisfaction.[15] Similarly, many relocated businesses found it difficult to maintain their customer base.[16]

In many cases, the "urban blight" targeted by the new road construction simply meant African-American communities—often thriving ones. A great body of work shows that urban freeways destroyed the hearts of African-American communities in the South Bronx, Nashville, Austin, Los Angeles, Durham, and nearly every medium to large American city.[17] In the South Bronx, for example, Robert Caro describes the planning of the Cross Bronx Expressway as an almost openly racist act.[18] Commenting on freeway construction through the African-American community of Hayti in Durham, NC, the Federal Highway Administration once dismissed displacement problems as "short-term adverse effects on man's environment."[19]

In Tennessee, plans for the construction of Interstate 40 were in fact redrawn to route the highway through the flourishing Jefferson Street corridor, home to roughly 80 percent of Nashville's African American-owned businesses. Not only did the construction of I-40 destroy this commercial district; it also demolished 650 homes and 27 apartment buildings while erecting physical barriers separating the city's largest African-American universities: Fisk University, Tennessee A&I University, and Meharry Medical College.[20]

Today, these roadways represent not only barriers to interaction but also conveyors of traffic, bringing noise, vibration, air pollution, eyesores, threats to public safety, and other detractions to existing communities. Grassroots environmental justice organizations such as West Harlem Environmental Action in New York City, PODER in Austin, Texas, Alternatives for Community and Environment in Roxbury, Massachusetts, and Air, Inc., in East Boston have actively protested injustices in highway building that resulted in heavy truck and car traffic, the siting of bus depots and truck transfer stations, and air pollution "hot spots" (areas of concentrated emissions) in low-income and minority communities.[21] Citing public health studies on childhood asthma in central cities, Clark Atlanta University professor Robert Bullard argues that the high incidence of tailpipe pollutants in urban areas constitutes evidence that suburban-serving freeways have significant negative impacts on inner-city neighborhoods, yet offer little benefit in return.[22]

Inner-City Disinvestment and Abandonment

Roadway construction to the suburbs was intended to enable people to live farther away from central city jobs, guaranteeing easy access to central business districts without requiring people to live near them. This had a "draining" effect on the wealth, resources, and spirit of central cities because the residential migration to the suburbs was soon followed by shopping and employment opportunities. Harvard professor William Julius Wilson argues that the forces of suburbanization "became part of a vicious cycle of metropolitan change and relocation. The flight of the more affluent families to the suburbs has meant that the central cities are becoming increasingly the domain of the poor and the stable working class."[23]

Perhaps the most alarming impact of urban outmigration is what Wilson calls "concentration effects." These effects are exhibited by poverty-stricken neighborhoods that do not possess the stable, working-class population necessary to maintain economic opportunities, local commerce, and decent living conditions. This concentration of poverty tends to isolate residents from mainstream society, making it increasingly difficult for them to have access to jobs, educational opportunities, medical services, and other prerequisites for a higher standard of living.[24]

While not using the term, some of today's political and spiritual leaders are concerned about concentration effects. Archbishop Anthony Pilla of the Catholic Diocese of Cleveland, for example, echoed Wilson's sentiments when he argued that "the poor and minorities have been isolated in concentrations that severely limit opportunities for a decent and secure life."[25] And Maryland Governor Parris Glendening recently lamented: "As residents and employers flee to the suburbs, they leave behind boarded-up storefronts, the jobless poor, higher welfare caseloads, and increased crime."[26] In 1960, central cities contained one-third of the nation's poor; in 1990, the central-city share had climbed to one-half, even though the central-city share of total population was only around 30 percent.[27]

These draining effects are also felt by businesses remaining in center cities and in smaller towns. Local "mom-and-pop" businesses have been seriously affected by the explosion of discount retailing (discussed above in chapter one) that accompanies sprawl—superstores, commercial strips, and malls located along major roadways—taking advantage of cheap land, cheap energy, cheap labor, and generous local tax breaks and incentives. A 1995 article in the *Kansas City Star* discussed the ways in which Interstate 70 dramatically changed the character of small towns after malls and discount outlets sprang up along its route. One long-time resident explained that "[the highway] killed our old downtown," arguing that it lost grocery stores, a cobbler, the bank, and other businesses because of competition from these superstores.[28]

CONSTANCE BEAUMONT

Abandoned buildings, such as this one in Spokane, Washington, are a consequence of inner-city disinvestment.

Research collected by Constance Beaumont of the National Trust for Historic Preservation provides quantitative evidence for this phenomenon.[29] For example, Beaumont reports that Wal-Mart stores in Iowa generated roughly $20 million in annual profit on average, but also that such profits were associated with an average $11 million loss in sales in adjacent downtown areas. Towns as far as 20 miles away experienced net sales losses of 19.2 percent.[30] She also cites research in Hagerstown, Maryland, and Plattsburgh, New York, that found a 31 percent decline in downtown retail sales and a 32 percent decline in downtown commercial property values, respectively, as a result of exurban competition.[31]

Predictably, the long-term effect of the transfer of economic activity and affluence to increasingly distant suburban locations is a diminished tax base and a sustained cycle of decline in many older communities. Research on "fiscal capacity," which refers to a municipality's ability to collect tax revenues, control the cost of its services, and maintain outside funding from state and federal sources, indicates that this disinvestment is both a cause and an effect of sprawl.[32] As municipalities lose their ability to maintain local services and tax revenues, they lose the qualities that people value in their locational decisions.[33] As already noted, those who are left behind tend to be of low income; as an area's income base declines further, additional poor people arrive to take advantage of declining rents. Once this decline has been established, it is increasingly difficult to attract new investors willing to take a risk on uplifting depressed communities, especially communities of color.[34]

Ironically, some of the fastest-growing and most sprawling suburbs are also suffering from decreased fiscal capacity. As chapter three highlighted, providing public services—such as roads, water and sewer facilities, and schools—to low-density, leapfrog development is significantly more costly than providing services to central cities and compact, higher-density suburbs. As a result, many fast-growing, sprawling areas are themselves increasingly saddled with high taxes and low levels of public service. It would appear that few, if any, jurisdictions' fiscal capacities have actually been improved by current patterns of development.

Isolation from Job Opportunities

There is no question that the draining of investment and economic activity to the fringe also means that residents of declining urban and inner-ring suburban neighborhoods have far fewer job opportunities. Unfortunately, the highways that provide access to sprawling areas and open the doors to economic development provide little help to the urban poor who cannot afford to own cars and cannot take transit because routes and service schedules often do not serve suburban workplaces well.

The separation of jobs from potential employees is called "spatial mismatch" in the academic and transit literature, which began discussing the subject in the 1960s and now provides a solid empirical base of supporting research.[35] Today, spatial mismatch debates are framed by recent reform efforts to find employment for welfare recipients following the passage of the Personal Responsibility and Work Opportunity Act of 1996. Unfortunately, most candidates for moving from welfare to work do not live close to available jobs. Instead, three-quarters of welfare recipients live either in center cities or rural areas, with urban poverty growing at the most rapid rate.

As discussed in chapter one, however, job openings are now overwhelmingly located in suburban areas. In some regions (Chicago, Cleveland, Dayton, Detroit, Greensboro, Louisville), suburban job growth accounted for 100 percent of overall metropolitan job growth during the first half of the 1980s.[36] In the greater Baltimore metropolitan area, overall employment rose by 7 percent between 1980 and 1985, while central city jobs declined by 8 percent. In Philadelphia, the central city unemployment rate is over 10 percent, while its suburban unemployment rate hovers at only 3 percent.[37]

Most efforts to provide access to jobs for potential employees now on welfare revolve around improving public transit service to suburban job locations.[38] While these efforts certainly have value, they are hampered by the fact that suburban jobs are increasingly located in areas that lack the population and activity densities that justify transit routes. Researchers at Case Western Reserve University, for example, found that only 8 to 15 percent of transit-dependent welfare recipients in inner-city Cleveland can reach jobs within 43 minutes.[39] In Boston, researchers studying entry-level job openings determined that no potential employers in the region's high-growth areas could be reached by welfare recipients using transit within a 30-minute commute, and only 14 percent could be reached within an hour.[40] In the Atlanta area, researchers have found that less than half of that region's entry-level jobs are located within a quarter-mile of a public transit route, and that almost no employment opportunities are accessible to transit in the jobs-rich Cobb and Gwinnett counties (3.9 and 2.1 percent, respectively).[41]

Another result of disinvestment, which only adds to the challenge of providing transit service to the working poor, is the tendency for suburban transit services to be better supported and funded than services for urban low-income areas. For example, UCLA professor Brian Taylor recently found that California operating-subsidy-allocation formulae heavily favored suburban transit services over urban ones, largely because of political factors.[42] Sociologist David Hodge presents similar findings with regard to the Seattle METRO transit system.[43] In recent years, civil rights cases have been launched against transit agencies in Los Angeles, New York City and Macon, Georgia, each charging discriminatory practices against low-income populations and people of color.[44]

These spatial and public transit dilemmas have generated great concern about continued metropolitan expansion among the nation's political leaders, Republicans and Democrats alike. The lack of reliable mobility choices especially hurts people who are trying to balance job demands with family responsibilities. For adults seeking to improve their financial situation, this can mean juggling day care, education, training, work (often shift work) and other duties, all of which require individuals to be assiduously prompt, with only poor transportation choices.

Communities Stuck in Place

Although this book argues that urban reinvestment is a prerequisite to addressing these ills, others have argued for an opposite solution to spatial mismatch and other inner-city problems: just get people to move out to the suburbs. While there is evidence that enabling low-income families to secure affordable housing in suburban locations does improve their standard of living and overall opportunities for jobs, education, and services, achieving this is not so easy.[45] (It is also not desirable, for the environmental and economic reasons discussed in our earlier chapters.) There is a long record of discrimination in zoning and mortgage lending practices that have barred low-income people and people of color from those communities.[46]

With respect to zoning, in particular, there is ample evidence that suburban jurisdictions have enacted exclusionary measures that inhibit the movement of low-income people and people of color to their communities.[47] Indeed, the instruments of exclusion often are also the instruments of sprawl, such as minimum lot sizes (which drive purchase prices higher) and the prohibition of multi-family housing units.[48] Some of these have been challenged in court: the well-known Mount Laurel cases in New Jersey, for example, challenged exclusionary zoning practices and eventually led to state legislation that resulted in the construction of roughly 15,000 affordable housing units.[49]

In addition, regardless of location, lending practices continue to present obstacles to the American dream for poor families, especially people of color. The Housing Discrimination Study conducted by the U.S. Department of Housing and Urban Development in 1989, for example, found that mortgage lenders were nearly twice as likely to reject African-American applicants as they were to reject similarly qualified white applicants.[50] The continuing plague of housing discrimination was also exposed in a 1992 study by the Federal Reserve Bank of Boston. Analyzing Home Mortgage Disclosure Act data, the study found that minority applicants had a 50 percent greater chance of getting their mortgage loan applications rejected than did comparable white applicants. [51]

The Spread of "Urban" Problems

Traditional thinking about suburbanization holds that sprawl is not just a form of development but also a process of moving away from urban ills. Much of this chapter supports that proposition. It is not so simple, however: problems once regarded as "urban" are now spreading to the suburbs, some of which are now experiencing their own cycle of decline and abandonment. While this continual movement of households to regions progressively farther from urban cores is easy to understand, it also generates significant social costs.[52]

In his book *Metropolitics*, Minnesota State Representative Myron Orfield presents maps showing how living conditions have changed over time within sprawling metropolitan areas.[53] In addition to showing the simple geographic progression of land development, he has demonstrated that problems such as unemployment, poor educational performance, and crime have spread from central city neighborhoods to inner-ring suburbs. With regard to Chicago, for example, Orfield notes that in 1991 9 suburbs had higher crime rates than that of Chicago proper, and 40 had rates above the regional average.[54]

In keeping with earlier theories of white flight, Orfield contends that the destabilizing effect of increasing poverty on schools and communities generates a flight of middle-class families (and the tax revenues they provide) at the same time these households are needed the most. Ironically, the new areas to which the middle class flees often lack the capacity to handle their arrival, and public services there decline as well. These migration patterns tend to inflict harms on regions as a whole, as infrastructure becomes more expensive to maintain, urban problems spread, and vital centers deteriorate.[55] The pattern of outward expansion leading to enlarged areas of economic and social abandonment in inner suburbs has been explicated also by Professor Tom Bier of Cleveland State University.[56]

Orfield and Bier are part of a vanguard of politicians and academics who are beginning to realize that avoiding or escaping these "urban" problems, once found mainly in center cities, is not a simple matter of moving to the next stable suburb. Rather, it is a matter of understanding and accepting the fact that the health of all jurisdictions is dependent on the health of the entire metropolitan area.

The Quality of Life on the Fringe

Our review of sprawl's social impacts on inner cities and older communities invites the question of whether outer suburbia lives up to its promises of affordable housing and a good quality of life for its own residents. There is little doubt that many

Americans like living in the outer reaches of metropolitan areas and would live nowhere else. But an examination of this issue reveals that suburbs—especially sprawling ones—have their own set of social problems.[57]

Many of these problems, of course, have been discussed in our preceding chapters: there are strong quality-of-life dimensions to such phenomena as dramatically increased traffic congestion, the isolation of residences from workplaces and shopping, the absence of facilities for walking, the health impacts of air and water pollution, rising taxes, and the stress resulting from nonsensical, ugly surroundings, to name a few. In a sense, these contributors or manifestations of environmental and fiscal problems are inherently "social" as well.[58] We revisit a few of these here, in the context of their impacts on individuals, and cite some additional impacts as well.

Sprawl and Community

One of the most common criticisms of fringe development concerns their deleterious effect on the sense of "belonging" and "social fabric" necessary to a feeling of community.[59] A helpful definition of these factors is offered by planner Stephen Cochrun, who contends that "People who have a strong sense of community feel like they belong in their neighborhoods, they believe they exert some control over what happens in their neighborhoods, while also feeling influenced by what happens in them, and they believe that their needs can be met through the collective capabilities of their neighborhoods."[60] While this factor is one of the most difficult to quantify, it also represents the cornerstone for a vast grouping of related impacts, including social alienation, increased stress, and a lack of civic engagement.[61]

The design of many suburban areas discourages interaction among residents and can be isolating for children and the elderly

The most common observation is that the design—and frequent chaos—of sprawl discourages interaction among residents. We noted in chapter one, for example, that many edge cities exhibit a lack of political cohesion and relatively few civic and cultural institutions to provide a unifying force. Cul-de-sac street design prevents individual developments from connecting with each other and, in some cases, walls and gates are erected for the very purpose of isolating developments from the outside world.

These factors, coupled with low residential densities and the lack of neighborhood stores, force people to leave their communities for basic shopping errands, social visits, and work. Since automobile travel is often the only means of achieving this, suburban residents tend to interact with their neighbors mainly through their windshields—a decidedly anti-social form of human interaction.[62] The relative absence of pedestrian activity is often identified as a threat to community cohesion, because walking is conducive to chance encounters and the creation of informal relationships within communities.[63]

Several researchers have documented this phenomenon. For example, in the 1980s psychologist Thomas Glynn developed psychological tools for assessing community cohesion,[64] allowing subsequent researchers using his techniques to demonstrate a relationship between the built environment and social fabric. A study by researchers Jack Nasar and David Julian used Glynn's methodology to evaluate a variety of neighborhoods in northwestern Columbus, Ohio, and determined that residents of mixed-use neighborhoods exhibited significantly greater sense of community than people who lived in single-use (i.e., only residential) areas.[65]

Other researchers extend this theory to the creation of formal social organizations. Urban planner William Shore, for example, argues that the lack of social connections in low-density suburbs hinders the creation of civic groups centered around common interests, such as the arts, sports, and music.[66] A number of other investigations seem to substantiate this view. Journalist and social observer Nicholas Lemann, for example, studied the Chicago suburb of Naperville and found that the creation of civic organizations was thwarted by the high turnover rate of its citizens.[67]

Driving All the Time—or Not

The lack of "community" in many outer suburbs is, in part, a result of our increasing dependence on automobiles. But it is hardly the only one. In chapter two, we described the dramatic increase in traffic volume that has accompanied the rapid geographic expansion of our metropolitan regions—as was noted there, traffic has essentially doubled in 20 years. While the implications for our environment have been profound, so too have been the implications for our social lives. In this section, we note a few of them.

Time scarcity and soccer moms As discussed in chapter two, there has been an increase over the past several decades in both the length of commutes and in overall time spent driving. Indeed, between 1983 and 1995, the average commute time increased by 14 percent and commute trip lengths rose by 37 percent.[68] According to a recent market research survey, Americans now spend roughly one out of eight waking hours in their cars.[69] Because drive time allows little other productive activity and greatly restricts meaningful social interaction, the additional time spent driving eats directly into leisure and professional time.[70]

This translates into "time scarcity," a term used to identify the stress associated with balancing work and personal responsibilities. Moreover, it is hardly comforting that the use of car phones and the increased popularity of "talking books" indicate strong consumer demand for ways to use their increased driving time productively: a recent study found that cellular phone use while driving, in particular, increases the risk of accidents by four to five times because it reduces drivers' ability to maneuver their vehicles and react to potential hazards.[71]

Studies of travel patterns and time-budget allocation have found that these demands are the greatest on working mothers.[72] The plight of so-called "soccer moms," for example, stems from the fact that many women not only hold full-time jobs but also perform more child care and household duties than their spouses. This requires women to make more automobile trips.[73] The 1995 Nationwide Personal Transportation Survey found that, while 45.5 percent of trips made by women tend to be family or personal errands, only 37 percent of men's trips are devoted to such tasks.[74] Further, a regional study in Washington, DC, found that women are twice as likely to take charge of family or personal errands as their male counterparts, and that men are much more likely to frequent bars and restaurants after work.[75]

According to Professor Sandra Rosenbloom of the University of Arizona, "Most women, and most women with children, are in the labor force, generally retaining substantial childcare and domestic obligations in addition to their jobs. At the same time, a growing number have also assumed duties for aging parents and in-laws."[76] Because fringe living forces most of these responsibilities to be met by driving automobiles longer and longer distances, the inevitable result is stress, fatigue, and less time with family.

Driver stress and aggressive driving   A wealth of research has been conducted on the stress induced by driving, especially under congested stop-and-go conditions for extended periods of time. A group of California psychologists, for example, found that congestion had major negative impacts on worker absenteeism, professional fulfillment, and overall health. These conditions, which included chest pains, high blood pressure, frustration, and dejection, were also shown to spill over into personal and family time.[77] A separate study, which examined stress levels of 600 nurses, found that those commuting by car exhibited much higher levels of stress than those traveling by transit when commute times were equal.[78]

The newest concern about such stress levels is that frustration over long commutes and gridlock has spawned violence on the nation's roads. This phenomenon, known as "aggressive driving," has been identified by federal, state, and local authorities as a serious threat to public health and safety, resulting in numerous initiatives to reduce its impact. The federal Department of Transportation's National Highway Traffic Safety Administration estimates that as many as one-third of traffic crashes, and roughly two-thirds of fatalities, are at least partially the result of such behavior. As NHTSA Administrator Ricardo Martinez recently testified, such behavior is partly caused by increased congestion levels and travel in metropolitan areas.[79]

Traffic congestion increases stress among drivers and vehicle occupants.

Personal transportation costs   Supporters of new suburban development contend that its combined impacts on society are minimal relative to its economic benefits, such as lower land prices and cheaper consumer goods at discount stores. Furthermore, some research suggests that individuals who live in suburban areas tend to exhibit a greater sense of economic well-being than their rural or urban counterparts.[80] But critics allege that the economic benefits of sprawl are overrated, partly because they do not consider externalities and indirect out-of-pocket costs.[81] Certainly, it is unfair to compare the average economic health of households living in suburban areas with those living in urban or rural areas, because suburban communities do not have comparable concentrations of low-income individuals.

In any event, recent research indicates that fringe development's low-density, single-use form is a double-edged sword in terms of monetary costs. While homes in such areas may tend to be relatively less expensive per square foot of space, transportation costs are typically much higher, because residents must make long trips exclusively by automobile, and thus tend to own and maintain more cars per person and per household. A study being conducted by a partnership of national non-profit organizations in conjunction with Fannie Mae, the national mortgage-lending institution, indicates that households located in auto-dependent areas spend a great deal more on transportation than households in "location-efficient" areas (i.e., areas that are compact, walkable, have a mix of uses, and are well served by transit).[82] For

Figure 4-1
Average Annual Household Expenditures by Major Category
Source: Bureau of Labor Statistics, U.S. Department of Labor, "Consumer Expenditures in 1996," Washington, DC: U.S. Department of Labor, 1998, USDL-98-415

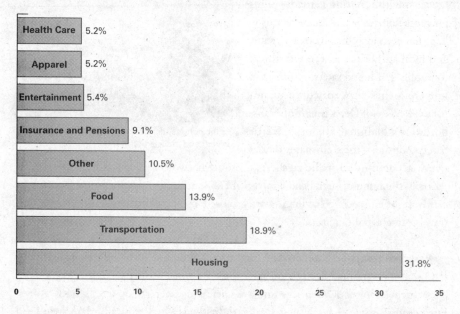

example, households located in compact, transit-rich neighborhoods in Chicago have been found to spend roughly $380 per month on transportation; their counterparts in sprawling, automobile-dependent locations in that region spend about $662 per month.[83]

The primary difference is the high cost of purchasing, maintaining, and operating cars. The American Automobile Association estimates that these costs amount to more than $6,700 per year for a new car, which on average carries a sticker price of $20,000.[84] Other research on U.S. consumer expenditures shows that households in metropolitan areas that invest heavily in building new highways spend a greater proportion of disposable income—well over one-fifth of all consumer expenditures—on transportation than areas that invest heavily in transit.[85] So, while residents of low-density suburbs may believe they are saving money on consumer goods and lower-cost housing, other big-ticket items appear to wipe out much of the savings.

The nondrivers left behind　In addition to claiming time, fueling stress, and costing money, the lack of real transportation choices in outer suburbia has a particularly negative impact on those who cannot drive, including the elderly, people with disabilities, low-income individuals, and youths.[86] Socially, this lack of opportunity has the effect of isolating nondrivers, preventing them from experiencing a diversity of people, places, and activities, and alienating them from mainstream society. It is an especially difficult problem to solve, given that sprawling areas are typically not dense enough to support frequent mass-transit service and lack pedestrian- and bicycle-friendly environs.[87]

Indeed, without transit services and opportunities to walk safely to nearby destinations, non-drivers must depend on families or friends, or costly taxi service, to give them rides—or else remain homebound. This is the plight of many older people, nearly ten million of whom do not drive.[88] The Nationwide Personal Transportation Survey found that 52.5 percent of people in the 65 to 74 age category, and 76.1 percent of people 75 or older didn't take any trips on the survey day.[89] Without access to the outside world, the physical and emotional health of elderly people suffers, as does the overall quality of their lives.

Figure 4-2
Relationship Between Auto Ownership and Neighborhood Density

Source: John Holtzclaw, "Using Residential Patterns and Transit to Decrease Auto Dependence and Costs, "San Francisco: Natural Resources Defense Council, 1994, p. 18.

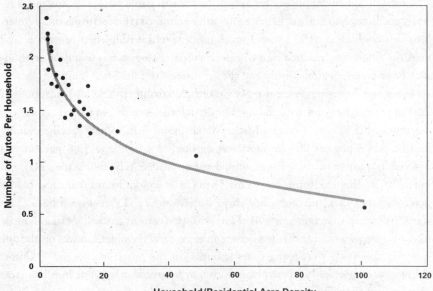

Young people are also affected. Too young to drive yet too old to want to stay home, adolescents often do not live close enough to friends and acquaintances to visit with great frequency unless they are driven by their parents or other "chauffeurs." And even when youths have better mobility, some research suggests that they might not have enough places to go or activities to keep them busy. The idle time that youths spend hanging out in public areas—often shopping malls and parking lots—is cited as a contributor to juvenile crime and mischief.

The Perception and Reality of Crime

One of the most powerful forces behind the suburban exodus has been the belief that there is more crime in urban areas. The belief is not groundless, given that residents of suburban areas do enjoy a degree of greater freedom from criminal attacks than their urban counterparts (albeit not as much as rural residents). According to surveys on crime, however, suburban and rural residents tend to greatly overestimate the risks of urban crime by as much as an order of magnitude.[90] For example, residents of two Minnesota counties believed their risk of victimization in urban areas was up to six times their actual likelihood.[91] In reality, the FBI Uniform Crime Report indicates that the difference between urban and suburban areas is not that great: criminal activity in the suburbs is 51.8 crimes per 1000, compared with 67.6 in urban areas.[92]

Certainly, urban density per se has little to do with crime rates. The Australian researchers Peter Newman and Jeffrey Kenworthy examined crime statistics in 26 American metropolitan areas and found no significant relationships between crime and density.[93] Moreover, research by environmental psychologists has found no relationship between population density and the seriousness of individual crimes.[94]

Minnesota State Representative Myron Orfield attributes these misperceptions at least in part to the popular media, specifically television news programs.[95] A national study by the Rocky Mountain Media Watch found that, on one specific evening in 1995, 28.5 percent of local news was devoted to crime, and 53.8 percent was devoted to stories of war, crime, and disaster—collectively called the "mayhem index."[96] Another study, this one in the Twin Cities region, found that there is a 71 percent chance that one of the first three stories on local TV news will be a crime story.[97] The result, according to Orfield, is that "perceptions harden, social and racial tensions increase, and the division between the city and the older suburbs on the one side and the newly developing outer suburbs on the other accelerates."[98] Unfortunately, as exaggerated as these perceptions may be, aversion to crime in urban areas continues to contribute heavily to people's locational decisions.[99]

The Societal Rationale for Smart Growth

As we first wrote in chapter one, even those who express a preference for suburban living do not necessarily wish for the kinds of low-density, single-use, sterile, and auto-dependent living, working, and shopping environments that they are getting. Indeed, consumers are beginning to demand neighborhoods that possess town centers and encourage more walking, social interactions, and "community." In response to these trends, some developers have begun to co-opt images of old-fashioned neighborhoods by using these terms in their advertising rhetoric. If enough smart developers catch on, soon home buyers will have more choices between the old-mold sprawl development that generates so many environmental, fiscal, economic, and social costs, and "smarter" suburban and urban development.

Politically, the social costs of metropolitan decentralization are finally beginning to resonate among decision makers from the right to the left, much like the political complacency that supported sprawl in the first place.[100] For example, leading Republicans (e.g., New Jersey Governor Christine Todd Whitman and California gubernatorial candidate Dan Lundgren) and Democrats (e.g., Maryland Governor Parris Glendening and Colorado Governor Roy Romer) have promoted "smart growth" agendas. We devote much of our final chapter to a discussion of what smart-growth communities might look like and how they might be encouraged.

It all comes down to quality of life. An improved quality of life is what environmentalists, urban activists, developers, and government bureaucrats all purport to want. But the vagueness of the term and the variety and extent of impacts allow for so much interpretation that the discussion is often rendered nonproductive.

In examining quality of life indicators related to sprawl development, this chapter has yielded several important conclusions. First, there is substantial evidence that suburban migration has had serious negative impacts on the quality of life in America's urban areas. The rapid spread of sprawl has also contributed to the spread of social problems to an expanding ring of older suburbs. It does not take much insight to realize that this continued pattern is

Walkable, mixed-use areas, such as this pedestrian plaza in Boulder, Colorado, increase social interactions and enhance a community's quality of life.

MATTHEW RAIMI

not sustainable, as increased driving, stress, the degradation of the natural and scenic environments, social segregation, and other problems overwhelm the original benefits of suburban living.

Second, there is ample evidence that sprawling areas are not immune to serious social problems of their own, related to their low densities, location at the outer edges of metropolitan areas, dependence on automobiles, and lack of accessible activities for children and the elderly. If these problems are to be mitigated, the smart growth agenda must include a commitment to suburban policies that increase transportation choices, encourage more human social interactions through walking, support the concentration and viability of small businesses, and ensure housing accessibility for a diversity of individuals and households.

Finally, there is a great need to erase the social chasms that divide our central cities from our suburbs, and our suburbs from each other. As sociologist William Julius Wilson writes in his book, *When Work Disappears: The World of the New Urban Poor,* "perhaps at no other time in the nation's history has it been more important to talk about the need to promote city and suburban cooperation, not separation."[101] He argues that, while suburban areas have weakened their urban cores by siphoning off resources and population, it is critical that the health of central cities be maintained because regional economies are so interdependent: "The more central cities are plagued by joblessness, dysfunctional schools, and crime, the more the surrounding suburbs undergo a decline in their own social and economic fortunes."[102] As long as Wilson's observation is valid, reducing sprawl and developing smarter ways to grow may be powerful tools to improving overall quality of life in America.

A Better Way
Visions of Smart Growth

As we write, our civilization is about to enter a new century. We have made it plain that we believe this new century must bring changes in the way we grow. Although the path that we have followed for the last half of the 20th century has been good in many ways, it has not been good in others. Our environment, economy, and social fabric are all threatened by what we have been doing to our greenfields.

While our story so far has not been a pretty one, we believe it can have a happy ending. At the beginning of this book, we wrote that we were offering our story of the consequences of dumb growth not just to recount a nightmare but also to outline and pursue a brighter dream. Indeed, we remain steadfast in our conviction that a future with personal comfort and a high standard of living, as well as a high quality environment for ourselves and our children, is well within our reach. This will require changes in the way we grow, but those changes will bring rewards.

In some ways we have already begun to take steps to rectify the ill effects of sprawl on our environment, economy, and social fabric. In this chapter we present eight "visions," each containing

With strong and attractive inner-city residential neighborhoods, the need to claim greenfields for development can be significantly reduced.

part of the answer. The first five outline some basic principles that we believe should guide twenty-first century development, to help avoid the mistakes of the past and

137

to begin the journey to a more sustainable future. The final three represent successful, real-world examples where a combination of practices are achieving multiple benefits.

Some Guiding Principles for Nonsprawling Land Use

There is no firm set of guidelines to dictate precisely how we should build the smarter growth of the future. Indeed, we would be the last to advocate fixed rules, since innovation and adaptation are essential. Nevertheless, there is an emerging consensus over a number of key (if flexible) elements that we believe we should strive for, including the following: strong central cities; compact and transit-oriented development; maintenance of agriculture and green space; better design of large-scale retail centers; and better design of suburban workplaces.

Strong Central Cities and "Infill" Neighborhoods

There is no question that one part of the solution must be the invigoration and maintenance of strong central cities and inner suburbs, along with more efficient utilization of land available for development within existing metropolitan areas. With central cities as hubs of economic and cultural activity, particularly when linked with strong inner residential neighborhoods, the need to drive long distances and claim new greenfields for development can be significantly reduced. Our cities and existing suburbs frequently have land available for development, too: the Maryland Office of Planning reports, for example, that the 20 percent population growth projected for metropolitan Washington, DC, from 1995–2020 could all be accommodated within the boundaries of existing developed areas.[1]

The real estate industry's 1997 *Emerging Trends* report lists the following desirable attributes of successful, vibrant "24-hour" cities:

- attractive housing, for both affordable and upscale markets
- nearby shopping
- ample recreation and entertainment
- personal security
- good schools
- access to transportation, with reduced automobile dependence
- a diversified tax base.[2]

Few American cities now possess all of these characteristics in abundance, and that is one reason why nearly all of them are losing some degree of market share to sprawl. But the industry's report contains some cause for optimism: it notes that the hottest U.S. "markets to watch" for metropolitan real estate investment are San Francisco, Seattle, Boston, New York, and Chicago, all cities with diversified, strong urban cores and established, thriving neighborhoods.[3]

Across the country, the signs of "reurbanization" suggest that our cities are ready once again to compete with greenfield development as centers of economic and social activity. More than a million new jobs have been created inside the 50 largest American cities since 1993, and unemployment has fallen substantially. [4] Violent crime in large cities declined sharply in the 1990s, with some cities experiencing a drop in homicides to rates not seen in two or three decades.[5] This is big news in a climate where a perception of crime is often cited as a reason for urban flight, and the decline in crime may partly explain why many cities, both large and small, began in the 1990s to reverse or slow the loss of population they suffered in the 1980s.[6]

Indeed, the Brookings Institution's Center on Urban and Metropolitan Policy predicts that downtown living will rise substantially in 19 of 20 large cities between 1998 and 2010.[7] The 1999 *Emerging Trends* report notes that the rejuvenation of core cities holds particular appeal for certain growing segments of the housing market:

> As baby-boomers become empty nesters, their children move into the expanding ranks of Generation Xers—single and looking to make it on their own. Both groups are gravitating to cities.[8]

If urban schools can be improved—a task beyond the scope of this book but one that, as a society, we must undertake—families with children will follow.

Among the places with hopeful signs of recovery is Detroit, one of a growing number of cities experiencing a resurgence of new homebuilding within the city.[9] Such "infill" sites are especially well-suited to smart-growth development strategies, because their locations do not claim new green space for buildings. Also in Detroit, General Motors recently expressed its confidence in the central city by purchasing the downtown Renaissance Center and announcing that it is moving its headquarters there.

Detroit is not alone. In other locations as well, downtowns are re-emerging as places of regional cultural activity and entertainment; major new downtown entertainment facilities either have been or are being raised, for example, in Fort Worth, Cleveland, Baltimore, Washington, DC, and New York. In Boston, inner-city crime has dropped and inner-city population is now on the rise, after a decline in the 1970s; Boston has

Inner-city Boston, with its rich history and vibrant public spaces, has recently experienced an urban revival after population declines in the 1970s.

experienced a significant increase in transit use per capita, and its rate of growth in automobile use per capita is now the lowest of major U.S. metropolitan areas.[10]

In New York City, Times Square has experienced a spectacular rebound from decades of decline to become a vibrant urban center once again, with the arrival of new hotels, new office buildings, and retail/entertainment centers from industry giants like Disney and Warner Brothers. Elsewhere in our nation's most populous city, retail and industrial expansion is taking place in the Bronx and, in several downtown neighborhoods, superstores previously associated primarily with sprawling suburban locations—K-mart and Sears among them—have opened stores to serve urban customers. New York's crime rate has declined dramatically, and tourism and real estate activity are on the rise.[11]

Things may be changing even in highly automobile-dependent Dallas, where new light rail transit and commuter rail facilities have far exceeded ridership projections, attracting high-density development around transit stations. The Continental Insurance Company is relocating 400 jobs from a suburban office park to a downtown Dallas location across the street from a rapid transit station, and a new $150 million Hotel—the Adam's Mark—is also being built downtown.[12]

By pointing to these hopeful signs regarding our central cities, we do not mean to suggest that urban vitality can itself be the solution to sprawl. Indeed, many of our examples here have also been examples of regions with sprawling, inefficient growth. What we do argue is that strong centers constitute *part* of the solution: making our central cities once again places where people want to live and shop, where businesses want to locate, and where investors want to place their capital is one of the keys to saving the countryside.

Compact and Transit-Oriented Development

How and what we build is just as important as where we build. We need to use our land more efficiently and sensibly, with a more diverse mix of housing and lot types in walkable, accessible neighborhoods. And we need to have our businesses and amenities as close as possible, integrated within rather than cut off and inaccessible from

The Importance of Regional Cooperation

Maintaining the strength of central cities can be extremely challenging in metropolitan regions where governance is complicated by a patchwork of highly independent jurisdictions. In chapters one and three, for example, we discussed how suburban governments frequently encourage sprawl, and weaken the core city and the region as a whole, by competing aggressively with each other for tax revenues that they hope will be generated by new businesses and residents. The Portland, Oregon region has achieved fame in responding to these concerns by establishing a directly-elected regional government and a metropolitan "growth boundary" within which development may occur. These mechanisms increase the opportunities for regional cooperation and reduce the incentives for destructive competition. As we discuss later in this chapter, the Portland approach is achieving substantial success in controlling sprawl while maintaining a strong urban core and a booming regional economy.

Additional help in forging regional cooperation is provided by the metropolitan planning mechanisms of federal transportation law, which since 1991 has required that regions establish institutions to plan cooperatively for highway and transit infrastructure in order to qualify for federal funds.[13] Although much of this book constitutes ample evidence that many regions still have far to go in coordinating transportation and land use, coordinating structures have been put in place and progress is beginning to be made.[14] It will be important that governments and stakeholders at all levels take advantage of the opportunities provided by this innovative legislation to plan transportation investments that contain sprawl and support central cities.

Yet another cooperative innovation is being provided in the Minneapolis-St. Paul region, where 40 percent of the growth in taxes from commercial and industrial property is now shared among communities in the region. The program has withstood a number of court challenges and should dampen somewhat the incentive for suburban jurisdictions to compete with the central cities and with each other for an expanded tax base. The Twin Cities region also has recently consolidated waste control, transit, and land-use management functions into a single regional agency, the Metropolitan Council.[15]

our homes. By doing this in the right places—suburbs as well as cities—with the right design, we need sacrifice none of the popular community attributes sometimes mistakenly thought of as inherently "suburban," such as privacy, safety, convenience, and open space.

Perhaps the most obvious characteristic of the smarter growth patterns that we advocate is that they be more compact, i.e., accommodating more people, businesses, and civic functions in a smaller overall space than sprawl development. The overall impact will be one of greater average density but, as Professor Reid Ewing (whose work we discussed earlier) points out, this need not be what we think of as "high" density: "compact development requires some concentration of employment, some clustering of housing, and some mixing of land uses (but not high-density nor monocentric development)."[16]

In many cases, we can begin with small steps by, for example, adding another floor above one-and two-story businesses in order to accommodate new apartments or businesses, especially in infill locations.[17] We also can target smaller-lot housing to the growing numbers of people who do not need or want to maintain a large yard, including those groups cited above by the authors of *Emerging Trends*, such as "empty nesters" and singles with or without children. We can utilize creative site design to provide ample, accessible open space in the overall development and community.[18] The impact of more compact development patterns on our lifestyle and housing preferences need not be overwhelming, particularly

New smart growth neighborhoods, such as the Kentlands in Montgomery County, Maryland, are an attractive antidote to "cookie cutter" suburban sprawl.

given that many of the greatest benefits, such as improved transportation efficiency, are realized as we change from sprawl to moderate densities.[19]

Indeed, as Anthony Downs has written, we could create an average density of between nine and ten dwelling units per acre—relatively high by today's standards and sufficient to support regular transit service—by allocating 32 percent of new residential development to multifamily housing and the other 68 percent to single-family homes on half-acre lots.[20] Newman and Kenworthy write that similar results can be achieved by designing a community either with all two-story townhouses or with a mix of two-and six-story apartments, townhouses, and single-family housing on separate lots. With the latter approach, we could even devote 30 percent of the developed area to open space and recreation, more than tripling the area so dedicated in a typical low-density, sprawling neighborhood. Newman and Kenworthy cite Toronto and Vancouver as examples of successful North American cities where the urban landscape juxtaposes pleasant high-rise development with more typical single-family housing, with no loss of attractiveness or citizen acceptance.[21]

One of the most comprehensively articulated set of principles to guide the more compact, smart-growth development of the future is that of architect and urban planner/designer Peter Calthorpe. In particular, Calthorpe designs both "neighborhood" (primarily residential) and "urban" (primarily business) transit-oriented developments (TODs), designed specifically to reduce traffic, conserve land, and preserve environmental quality. Calthorpe's TODs attempt to do or assist the following things:

• Help organize growth on a regional level to be compact and transit-supportive.
• Place shopping, housing, jobs, parks, and civic uses within walking distance of transit stops.
• Create pedestrian-friendly street networks that directly connect local destinations.
• Provide a mix of housing types, densities, and costs.
• Preserve sensitive habitat, riparian zones, and high quality open space.
• Make public spaces the focus of building orientation and neighborhood activity.
• Encourage infill and redevelopment along transit corridors within existing neighborhoods.[22]

Calthorpe emphasizes that the key is neighborhood walkability, from transit to one's primary destination (such as home or employment) and from the primary destination to others (such as retail, day care, parks, and civic services). Destinations likely to attract the most visits should be placed at the center of the TOD, at or near the transit stop. Surrounding the core area can be a secondary area for single-family residences, larger businesses, schools, and major parks.[23] To preserve and enhance walkability, the development should be designed with the following: close and varied destinations; direct pedestrian links free of cul de sacs, large parking lots, and massive intersections; safe, interesting, and comfortable sidewalks with shade trees; and human scale in attractively designed buildings that line the street and orient to the pedestrian.[24]

In order to enhance walkability, TODs should have direct pedestrian links free of cul-de-sacs and place the highest concentrations of housing and commercial activity near the transit stop.

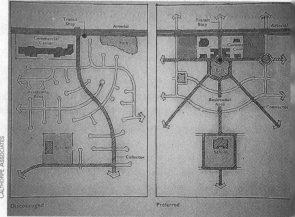

143

The TOD concept is also strongly promoted by transportation researchers Michael Bernick and Robert Cervero of the University of California at Berkeley, whose work we reported in chapter two. In their book, *Transit Villages in the 21st Century*, Bernick and Cervero articulate design guidelines very similar to Calthorpe's (although the Berkeley researchers focus exclusively on communities built around rail, as distinguished from bus, transit), and note that the results can include not only environmental benefits but also social ones, including the provision of affordable housing and enhanced public safety. They also observe that such communities pose no threat to those portions of the housing market that will continue to prefer low-density living, since TODs will only relieve the pressure to intensify other suburban neighborhoods.[25]

Like Calthorpe and others, Bernick and Cervero find comforting antecedents for TODs in such walkable, smaller American cities as Princeton, New Jersey, and Annapolis, Maryland, and in prewar "streetcar suburbs" such as Shaker Heights, Ohio, and Pasadena, California.[26] They note that neighborhoods with the desired characteristics can develop incrementally within existing, already-developed areas as well as in new communities, and they recount a number of ingredients that can make such developments more likely to occur: supportive zoning, market-based planning, strong community leadership, and a receptive private sector.[27]

The Location-Efficient Mortgage: An Incentive for Smart Development

Compact neighborhoods that are walkable and convenient to public transit not only provide an alternative to sprawl; they also save household income. The reason is that residents of transit- and pedestrian-oriented neighborhoods drive much less than their counterparts in sprawling developments, as we have discussed. This enables households in many inner-city and other efficient locations to save substantial sums of money that would otherwise go toward transportation by, for example, getting by with one car instead of two, with two instead of three, or with no car at all.

In order to help the marketplace more accurately account for these savings, a partnership of nonprofit organizations (including NRDC, STPP, and the Center for Neighborhood Technology) is working with Fannie Mae, the federally chartered mortgage lending institution, and private banks to develop and test the "location-efficient mortgage" (LEM). The LEM allows homebuyers in neighborhoods meeting research-based tests of higher density and good transit access to qualify for larger loans at a given level of income, because of the transportation savings available to apply to larger monthly mortgage payments.[28]

While urban and suburban infill sites provide the ideal locations for successful TODs, these principles may also be used to design new growth areas and new towns where infill locations are insufficient to accommodate growth.[29] Indeed, at some point in the growth of large metro areas it may become environmentally desirable—particularly in reducing traffic—to establish well-designed "subcenters" in a region's suburbs, linked by transit to the core and each other.[30] What TODs must not do, however, is repeat the mistakes of sprawl. Calthorpe particularly warns against such maladies as segregating places of activity, isolating pedestrians from the street, and allowing major arterial roadways to dominate the landscape and one's transportation choices.[31]

There are signs that the necessary ingredients are starting to fall into place. Noting that such developments are the most attractive not only for residents but also for suburban investors, the authors of *Emerging Trends* see the building of compact, diverse villages as a promising trend:

> Increasingly, better suburban areas look like smaller versions of traditional cities, featuring attractive neighborhoods, easily accessible retail and office districts, and mass transportation alternatives to the car.[32]

In greater Chicago, for example, a highly successful development called Market Square has sprung up in the community of Lake Front, on the North Shore Line of the local suburban transit entity, Metra. In the City of Chicago itself, developments have formed at Lincoln Square on the CTA's Brown Line and at Pulaski Station on the Green line.[33] A study commissioned by the American Lung Association projects that the Pulaski project, which includes enhanced transit amenities along with commercial revitalization and a variety of housing types, may reduce neighborhood automobile use by as much as 20 percent, reducing potential emissions by over seven tons of hydrocarbon air pollutants and over three tons of nitrogen oxide pollutants per year.[34] In their book, Bernick and Cervero discuss a number of successfully emerging transit villages around rail stops in metropolitan San Francisco, San Diego, Los Angeles, and Washington, DC.[35]

As *Emerging Trends* has observed, the consumer market is already shifting away from the old automobile-dependent model:

> Residential locations that are not totally independent—where you can walk or ride bicycles to recreation and essential shopping—will become more desirable as people grow increasingly fed up with the traffic hassles. The more pedestrian-friendly an area is, the better.[36]

A number of studies have confirmed that residents are just as satisfied with housing at six or seven units per acre as they are at three or four units per acre and, in

high-priced housing markets, the most popular products are often townhouses, courtyard, and other small-lot houses. People are particularly willing to accept higher densities when other amenities, such as neighborhood parks, are provided. For shopping, consumers favor compact neighborhood and city commercial centers over strip development by a wide margin.[37]

Research has also found that cluster development can appreciate faster than sprawl subdivisions over time and that a significant portion of the housing market prefers and is willing to pay a premium for living within walking distance of rail transit, trading off other amenities if necessary.[38] For commercial development, rents in transit-oriented locations compete favorably with those near freeways.[39]

Small-lot houses within walking distance to shops, such as these in Boulder, Colorado, are becoming more desirable for people who wish to escape the hassles of suburban living.

Maintaining Agriculture and Open Space

At the same time that we build more sensibly, we must also conserve for future generations the best of our natural areas and working agricultural landscape. There is room for the application of both small steps and large ideas in addressing this issue.

For example, in West Windsor, New Jersey, a modest portion of property tax revenue is being used to fund a program to buy and preserve nearby open space. The fund works in tandem with an incremental-growth zoning law that favors close-in development and allows new construction in outer zones only if developers agree to reduce land consumption and pay for infrastructure.[40] Also in New Jersey, an amendment to the state constitution was approved by voters in 1998 to enable enough borrowing to save up to half the state's undeveloped land either by direct purchase or by purchase of development rights. Additional open-space measures were approved by voters in 1998 in Alabama, Arizona, Florida, Minnesota, Oregon, and Rhode Island.[41] Around Washington, DC, some conservationists are beginning

---

Prairie Crossing and the Paradox of "Natural" Developments

In many ways, the new development of Prairie Crossing, north of Chicago in Lake County, Illinois, typifies what can be good about environmentally sensitive development. Its residential areas are accessible to pedestrians and cyclists, with neighborhood centers and convenience stores; it preserves open space and native vegetation by clustering housing. The development has even won awards from some sectors of the environmental community.[42]

There is, however, a problem: Prairie Crossing is some 45 miles north of the Chicago Loop and is itself expanding the urban fringe. It, and developments like it elsewhere, could end up drawing other development to nearby greenfields, thereby increasing traffic and furthering the problems associated with sprawl. Research suggests that even the best-designed suburban communities, if built in and among sprawl development, may have difficulty achieving trip reductions equivalent to comparably designed neighborhoods in inner suburbs and other infill areas.[43] While Prairie Crossing does have the benefit of a commuter rail line into Chicago, it remains to be seen whether the development—studied not in isolation but in the context of Lake County and the Chicagoland region—can produce net environmental benefits.

---

to conceive a 10-mile wide "greenbelt" of protected parks, forests, and agricultural land, modeled after the greenbelt around London.[44]

A greenbelt around Washington would be a challenge to assemble, but the task would enjoy the advantage of building upon the country's most successful farmland protection program in nearby Montgomery County, Maryland. In particular, the county—notwithstanding a population of over 800,000 people and a shared border with Washington—has legally protected more than half of its 93,252 acres of farmland through an innovative and mutually reinforcing combination of conservation easements (by which owners donate or sell development rights to a land trust), transfer of development rights (by which owners sell the rights to owners seeking to build in parts of the county targeted for growth), and 25-acre agricultural zoning within the area designated for preservation.[45]

Altogether, Montgomery is seeking to protect about one-third of its total land base of 317,000 acres from non-agricultural development, and so far leads the nation in the amount of land that has been legally protected. Similar programs are having an impact in Marin and Sonoma Counties in California, in Lancaster County, Pennsylvania, and in a number of other counties in Maryland.[46] The state of Oregon has also achieved success in reducing farmland losses, from 30,000 acres per year to

Using innovative land use strategies, Montgomery County, Maryland, has successfully protected over 90,000 acres of farmland and open space.

only around 2,000 acres per year, through application of urban growth boundaries and other statewide growth management measures.[47]

The contrast between outer Montgomery's still-green spaces and the more haphazard development just across the Potomac River in Fairfax County, Virginia, is striking. But even in Montgomery there is reason for continued vigilance. Some of the land in the county's agricultural preserve is owned not by farmers but by speculators, presumably poised to take advantage of any relaxation in local preservation laws. In addition, many Montgomery farmers must augment their farm income with other activities or investments in order to remain economically viable.[48] Still, the success of the preserve so far is impressive and undeniable.

The most comprehensive strategic thinking about farmland is that conducted by the American Farmland Trust. As discussed above in chapter two, the Trust has undertaken an extensive national inventory of highly productive and unique farmland and identified the land most in danger of being lost to sprawl.[49] In connection with that inventory, the Trust recommends a number of measures to address the threats, including the following:

• Local communities should analyze development trends in areas where productive farmland is in the path of development, attempt to reach consensus on criteria to identify land worth protecting, undertake a review of the adequacy of existing policies, and attempt to reach consensus on additional measures needed, such as those in effect in Maryland and Oregon.
• States should provide technical and financial assistance to local efforts to establish a farmland inventory and tracking system, as well as review state laws and policies that affect agricultural conservation.
• At the federal level, Congress should strengthen and the executive branch should implement fully the Federal Farmland Protection Policy Act, which attempts to minimize the negative impacts that federal programs can have on farmland conversion. Among other needed federal actions identified by the Trust are farmland research, measures to assure that federal construction and land management programs do

not unnecessarily further or encourage farmland conversion, expansion of financial aid to state and local conservation easement programs, and reform of estate taxes to lessen the cost of intergenerational transfers of land within farm families.[50]

The same types of community measures—taking inventory, setting targets, and employing consensus-building to select approaches, for example—can and should be used not only for farmland but also to protect threatened habitat and historic and scenic resources.[51] To some extent they are required by law,[52] although implementation has been spotty at best. In addition, many of the same legal instruments employed to conserve farmland, such as easements, purchase of development rights, and outright purchase, may be appropriately applied to conserve biologic, historic, and scenic resources. Sensitive planning and design approaches also may be employed to protect important corridors and resources within and among new development, in addition to those measures used to protect areas from development.[53]

Taming Superstores

Perhaps no greater challenge is presented to smart-growth advocates than that of the so-called "big-box retailers" and other superstores that flocked in the 1990s to the exurban fringe. These stores often occupy two or more football fields' worth of single-story retail space, are surrounded by vast parking lots covering as much land as 10 or more football fields, and are basically accessible only by automobile.[54] Retailing on this scale may simply not be compatible with the principles of strong town centers and compact growth. Or is it?

A 1997 publication from the National Trust for Historic Preservation demonstrates that, in fact, large-scale retailing may be more compatible with nonsprawling development and community renewal than the typical, sprawling big-box development suggests. Writing in *Better Models for Superstores*,[55] the Trust's Constance Beaumont provides an encouraging sequel to her earlier work, discussed in chapter four, documenting the harms that superstore sprawl can bring to communities. In *Better Models*, Beaumont points out that a few large-scale retailers are beginning to demonstrate in some communities that, with creativity and flexibility, they can indeed recycle existing buildings, respect the environment, and make money at the same time.

For example, in the late 1990s Target, the discount chain of over 500 stores owned by the Dayton-Hudson Corporation, opened a store in downtown Pasadena, California, refurbishing a 164,000-square-foot building that had housed a traditional department store for many years but had been vacated in 1992. The Pasadena store is the first Target in the country with more than one floor of retail space and the first in a downtown rather than on the suburban fringe. The Pasadena project required thinking "outside the box," so to speak, in a number of respects, including the installation of a system of custom elevators and moving stairs to transport customers and merchandise between floors, and compromises with city planners regarding street-facing windows and exterior signage.

The Pasadena store cost Target approximately $50 dollars per square foot to build—significantly more than the cost in the usual suburban location—but the city of Pasadena contributed tax incentives to soften the pain. The good news for the retailer and its customers is that, since opening in 1994, the Pasadena store has been a rousing commercial success: sales have been running some 30 to 35 percent higher than anticipated and substantially higher than Target's national average.[56]

Even the most vilified of all superstore chains, Wal-Mart, has invested in a downtown location in Rutland, Vermont, where it is recycling a site that had been abandoned by K-Mart. Wal-Mart was persuaded to do so because a lively debate over the merits of large-scale retailing in that particularly scenic state prompted local preservationists to engage the company directly in an effort to find viable, win-win alternatives to the typical greenfields location. While the store—at 75,000 square feet—is smaller than most new Wal-Marts, both the company and local citizens are optimistic that it will do well. Although the Rutland initiative represents a significant first step, in other Vermont communities (and in communities across the country), the debate continues to rage, as the chain appears committed to building big boxes on the fringe.

In Santa Monica, California, Toys R Us has seen a downtown location for its store made more attractive and viable for retailing by the city government's commitment to the downtown. In particular, the company was able to take advantage of a program through which downtown businesses were assessed and funds raised to pay for maintenance and repair of infrastructure, cleaning of parking facilities and sidewalks, landscaping, and insurance. Such "business improvement districts" have become a popular tool for urban revitalization efforts across the county. In Santa Monica, the city also has adopted special zoning provisions to attract residential housing downtown in order to keep the business district viable at night. These policies succeeded in attracting the retailer into establishing a 55,000 square-foot store with two stories, display windows, and many attractive design features intended to mesh with the urban streetscape. No additional parking lots were required because of the adequacy of nearby parking garages. The store is doing well financially and local citizens are pleased with its success.

Beaumont's book describes other superstore success stories in downtown locations as diverse as Chicago, San Diego, Denver, Indianapolis, and New York City. The

Trust recommends that communities take a number of steps to assure that superstores support existing downtowns rather than sprawl; chief among the steps are zoning ordinances, size guidelines, design standards, mandatory review of developments that have regional impacts, impact fees, and local business retention zones.[57] Additional measures that are helping soften the impact of big-box stores in some regions include a requirement that retailers recycle and use existing, abandoned structures before building new ones, and guidelines that encourage the use of pedestrian amenities and other features to break up the expansiveness of large parking lots.[58]

Big-box retailers are beginning to discover that locating in transit-accessible and walkable areas and reusing existing buildings can be financially successful. (These photos show the Dry Goods Building in Denver and the Tenleytown area of Washington, DC.)

Better Suburban Workplaces

Controlling sprawl does not mean forsaking the suburbs as places to live, work, and shop. In fact, as discussed above, in regions of a certain size it can be desirable to supplement the central business district with subcenters of commercial and residential activity outside the core.

The key task is to apply smart-growth principles to the suburban subcenters.

Robert Cervero has developed a set of cohesive principles designed to make suburban workplaces more supportive of environmentally responsible transportation practices. These principles, which are highly compatible with Calthorpe's more generally applicable guidelines for transit-oriented development, include the following:

• Higher densities that include multi-story buildings, shared-use parking, and reduced parking space dimensions where feasible.
• Better coordination of job and housing growth to minimize the travel distance between the two activities, including the construction of mixed-use developments that site workplace locations among housing, child-care facilities, and retail functions.

- Office developments that feature a well-defined, centralized core, with people-oriented facilities, such as restaurants, shops, and banks to serve as a focus for surrounding development.
- Site design, building orientation, and pedestrian amenities that facilitate walking between buildings and developments.
- On-site roads and trailpaths that link directly with nearby off-site facilities rather than only with arterials or other main roads.
- Transit stops positioned to minimize walking distances for the greatest number of passengers, with bus connection points near the front entrances of major buildings and full amenities at drop-off points for carpools and vanpools.[59]

Three Models to Watch and Learn From

There are many places around the country and, indeed, around the world that are beginning to apply various combinations of these principles. It is beyond the scope of this book to document them all. In this section, we offer three examples that we believe to be particularly instructive and promising: Portland, Oregon; the state of Maryland; and the European Union.

Putting It All Together in Portland

Many of these principles—and others—are being put to the test in the Portland, Oregon, region, where state and local leaders have been implementing a variety of growth-management techniques since the early 1970s. Indeed, Portland has become a sort of "living laboratory" for efficient urban planning and living. The results are benefiting both the environment and the region's economy. While Portland's achievements have been widely reported—and perhaps suffer from overexposure among those who make their living in the planning field—its experience holds great promise for other metropolitan regions.

In particular, the state of Oregon adopted a statewide planning program in 1973, under the leadership of then-governor Tom McCall, a Republican. The program incorporates protective zoning for about 40,000 square miles (25 million acres) of farmland and private forest land. It requires cities and counties to zone for affordable housing, in effect increasing average residential densities. And, perhaps most importantly, it requires urban growth boundaries (UGB) around every city in the state.

The law encourages urban development within UGBs and strongly discourages it on the outside.[60]

The Portland metropolitan UGB encompasses 24 cities, parts of three counties, and some 1.3 million people as of this writing. It is just over 200,000 acres in size. The Portland region also supplements its municipal and county governments with a directly elected regional council, called Metro, responsible for long-range land use and transportation planning, among other functions.

These measures are having an impact. In contrast to cities like Chicago, where the growth in developed land has outpaced the growth in population more than tenfold, Portland has accommodated a 50 percent increase in population since the early 1970s with only a 2 percent increase in its land base.[61] Between 1960 and 1990, the density of metropolitan Portland actually increased by nearly 10 percent, while that of other regions fell sharply. Moreover, the share of regional employment in Portland's lively downtown has held steady, despite booming growth in the region as a whole.

With the help of a regional light rail transit system, downtown Portland has maintained its position as the center of activity.

Although "car dependency remains high," according to some reports,[62] Portland's downtown has accommodated 30,000 new jobs in the last two decades without a significant increase in the number of parking spaces or vehicle trips. Assisted in part by the region's excellent light-rail system, there has been a 50 percent increase in public transit trips to downtown, and 43 percent of all work commuting trips in Portland— many times the national average—are now made on public transit. Air quality is improving.[63]

The regional economy is in good shape, too. Newer companies in or near Portland, such as Hewlett-Packard, Intel, and Nike, have located there precisely because of the attraction of a diverse urban lifestyle in close proximity to a preserved, scenic natural and rural environment.[64] The region was one of two that topped the real estate industry's 1997 list of smaller-market regions most attractive to investors.[65]

For the future, the Portland region has prepared a "Metro 2040" plan that promises to extend these gains into the next century. Essentially, the plan incorporates the findings of the LUTRAQ study described in chapter two and applies them region-wide, emphasizing pedestrian-friendly and transit-oriented development, downtown revitalization, investment in public transit, and increased densities in presently underutilized commercial centers. Under the plan, the region expects to be able to accommodate a population increase of one million persons over 50 years, with only a 6 percent expansion of the urban growth boundary.[66]

Notwithstanding Portland's obvious successes, and the region's undeniable popularity with residents and businesses, its approach to land use does have its detractors, including property-rights advocates and developers who feel constrained by the UGB. They point to rapidly increasing housing prices and the city's recent ranking by the National Homebuilders Association as the nation's fifth least affordable.[67] This may be due in part, however, not to the UGB but to the fact that a depressed market for timber—still a major factor in the region's overall economy—kept wage growth at a relatively modest level in the 1990s. The average sale price of a home in greater Portland, at about $150,000 as of this writing, remains roughly comparable to average prices in other western cities such as Reno and Denver, and is less than the average price in San Diego, Seattle, and San Francisco. In fact, a benefit of the Portland approach is that its homes have held their value, in contrast to the situation in many other regions where sprawl and residential overbuilding have weakened the investments families have made in their urban homes.

Other regions, encouraged by Portland's success, are taking steps to emulate it. The list of cities that either have recently adopted or are seriously considering adopting their own urban growth boundaries now includes Boulder; Minneapolis; Seattle; Madison, Wisconsin; Lexington, Kentucky; and San Diego, San Jose, and Ventura County, California, as well as several smaller cities in the San Francisco Bay region.[68] As John Fregonese, former chief growth planner for Portland's Metro, notes, cities

Success in Toronto, Too

Portland is not the only North American city enjoying the benefits of growth management. Another encouraging example is Toronto, which emphasizes clustered, higher density, mixed-use development within easy walking distance of transit stations. Among the results are the following: 17 percent of all travel and 31 percent of all work commuting in the city are by public transit; 15 percent of all residents of downtown Toronto walk to work; and an impressive 80 percent of all people attending sports events at the city's Sky Dome stadium arrive by transit.[69]

will follow suit when they realize that they are "using up the one thing that nobody's making more of, and that's land."[70]

Smart Growth Under Maryland's Program

If Oregon paved the way with innovative and successful growth management legislation in the 1970s, Maryland is hoping to become a model for the late 1990s onward. Under the leadership of Governor Parris Glendening, the state has enacted a legislative package collectively known as the "Neighborhood Conservation and Smart Growth Initiative." In discussing the package, Glendening stated in an interview with *The Washington Post* that, except for education, "controlling sprawl is the most important issue facing us in terms of what our quality of life is going to be."[71]

Unlike the Oregon legislation, the guiding principle of the Maryland initiative is not regulatory prescription, but selective use of the state purse. In particular, beginning in October 1998 the state is prohibited from contributing funds to "growth related" projects such as highways, sewer and water construction, housing, and economic development assistance, except in "priority funding areas" designated by county governments in accordance with the legislation.[72]

In order to be eligible for designation, future residential communities must exhibit at least a minimum average density of 3.5 dwellings per acre and must be included within a 10-year water and sewer plan. Existing municipalities, areas within the Washington and Baltimore beltways, enterprise zones, and certified "heritage" areas automatically qualify, as do designated "rural villages." Designation of priority funding areas meeting these criteria is left to local jurisdictions, but localities may not "overdesignate": there must be a showing of demand for development sufficient to justify the amount of land being designated.[73] Local governments or the private sector may continue to fund infrastructure and other projects outside the priority areas, but the state may not do so under the law.[74]

In addition to the restriction of state funds to priority areas, Maryland's Smart Growth legislation embraces a number of complementary programs. In particular, the Rural Legacy Program helps maintain contiguous blocks of farmland, forests, and natural areas by using revenue from a state sales tax and from the sale of state bonds to purchase properties and easements in response to competitive proposals submitted by local governments and nonprofit land trusts. The Job Creation Tax Credit Act provides an income tax benefit to employers who create at least 25 full-time jobs within priority funding areas. The Live Near Your Work program provides home-buying assistance to purchasers in targeted areas where participating employers provide matching resources. A brownfields program limits liability for those redeveloping abandoned or underutilized industrial sites unless they increase contamination or create new pollution. In addition, pre-existing legislation in Maryland protects certain sensitive areas, including streams and stream buffers, 100-year floodplains, habitat for endangered species, and steep slopes.[75]

Maryland's package of initiatives is not a panacea. The minimum-density requirement for priority funding areas is modest,[76] and lower-density development may proceed if built without state funding. The large amount of discretion afforded county governments in designating priority funding areas could lead to abuse.[77] In addition, at the time of enactment, citizens were concerned about the damage that could be done by development projects already in the works before the legislation was passed, including a six-lane highway proposed for the northern fringe of greater Washington and a mega-development planned for 2,250 acres of currently rural property in a sensitive watershed in the southern part of the state.[78]

In addition, although Governor Glendening has been committed fully to the program, it remains to be seen whether future administrations will follow suit. At the moment, no one knows how successful the initiatives will be in reshaping growth patterns. But we believe Maryland's legislation is a step in the right direction, and other states would do well to emulate and build upon it.

The European Experience

Land use in Western Europe tends to be strikingly different from the patterns we have described for the United States. Urban areas are more urban; rural areas are more rural. Anthony Downs puts it this way:

> In Western Europe, travelers leaving a metropolitan area suddenly pass from densely settled urbanized neighborhoods to uninterrupted, open farmland. In the United States, there is a gradual transition from the former to the latter through a broad region of scattered patchwork subdivisions and small outlying residential and commercialized areas.[79]

Indeed, we observed in chapter one that metropolitan areas in Europe are three to four times more dense than the typical American city, even in their newer, outer suburbs. We also noted in chapter two that Western Europeans are much more likely than Americans to travel by walking, public transit, and cycling.

While there are significant cultural differences between our country and those across the Atlantic, it is still worth taking a brief look at how land is used in Europe to understand better what the range of possibilities includes. Entire books have been written on the subject, but here we will make just a few observations.

At least some of the differences in development patterns between the United States and Europe can be explained by history. Many U.S. cities developed largely in the age of the automobile, allowing development to be at lower densities. By contrast, as noted by the Office of Technology Assessment, ". . . most European cities are substantially older than U.S. cities, and built for foot and animal traffic rather than for automobiles. Their greater residential density and lower travel requirements are due at least in part to this history. . . ."[80] In addition, the relative scarcity of land for agricultural production in Europe has created both market and political forces that tend to favor retaining land in agriculture.[81] This has tended to increase the value of urban land as well, creating another market incentive for it to be intensively used.[82]

Beyond the influence of history and the market, the role of cultural attitudes and public policy in European land use also is substantial. Western Europeans regard land as a scarce, valuable, civic resource and expect their governments to protect it.[83] Indeed, in contrast to the American practice whereby jurisdiction may be fragmented among hundreds of authorities in a single metropolitan region, and national and state governments typically play little if any role, nearly all national governments in Western Europe exercise some direct authority over land use. Many of them have coherent national policies concerning patterns of development, both among and within metropolitan areas.[84]

In the United Kingdom, for example, this structure was manifested in the Town and Country Planning Act of 1947, which established a national framework for the planning and development of land and set the stage for the creation of the now-famous greenbelts surrounding London and other British cities. Although the 1947 law has been modified significantly over the years, British law still requires localities to present long-term land use plans to the national government. Current British law also requires local authorities to assure that significant retail development will be accessible by a variety of transportation modes and will not result in an unacceptable increase of carbon dioxide and other polluting emissions.

Local authorities are also required by British transportation planning law to do the following:

- Promote development within urban areas, at locations highly accessible by means other than the private car.
- Locate major generators of travel demand in existing centers which are highly accessible by means other than the private car.
- Strengthen existing local centers—in both urban and rural areas—that offer a range of everyday community, shopping and employment opportunities, and aim to protect and enhance their viability and vitality.

- Maintain and improve opportunities for people to walk, cycle, or use public transport rather than drive between homes and facilities that they visit regularly.
- Limit parking for developments and other on or off-street parking to discourage reliance on the car for work and other journeys where there are effective alternatives.[85]

In addition, the "maximum amount" of new housing must be located in existing urban areas accessible to a mixture of uses and transportation modes.[86]

Other European countries also place restrictions on development, limiting out-of-town retail establishments in order to keep their city centers strong. The French national government, for example, requires its approval for construction of food stores even as small as 3,000 square feet. Spain has a similar requirement, while Germany has long had a practice of limiting suburban shopping centers.[87] In the Netherlands, the "Right Business in the Right Place" policy encourages the siting of labor- or visitor-intensive facilities at locations easily accessible by public transit and away from locations accessible easily by automobile only.[88] In Stockholm, Sweden, transit usage is very strong, partly as a result of strategic increases in density in the city center and certain suburbs (see box).[89]

The preservation of greenbelts around major cities has proven to be a particularly useful mechanism for keeping cities strong and maintaining nearby rural areas. In 1990, the British Department of the Environment inventoried 3.8 million acres of greenbelt land, most of it farmland, around London and other major cities. Indeed, greenbelts now cover 12 percent of England.[90]

Frankfurt, Germany, is proposing its own greenbelt, which would include meadow and farmland landscapes, as well as orchards and forests. According to the German Federal Ministry for Regional Planning, Building, and Urban Development, "the objective of the Green Belt planning is [to] lastingly safeguard the existing open spaces and stabilize them in their structure, to reduce existing strains and improve their quality as habitat and natural place."[91]

While land-use policies are having an impact on transportation, the reverse also has been true: European transport policies and investments have helped control land use, with European nations emphasizing high gasoline taxes coupled with continued improvement and reliance upon railroads and local mass transit systems in recent decades. Western Europe did not experience nearly as great an expansion of its highway facilities as did the United States in the post-World War II era.[92]

Although the European experience is instructive, Americans cannot assume that it is definitive. Europeans, too, are experiencing sprawl and growing traffic. In the

Scandinavia: Home of the Transit Metropolis

Stockholm, the Swedish capital, has been characterized by Bernick and Cervero as "arguably the best example anywhere of coordinated planning of rail transit and urban development."[93] What makes the example particularly instructive is that it occurred in one of the world's most affluent countries, with one of the highest rates of automobile ownership in Europe, and around a city that grew rapidly after World War Two and easily could have followed the American pattern of outward, highway-oriented expansion. Instead, the region is remarkably compact and pleasant, based largely on moderate densities around urban and suburban transit stops, and impressively not automobile-dependent. Another Scandinavian capital, Copenhagen, has achieved similar results. Bernick and Cervero describe the two regions:

> In Scandinavia's two largest metropolises, Stockholm and Copenhagen, dozens of compact, mixed-use satellite communities are interconnected by regional rail systems. All are built on a scale that encourages pedestrian circulation. Most rail stops focus on town centers with a public square and an outdoor marketplace. The accent on livability is showcased by pedestrian amenities—park benches, newspaper kiosks, bus shelters, sidewalk cafes, open-air markets, flower stands, and arcades designed to protect pedestrians from the elements. In Vällingby, one of Stockholm's rail-served satellites, the rail station shares space with a supermarket, where returning commuters can do their daily shopping on the way home. The station is adjacent to a car-free village square lined with more shops and service establishments, including several day-care centers. More than 50 percent of Vällingby's employed residents commute by transit despite the fact that Sweden has one of the highest per capita car ownership rates in Europe.[94]

United Kingdom, a million acres of farmland and close to two million acres of countryside have been lost since World War II.[95] There are pressures to relax land use controls in some places. Moreover, problems of disinvestment and economic decline plague such European cities as Copenhagen, where a planner complains that "we have the oldest and the poorest housing. We have the students, the poor, and the unemployed. The suburbs have the rich. We have the problems."[96] In Barcelona, the central city has lost 150,000 people since 1980, while the metropolitan area's population has increased.[97]

Still, there is reason to believe that the problems of sprawl are not nearly so advanced in Europe as in the United States. The loss of a million acres of farmland since the mid-1940s would not appear as grave as the loss of nearly a million acres *every two years,* as we have been experiencing in America. As noted, even the newer and outer suburbs of European cities, while more sprawling than the central cities, are several times more compact than their American counterparts. Writer Alex Marshall summarizes the European experience:

> [F]or many reasons, European cities are unlikely to drop as hard or as far as American center cities. . . . Super-high gas taxes keep the lid on driving, and consistent public investment makes mass transit a far more attractive option than in the U.S. . . . European cities enjoy much greater public loyalty to their centers. Governments are stronger, bigger, and more generous, and that, too, helps the center hold. Finally, the cities still generate huge tourism revenues—plenty to support the maintenance of museums and historical sites.[98]

We may well have much to learn from their experience.

Epilogue
The Brighter Dream

In this book, we have tried to collect and present some of the most compelling evidence that our greenfields—and, indeed, our society—are in trouble because of sprawl development. We hope that readers will be as persuaded by this overwhelming body of evidence as we were when we researched it. At a minimum, we hope readers will utilize the references we provide in the narrative and notes to read more and form their own conclusions.

We do not pretend that the rewards of smart growth will come easily, and they certainly cannot all come quickly. Our patterns of metropolitan development and sprawl have evolved over many decades, and it will take many years to reverse their negative impacts. The international Organization of Economic Cooperation and Development warns that land use in mature economies inevitably changes slowly: annual levels of new housing construction in the United States, for example, represent less than 1 percent of existing housing stocks.[1]

And there is no one "magic" answer that can cure the problems of sprawl. As suggested above in this final chapter, a more sustainable future will take many approaches, and many incremental changes. Some will be made by local governments; some will be made by an enlightened private sector, when developers and companies perceive that smart-growth locations and practices serve their interests; many will be made by consumers, who will seek to better their own welfare. Moving forward will require many simultaneous approaches adding up to a collective solution.

But we are excited to be among those working on the brighter dream. In the last verse of the song for which this book is named, the Brothers Four sang, "[the] greenfields are gone now." This is not literally true: many of America's greenfields may be gone, but not all of them. Not yet. All of our research, and all of the good work being done on the subject by others, only reinforces our conviction that the time to act is now. We enter the twenty-first century full of hope, energy and optimism.

Endnotes

Introduction

1 "Greenfields," words and music by Terry Gilkyson, Richard Dehr, and Frank Mille, copyright 1956 by Blackwood Music, Inc. "Greenfields" was released on the album The Brothers Four in 1959 and reached number one on the popular music charts in 1960. It has been reissued on *Greatest Hits*, by The Brothers Four, Columbia Records CK-8603.

Chapter 1

1 Equitable Real Estate Management, Inc., and Real Estate Research Corporation, *Emerging Trends in Real Estate: 1997*, Chicago: Real Estate Research Corporation, October 1996, p. 24. Lend Lease Real Estate Investments and PricewaterhouseCoopers, *Emerging Trends in Real Estate 1999*, New York: Lend Lease Real Estate Investments, October 1998, p. 24. Before the 1999 edition was published, Lend Lease acquired RERC. Both reports were authored by Jonathan Miller of RERC/Lend Lease.

2 Henry L. Diamond and Patrick F. Noonan, *Land Use in America*, Washington, DC: Island Press, 1996, p. 85.

3 U.S Bureau of the Census, *Estimates of the Population of Metropolitan Areas* (MA-96-9), December 1997. There were 323 "metropolitan statistical areas" designated by the Census in 1990. By definition, such areas include one or more core cities or areas with at least 50,000 inhabitants, the county or counties that contain them, adjoining counties with at least 50 percent of their population in the urbanized area, and additional counties that meet certain tests related to community and metropolitan character. See Rutherford H. Platt, *Land Use and Society*, Washington, DC: Island Press, 1996, pp. 19–21.

4 Michael A. Stegman and Margery Austin Turner, "The Future of Urban America in the Global Economy," *Journal of the American Planning Association*, vol. 157, Spring 1996, p. 62. See also Platt, *op. cit.*, p. 6.

5 Terry Moore and Paul Thorsnes, *The Transportation/Land Use Connection*, Chicago: American Planning Association, Planners Advisory Service Rept. No. 448/449, 1994, p. 24.

6 Platt, *op. cit.*, p. 19; Moore and Thorsnes, *op. cit.*, p. 8.

7 Platt, *op. cit.*, pp. 306, 307, 21.

8 Anthony Downs, *Stuck In Traffic: Coping With Peak-Hour Traffic Congestion*, Washington, DC: The Brookings Institution; Cambridge, MA: The Lincoln Institute of Land Policy, 1992, pp. 8–9. Among the smaller metropolitan regions in Florida reported by Downs as experiencing rapid growth are Fort Myers-Cape Coral (66%), Fort Pierce (66%), Ocala (59%), and Naples (77%). Also cited is Bangor, Maine, which grew 75% in the 1980s.

9 Platt, *op. cit.*, pp. 306, 307.

10 D'Vera Cohn, "DC Population Still Declining In Latest Count," *The Washington Post*, December 31, 1996, pp. A1, 10.

11 U.S. Bureau of the Census, *op. cit.*.

12 Judith Evans, "Home Buyers Favor Suburbs Over Cities," *The Washington Post*, June 29, 1996, p. E1; Roger K. Lewis, "Future Shock: A Bold Vision For Aging Cities," *The Washington Post*, July 20, 1996, pp. E1, 20. Both authors cite an annual analysis of housing trends prepared by the Joint Center for Housing Studies at Harvard University.

13 Moore and Thorsnes, *op. cit.*, p. 24.

14 Economic and Statistics Administration , U.S. Census Bureau, U.S. Department of Commerce, *Geophysical Mobility: March 1995 to March 1996*, P20-497, Table A-3, December 3, 1997.

15 Stegman and Turner, *op. cit.*, p. 158.

16 Diamond and Noonan, *op. cit.*, p. 87.

17 See, e.g., Michael J. Ybarra, "Putting City Sprawl on a Zoning Diet," *The New York Times*, June 16, 1996, section 4, p. 4.

18 Diamond and Noonan, *op. cit.*, p. 68. Professor Platt complains that the federal government does not maintain good, detailed inventory data on urban land, as it does for agricultural and natural resource lands. Instead, such data are maintained, if at all, at the state and local levels. Platt, *op. cit.*, p. 18.

19 Judy S. Davis, Arthur C. Nelson, and Kenneth J. Ducker, "The New 'Burbs: The Exurbs and Their Implications for Planning Policy," *Journal of the American Planning Association*, vol. 60, Winter 1994, pp. 45–46.

20 Evans, *op. cit.*.

21 Cohn, *op. cit.*.

Chapter 1 (continued)

22 Janet Pelley, *et al.*, *Sprawl Costs Us All*, Annapolis, MD: Sierra Club Foundation, 1997, p. 7.

23 Karl Blankenship, "Chewing Up the Landscape," *Bay Journal*, Baltimore: Chesapeake Bay Foundation, December 1995, p. 6. The author reports that, of the .1.2 million new residents of central Maryland, about a third—some 425,000 persons—represent outmigration from nearby cities.

24 *Ibid.* Average lot size in central Maryland is now 0.57 acres per household

25 *Ibid.* Population is projected to grow by 39.6 percent over 25 years, while converted land is projected to grow by 104 percent.

26 Carroll County Bureau of Planning, *Managing Growth*, Issue No. 1, March 1996, cited in Pelley, *op. cit.*.

27 Diamond and Noonan, *op. cit.*, pp. 88–89.

28 Platt, *op. cit.*, p. 131.

29 Northeastern Illinois Planning Commission (NIPC), *Strategic Plan for Land Resource Management* (1992), p. 4.

30 Ybarra, *op. cit.*; Timothy Egan, "Urban Sprawl Strains Western States," *The New York Times*, December 29, 1996.

31 Thomas E. Bier, "Housing Dynamics of the Cleveland Area, 1950–2000," in *Cleveland: A Metropolitan Reader*, Kent State University, 1995, p. 251.

32 *Ibid.* pp. 245, 246.

33 Lincoln Institute of Land Policy, *Alternatives to Sprawl* (policy report based on the conference "Alternatives to Sprawl," sponsored by the Lincoln Institute, The Brookings Institution, and the National Trust for Historic Preservation, Washington, DC, March 1995), Cambridge, MA: Lincoln Institute of Land Policy, 1995, p. 5 (citing Anita A. Summers).

34 Eco City Cleveland, "Sprawl Without Growth," in *Moving to Corn Fields: A Reader on Urban Sprawl and the Regional Future of Northeast Ohio*, 1996, pp. 9, 12.

35 Chris Lester, Jeffrey Spivack, Gregory Reeves, Steve Nicely, "Divided We Sprawl," *Kansas City Star*, December 17–22, 1995, reprint, pp.1–20.

36 Lincoln Institute, *op. cit.*, pp. 22-23. *See, generally*, Myron Orfield, *Metropolitics*, Washington, DC: Brookings Institution Press and Cambridge, MA: The Lincoln Institute of Land Policy, 1997.

37 Equitable Real Estate Management, *op. cit.*, p. 2.

38 Jeff Gersh, "Subdivide and Conquer," *The Amicus Journal*, vol. 18, Fall 1996, pp. 14–20.

39 Egan, "Urban Sprawl Strains Western States," *op. cit.*.

40 See Sue Anne Pressley, "Atlanta's Booming Growth Is No Easy Ride," *The Washington Post*, December 4, 1998, p. A3.

41 Christopher B. Leinberger, "The Metropolis Observed," *Urban Land*, vol. 57, October 1998, pp. 28–33.

42 Moore and Thorsnes, *op. cit.*, p. 24.

43 U.S. Bureau of the Census, *op. cit.*; Rene Sanchez, "Population Increase Highest in Western States," *The Washington Post*, January 1, 1998, p. A14.

44 Randall Arendt, *et al.*, *Rural by Design: Maintaining Small Town Character*, Chicago: American Planning Association, 1994, p. 19.

45 Platt, *op. cit.*, p. 131.

46 Diamond and Noonan, *op. cit.*, p. 88.

47 Arendt, *op. cit.*, p. 19.

48 Todd Shields, "On Edge," *The Washington Post Magazine*, February 16,1997, pp. 23, 24.

49 Tony Hiss, *The Experience of Place*, New York: Alfred A. Knopf, 1990, pp. 130–31.

50 Reid H. Ewing, "Characteristics, Causes, and Effects of Sprawl: A Literature Review," *Environmental and Urban Issues*, Florida Atlantic University/Florida International University, 1994, pp. 2–4; Reid H. Ewing, "Is Los Angeles-Style Sprawl Desirable?" *Journal of the American Planning Association*, vol. 63, Winter 1997, pp. 107–110.

51 Lee R. Epstein, "Where Yards Are Wide: Have Land Use Planning and Law Gone Astray?" *William and Mary Environmental Law and Policy Review*, vol. 21, 1997, pp. 345, 347.

52 Platt, *op. cit.*, p. 138.

53 Anthony Downs, *New Visions for Metropolitan America*, Washington, DC: The Brookings Institution; Cambridge, MA: Lincoln Institute of Land Policy, 1994, pp. 5–7.

54 Arendt, *op. cit.*, p. 5; see, generally Moore and Thorsnes, *op. cit.*

55 Platt, *op. cit.*, p. 139.

56 Platt, *op. cit.*, pp. 23–24. *The Kansas City Star* tracked that region's decline in overall density from an average of over 8,000 persons per square mile in 1920 to just over 2,000 persons per square mile in 1990. See Lester, *et al.*, *op. cit.*, at p. 6.

57 Platt, *op. cit.*, pp. 23–24.

58 The impact of current development trends on farmland is discussed in chapter two.

Chapter 1 (continued)

59 Diamond and Noonan, *op. cit.*, p. 88.

60 Peter W.G. Newman and Jeffrey R. Kenworthy, *Cities and Automobile Dependence: A Sourcebook*, Aldershot, UK, and Brookfield, VT: Gower Publishing Co., 1989, p. 40–44. Looking beyond Europe, the spatial characteristics of contemporary American settlement become even more striking: Springfield, IL, at around 2.4 persons per acre, has half the population density of rural Java. Peter W.G. Newman and Jeffrey R. Kenworthy, "Is There a Role for Physical Planners?" *Journal of the American Planning Association*, vol. 58, Summer 1992, pp. 3, 353–362.

61 Diamond and Noonan, *op. cit.*, p. 85.

62 Arendt, *op. cit.*, p. 19.

63 Tom Schueler, *Site Planning for Urban Stream Protection*, Washington, DC: Metropolitan Council of Governments, Environmental Land Planning Series, 1995, p. 73.

64 Downs, *Stuck in Traffic, op. cit.*, pp. 17–18.

65 Peter W.G. Newman and Jeffrey R. Kenworthy, "Gasoline Consumption and Cities: A Comparison of U.S. Cities With a Global Survey," *Journal of the American Planning Association*, vol. 55, Winter 1989, pp. 24, 25.

66 Platt, *op. cit.*, pp. 138–39 (using the term popularized in Joel Garreau's book, *Edge Cities*). See also Robert Cervero, *America's Suburban Centers: The Land Use-Transportation Link*, Boston: Unwin Hyman, 1989, pp. 4–5; Robert Cervero, "Congestion Relief: The Land Use Alternative," *Journal of Planning Education and Research*, vol. 10, 1991, pp. 119,121.

67 See Peter Calthorpe, *The Next American Metropolis*, New York: Princeton Architectural Press, 1993, p. 19.

68 Diamond and Noonan, *op. cit.*, p. 94.

69 Stegman and Turner, *op. cit.*, p. 158; See also Davis, *op. cit.*, p. 45–46; Organization for Economic Cooperation and Development and European Conference of Ministers of Transport, *Urban Travel and Sustainable Development*, 1995, p. 42.

70 Cervero, "Congestion Relief," *op. cit.*, p. 121; Cervero, *America's Suburban Centers, op. cit.*, pp. 4–5.

71 Platt, *op. cit.*, pp. 138–39.

72 Cervero, *America's Suburban Centers, op. cit.*, pp. 4–5.

73 Cohn, *op. cit.*, 10; Peter Behr, "Northern Virginia Is Still Where The Jobs Are," *The Washington Post*, August 31, 1996, p. F1.

74 Larry Van Dyne, "Job Wars," *Washingtonian*, vol. 32, January 1997, p. 4.

75 D'Vera Cohn, "Numerical Order," *The Washington Post Magazine*, February 16, 1997, p. 12. From 1990 to 1998, the share of employment claimed by Washington's outer suburbs increased from 39 to 50 percent. Mark Rubin and Margery Austin Turner, *Patterns of Employment Growth in the Washington Metropolitan Area* (publication pending as this book goes to press).

76 Downs, *Stuck In Traffic, op. cit.*, pp. 18–19.

77 Edward E. Hill and John Brennan, *Where is the Renaissance? Employment Specialization Within Ohio's Metropolitan Areas*, paper presented at the Conference on Interdependence of Central Cities and Suburbs, sponsored by the Brookings Institution, the Lincoln Land Institute, and the University of Illinois at Chicago, September 24, 1998.

78 Cervero, "Congestion Relief," *op. cit.*, p. 120.

79 Downs, *Stuck In Traffic, op. cit.*, pp. 18–19.

80 Cervero, *America's Suburban Centers, op. cit.*, pp. 43–45.

81 Platt, *op. cit.*, pp. 138–139.

82 Arendt, *op. cit.*, p. 136.

83 Jackie Spinner, "In Charles County, All Roads Lead to the Mall," *The Washington Post*, September 1, 1996, p. B1.

84 See Calthorpe, *op. cit.*, p. 22.

85 George Abney, "The Statehouse," *Historic Preservation News*, vol. 34, December 1994/January 1995, p. 18.

86 Frank Jossi, "Rewrapping the Big Box," *Planning*, vol. 64, August 1998, p. 16.

87 *Ibid.*

88 *Ibid.* See also Margaret Webb Pressler, "Toys R Us to Close 90 Stores," *The Washington Post*, September 17, 1998, p. C1.

89 Land Lease Real Estate Investments, *op. cit.*, pp. 6–7.

90 Platt, *op. cit.*, pp. 129–31.

91 *Ibid.* pp. 197, 220–22.

92 Donald M. Rothblatt, "North American Planning: Canadian and U.S. Perspectives," *Journal of the American Planning Association*, vol. 60, Autumn 1994, pp. 501, 506–7.

93 Platt, *op. cit.*, p. 139.

94 Center for Neighborhood Technology, *Community Green Line Initiative* (undated), p. 2.

Chapter 1 (continued)

95 Environmental Law and Policy Center of the Midwest, *Portrait of Sprawl: Northeastern Illinois Population Change* (map, undated). Chicago's traditional central business district is called "the Loop" because of the configuration of the city's mass transit system.

96 Orfield, *op. cit.*, pp. 160–164.

97 NIPC, *op. cit.*, p. 3.

98 *Ibid.* at 4.

99 Downs, *New Visions, op. cit.*, p. 145.

100 Newman and Kenworthy, *Cities and Automobile Dependence, op. cit.*, 299. Jeff Kenworthy, Felix Laube, *et al.*, *Report for the World Bank*, Perth, Australia: Murdoch University, February 1997, p. 6; see also Wendell Cox, *Demographic Briefs: U.S. Urbanized Area Population and Density Trends: 1950–1990*, Belleville, IL: Wendell Cox Consultancy, 1996.

101 Downs, *New Visions, op. cit.*, pp. 142–3, Downs, *Stuck In Traffic, op. cit.*, p. 90.

102 NIPC, *op. cit.*, p. 3.

103 Alex Rodriguez, "Not Much 'Rush' In Rush Hour," *Chicago Sun-Times*, February 23, 1997, p. 8.

104 Sue Ellen Christian, "Growth Without Pain: McHenry Seeks An Elusive Mix," *Chicago Tribune*, McHenry County edition, April 11, 1995.

105 See *Village of Schaumburg*, information from the Roosevelt University web site, http://www.roosevelt.edu/metro/vschaumb.htm, January 6, 1999. Roosevelt has a campus in Schaumburg. See also Platt, *op. cit.*, p. 138.

106 The Sears Tower is the tallest office building in the United States.

107 Phil Borckman, "Motorola On Board Elgin's Revival," *Chicago Tribune*, Metro Northwest Section, August 15, 1996; Valerie Berton, "Growing Pains," *American Farmland*, vol. 16, Fall 1995, p. 8.

108 *Ibid.* pp. 8–10; Christian, *op. cit.*.

109 Ray Quintanilla, "Tollway No Longer Stopping Point for Annexations," *Chicago Tribune*, April 3, 1996.

110 Berton, *op. cit.*, pp. 8–10.

111 Dionne Searcy, "Barrington Area Goals Put To Test," *Chicago Tribune*, Metro Northwest Section, August 11, 1996.

112 Christian, *op. cit.*.

113 "Southwest Suburbs Witnessing a Boom," *Chicago Sun-Times*, January 27, 1995.

114 NIPC, *op. cit.*, p. 5.

115 William Presecky, "Ballot Issues Put Price Tags On Growth," *Chicago Tribune*, Metro Southwest Edition, January 19, 1996.

116 Alex Rodriguez, "Transit Plan Looks Ahead to 23 Years of Suburb Growth," *Chicago Sun-Times*, February 14, 1997, p. 3.

117 Michael Gillis, "Judge Stalls Tollway," *Chicago Sun-Times*, January 17, 1997, p. 1. The litigation was brought by the Environmental Law and Policy Center of the Midwest, Business and Professional People for the Public Interest, and the Sierra Club. See *Sierra Club v. U.S. Department of Transportation*, 962 F. Supp. 1037 (N.D. Ill. 1997). The I-355 extension is only one controversial extension of the region's tollway system; another project that would extend Route 53 to the north is opposed by many citizens and politicians in Lake County. See, e.g., Timothy S. Rooney, "Traffic Jam Forms Against Route 53," *Chicago Daily Herald*, January 17, 1996, p.1.

118 William Presecky, "Peotone Airport Glows In Study—Third Regional Airport Is Called a Remedy to Sprawl," *Chicago Tribune*, August 24, 1996.

119 Julie Dendoff, "Harvey's Hope Could Rise From Mall's Rubble," *Chicago Tribune*, Metro Chicago edition, August 22, 1996.

120 Orfield, *op. cit.*, p. 160.

121 Cervero, *America's Suburban Centers, op. cit.*, p. 176.

122 Orfield, *op. cit.*, p. 160.

123 Newman and Kenworthy, *Cities and Automobile Dependence, op. cit.*, p. 299.

124 NIPC, *op. cit.*, p. 3. See also Orfield, *op. cit.*, p. 163.

125 Cervero, *America's Suburban Centers, op. cit.*, pp. 179–184.

126 NIPC, *op. cit.*, p. 4.

127 William Grady, "Growth Shows Another Side," *Chicago Tribune*, Metro DuPage section, December 17, 1996.

128 Howard Reich and Desiree Chen, "Sprawling Culture Scene Puts Suburbs In Starring Role," *Chicago Tribune*, August 5, 1996.

129 Moore and Thorsnes, *op. cit.*, pp. 9–10, 16–18.

130 California Air Resources Board (CARB), *Transportation-Related Land Use Strategies to Minimize Motor Vehicle Emissions*, June 1995, citing John Shaw, p. B-64; Downs, *Stuck In Traffic, op. cit.*, p. 17.

131 Downs, *Stuck In Traffic, op. cit.*, p. 101.

132 See Diane Ravitch, *A New Era in Urban Education?* Washington, DC: The Brookings Institution,

Chapter 1 (continued)

Policy Brief #35, August 1998. Ravitch, who was an assistant secretary in the U.S. Department of Education in the Bush administration, lays much of the blame on the governance structure of urban school systems, and advocates the use of charter schools and vouchers as remedies.

133 See, e.g., Epstein, *op. cit.*, at 350–51 and 355–56; Joel Kotkin, "White Flight to the Fringes," *The Washington Post*, March 10, 1996, C1.

134 Michael Newman, "Utopia, Dystopia, Diaspora," *Journal of the American Planning Association*, vol. 57, Summer 1991, pp. 344–347; See also Ewing, "Is Los Angeles-Style Sprawl Desirable?" *op. cit.*.

135 Kevin Lynch, "What Is the Form of a City, and How Is It Made?" in Jay M. Stein, ed., *Classic Readings in Urban Planning*, New York: McGraw-Hill, 1995, pp. 179–187.

136 Hiss, *op. cit.*, pp. 131–32.

137 Epstein, *op. cit.*, pp. 356–62.

138 See, e.g., Lincoln Institute, *op. cit.*, 5–6; Arendt, *op. cit.*, pp. 135–139; Moore and Thorsnes, *op. cit.*, pp. 42–43, 64; Ewing, "Characteristics, Causes and Effects," *op. cit.*, pp. 4–5.

139 Van Dyne, *op. cit.* We discuss the Disney project again in our next chapter. See also Michael D. Shear, "Prince William Shifts From Big to Small," *The Washington Post*, September 30, 1996, p. B1. Van Dyne points out that another factor contributing to the suburban flight of large businesses is opposition to expansion by city neighbors. The insurance giant GEICO, for example, faced nearly two decades of opposition to its on-site expansion plans before fleeing its inner-suburb, transit-accessible location in metro Washington, DC, for a semi-rural site 40 miles south of the city.

140 As noted, Metropolitan Chicago alone has over 260 local governments with jurisdiction over land use.

141 Loudoun's growth is profiled at length in Glenn Frankel and Peter Pae, "In Loudoun, Two Worlds Collide," *The Washington Post*, March 24, 1997, pp. A1, 10–11. The authors quote one developer's assertion that the environmental group's proposal smacked of "the socialistic power that they might have over in Maryland. Here in Virginia, I think land rights are a hell of a little more sacred."

142 Epstein, *op. cit.*, pp. 353–55, 364–65.

143 Downs, *New Visions*, p. 5.

Chapter 2

1 Gregg Easterbrook, *A Moment on the Earth: The Coming Age of Environmental Optimism*, New York: Penguin Books USA, 1996.

2 Quoted in Timothy Egan, "Urban Sprawl Strains Western States," *The New York Times*, December 29, 1996, p. 1. Melnick is the director of the Morrison Institute for Public Policy at Arizona State University.

3 Lee R. Epstein, "Where Yards Are Wide: Have Land Use Planning and Law Gone Astray?" *William and Mary Environmental Law and Policy Review*, vol. 21, 1997, p. 349.

4 Margo Oge, Director, Office of Mobile Sources, U.S. Environmental Protection Agency, *Automotive Emissions: Progress and Challenges*, presentation to Automotive Management Briefing Session, Traverse City, MI, August 9, 1995. See also Office of Mobile Sources, U.S. Environmental Protection Agency, *Automobiles and Ozone*, Fact Sheet OMS-4, January 1993.

5 Don Pickrell, *Description of VMT Forecasting Procedure for "Car Talk" Baseline Forecasts*, Volpe Center, U.S. Department of Transportation, Table 2. See also Energy Information Administration, *Annual Energy Outlook 1996*, DOE/EIA-0383 (96), January 1996, p. 24.

6 Organization for Economic Cooperation and Development and European Conference of Ministers of Transport, *Urban Travel and Sustainable Development*, 1995, p. 16.

7 U.S. Department of Transportation, 1990 National Personal Transportation Survey (NPTS), *Travel Behavior Issues in the 90s*, 1992, p. 11.

8 *Ibid.* pp. 11-13; see also U.S. Department of Transportation, *Our Nation's Travel: 1995 NPTS Early Results Report*, September 1997.

9 Anthony Downs, *Stuck In Traffic: Coping with Peak-Hour Traffic Congestion*, Washington, DC: The Brookings Institution; Cambridge, MA: The Lincoln Institute of Land Policy, 1992, p. 14.

10 Pickrell, *op. cit.*, Table 2; NPTS, *op. cit.*, pp. 11, 13.

11 Peter Calthorpe, *The Next American Metropolis*, New York: Princeton Architectural Press, 1993, pp. 20, 47–48.

12 U.S. Department of Transportation, *Our Nation's Travel, op. cit.*, p. 32.

13 Pickrell, *op. cit.*, Table 7.

14 Puget Sound Council of Governments, *Vision 2020: Growth and Transportation Strategy for the Central Puget Sound Region*, October 1990, p. 6.

Chapter 2 (continued)

15 Chesapeake Bay Foundation, *A Dollars and Sense Partnership: Economic Development and Environmental Protection*, Annapolis: Chesapeake Bay Foundation, 1996 (cited in Janet Pelley, *et al.*, *Sprawl Costs Us All*, Annapolis, MD: Sierra Club Foundation, 1997, p. 6).

16 California Air Resources Board (CARB), *The Land Use-Air Quality Linkage*, 1994, p. 1.

17 Chris Lester, Jeffrey Spivack, Gregory Reeves, Steve Nicely, "Divided We Sprawl," *The Kansas City Star*, December 17–22, 1995, p. 9, reprint, pp.1–20.

18 Center for Neighborhood Technology, *Community Green Line Initiative: Land Use Planning, Community Development and Public Transit—the Pulaski Station Project* (undated).

19 Jeff Kenworthy, *et al.*, *Report for the World Bank*, Perth, Australia: Murdoch University, February 1997, p. 6; Peter W.G. Newman and Jeffrey R. Kenworthy, *Cities and Automobile Dependence: A Sourcebook*, Aldershot, UK, and Brookfield, VT: Gower Publishing Co., 1989, p. 299.

20 Federal Highway Administration, *Highway Statistics 1989*, Washington, DC: U.S. Department of Transportation, 1990; Federal Highway Administration, *Highway Statistics 1994*, Washington, DC: U.S. Department of Transportation, 1995 [cited in 1000 Friends of Oregon, *Making the Connections: A Summary of the LUTRAQ Project*, Portland, OR: February 1997, p. 3 (prepared by Parsons Brinckerhoff)].

21 Center for Neighborhood Technology, *op. cit.*

22 "Pace Planning Expansion But Riders Still Shun Buses," *Chicago Sun-Times*, March 6, 1995, p. 1.

23 Surface Transportation Policy Project, *An Analysis of the Relationship Between Highway Expansion and Congestion in Metropolitan Areas: Lessons from the 15-Year Texas Transportation Institute Study*, Washington, DC: Surface Transportation Policy Project, November 1998. Chicago's congestion has worsened; only two years ago, the region ranked as the country's fifth-most congested. See Alex Rodriguez, "Not Much 'Rush' In Rush Hour," *Chicago Sun-Times*, February 23, 1997, p. 8.

24 Kenworthy, *et al.*, *op. cit.*, p. 6; Newman and Kenworthy, *Cities and Automobile Dependence*, *op. cit.*, p. 188.

25 Michael Bernick and Robert Cervero, *Transit Villages in the 21st Century*, New York: McGraw-Hill, 1996, p. 60.

26 Neal R. Peirce, "New Friends Plead the Case for Mass Transit," *The Baltimore Sun*, April 10, 1995, p. 9A.

27 Northeastern Illinois Planning Commission (NIPC), *Strategic Plan for Land Resource Management*, 1992, p. 28.

28 Robert Cervero, "Jobs-Housing Balancing and Regional Mobility," *Journal of the American Planning Association*, vol. 55, Spring 1989, pp. 136, 138–141.

29 Alex Rodriguez, "Transit Plan Looks Ahead to 23 Years of Suburb Growth," *Chicago Sun Times*, February 14, 1997, p. 3.

30 Sue Anne Pressley, "Atlanta's Booming Growth Is No Easy Ride," *The Washington Post*, December 4, 1998, p. A3.

31 U.S. Department of Transportation, *Our Nation's Travel*, *op. cit.*, p. 13.

32 Reid H. Ewing, "Is Los Angeles-Style Sprawl Desirable?" *Journal of the American Planning Association*, vol. 63, Winter 1997, pp. 107, 113.

33 Alice Reid, "Work Patterns Shifting Commute, Traffic Study Says," *The Washington Post*, August 15, 1996, p. C1 (citing research by the American Association of State Highway and Transportation Officials).

34 Alan Pisarski, *New Perspectives in Commuting*, Washington, DC: Federal Highway Administration, Office of Highway Information Management, July 1992 (cited in 1000 Friends of Oregon, *Making the Connections: A Summary of the LUTRAQ Project*, Portland, OR: February 1997) (prepared by Parsons Brinckerhoff).

35 See e.g., Robert Cervero, *America's Suburban Centers: The Land Use-Transportation Link*, Boston: Unwin Hyman, 1989, p. 7; Robert Cervero, "Congestion Relief: The Land Use Alternative," *Journal of Planning Education and Research*, vol. 10, 1991, pp. 120–121.

36 Susan Handy, *How Land Use Patterns Affect Travel Patterns: A Bibliography*, Council of Planning Librarians, 1992, p. 26–27 (citing 1987 research by Alan Pisarski). Professor Handy reports Pisarski's research as finding that, in the 1980s, suburb-to-suburb commuting did hold an advantage over suburb-to-city commuting in both reduced trip time and reduced trip length. Given the trends, the advantage is unlikely to be maintained for long. Professor Ewing notes that, by the end of the 1980s, average commute times were significantly greater in suburbs than in central cities. Ewing, "Is Los Angeles-Style Sprawl Desirable?" *op. cit.*

37 Cervero, *America's Suburban Centers*, *op. cit.*, p. 8.

38 Bernick and Cervero, *op. cit.*, p. 42.

39 Jeff Kenworthy, Felix Laube, *et al.*, *Report for the World Bank*, Perth, Australia: Murdoch University, February 1997, p. 8.

40 U.S. Department of Transportation, *Our Nation's Travel*, *op. cit.*, p. 17; see also U.S. DOT, *1990 NPTS*, *op. cit.*, pp. 17–25. Transit claims over 50 percent of commuting trips in New York, and significantly high

Chapter 2 (continued)

shares of work trips in Chicago and in many Eastern cities. See Bernick and Cervero, *op. cit.*, pp. 60–61.

41 Kenworthy, *et al.*, *op. cit.*, p. 8.

42 Calthorpe, *op. cit.*, p. 47. See also John Pucher, "Urban Travel Behavior as the Outcome of Public Policy: The Example of Modal-Split in Western Europe and North America," *Journal of the American Planning Association*, vol. 54, 1988, pp. 509–520; John Pucher, "Urban Passenger Transport in the United States and Europe: A Comparative Analysis of Public Policies," *Transport Reviews*, vol. 15, 1995, pp. 211–227.

43 Terry Moore and Paul Thorsnes, *The Transportation/Land Use Connection*, Chicago: American Planning Association, Planners Advisory Service Rept. No. 448/449, 1994, p. 37.

44 Pelley, *et al.*, *op. cit.*, p. 6.

45 Downs, *Stuck in Traffic, op. cit.*, p. 2.

46 U.S. Department of Transportation, *Our Nation's Travel, op. cit.*, p. 22.

47 Downs, *Stuck in Traffic, op. cit.*, pp. 26–30. See also Transportation Research Board, National Research Council, *Special Report 245: Expanding Metropolitan Highways*, 1995, pp. 221–222; Valdus Adankus, former Regional Administrator, U.S. Environmental Protection Agency, quoted in Environmental Law and Policy Center, "Anti-Sprawl Groups Respond to UIC/Tollway Study on Highways and Sprawl," press release, November 9, 1998 ("The link between added highway capacity, particularly new multi-lane highways in relatively rural areas, and significantly increased development in these areas has been well documented."); Alan Sipress, "Widen the Roads, Drivers Will Come," *The Washington Post*, January 4, 1999, B1.

48 Holtzclaw has worked extensively as a transportation consultant to the Natural Resources Defense Council. His most recent work has been sponsored by a partnership of organizations involved in developing the "location-efficient mortgage" (LEM), which would credit borrowers for the reduced transportation costs made possible by living in transit- and pedestrian-accessible neighborhoods. The LEM partnership comprises NRDC, the Surface Transportation Policy Project, and the Center for Neighborhood Technology. We discuss the LEM more specifically in chapter Five.

49 See, John Holtzclaw, *et al, Location Efficiency: Neighborhood and Socio-Economic Characteristics Determine Auto Ownership and Driving: Studies in Chicago, Los Angeles, and San Francisco*, monograph, publication pending; John Holtzclaw, *Using Residential Patterns and Transit to Decrease Auto Dependence and Costs*, San Francisco: Natural Resources Defense Council and Costa Mesa, CA: California Home Energy Efficiency

Rating Systems, 1994; John Holtzclaw, *Explaining Urban Density and Transit Impacts on Auto Use*, paper presented to the California State Energy Resources Conservation and Development Commission, 1990. Refinements to the Holtzclaw research are on file with the author and with the LEM partnership. (Except when our use of this body of work relies on a single portion of it, we cite it collectively herein as "Holtzclaw.") See also Greig Harvey, *Relation of Residential Density to VMT Per Resident*, Oakland, CA: Metropolitan Planning Commission, 1990.

50 Bernick and Cervero, *op. cit.*, pp. 82–83.

51 "Net" density refers to the number of persons or households per unit of land specifically devoted to housing, and is usually expressed in America as a per-acre measurement. "Gross" density includes all land uses, including public space, roads, and commercial land, and is generally expressed in America as persons per square mile.

52 California Air Resources Board (CARB), *Transportation-Related Land Use Strategies to Minimize Motor Vehicle Emissions*, 1995, p. 5-5.

53 Conversion of gross population density to net residential density is necessarily imprecise. Nevertheless, a common conversion ratio is one household per residential acre to every 800 persons per square mile. See, e.g., Anthony Downs, *New Visions for Metropolitan America*, Washington, DC: The Brookings Institution; Cambridge, MA: Lincoln Institute of Land Policy, 1994, p. 145.

54 Robert Dunphy and Kimberly Fisher, "Transportation, Congestion, and Density: New Insights," *Transportation Research Record No. 1552*, Washington, DC: Transportation Research Board, 1996, pp. 89–96.

55 Downs, *New Visions, op. cit.*, p. 149.

56 Newman and Kenworthy, *Cities and Automobile Dependence, op. cit.*, p. 129.

57 Kenworthy, *et al.*, *op. cit.*, p. 17.

58 Nelson Nygard Consulting Associates, "Land Use and Transit Demand: The Transit Orientation Index," in *Primary Transit Network Study*, Portland, OR: Tri-Met, 1995, Chapter 3.

59 In particular, for light rail a 10 percent higher residential density is associated with 5.9 percent more riders per station, and a 10 percent higher CBD employment density is associated with about 4 percent more riders per residential station. For commuter rail, a 10 percent higher CBD employment density is associated with an average of 7.1 percent more riders at residential stations, while a 10 percent higher residential density yields about 2.5 percent more riders. Residential density has a proportionally lower impact on commuter rail ridership partly because of the popularity of park-and-ride lots.

Chapter 2 (continued)

Parsons Brinckerhoff Quade and Douglas, *Commuter and Light Rail Transit Corridors: The Land Use Connection*, 1996, cited in 1000 Friends of Oregon, *Making the Connections, op. cit.*, at 11–15. See also Bernick and Cervero, *op. cit.*, pp. 75–81.

60 Boris Pushkarev and Jeffrey Zupan, *Public Transport and Land Use Policy*, Bloomington, IN: Indiana University Press, 1977.

61 Holtzclaw, *op. cit.*

62 See, *e.g.*, Downs, *New Visions, op. cit.*, pp. 158–161; Newman and Kenworthy, *Cities and Automobile Dependence, op. cit.*, pp. 127–129 (placing the threshold at 30–40 persons per hectare gross); L.D. Frank and G. Pivo, "Impacts of Mixed Use and Density on Three Modes of Travel," in *Issues in Land Use and Transportation Planning, Models and Applications*, Washington, DC: Transportation Research Record No. 1466, 1994, pp. 44–52; T. Messenger and R. Ewing, "Transit-Oriented Development in the Sunbelt," *Transportation Research Record No. 1552*, 1996, pp. 145–152.

63 See, *e.g.*, Downs, *Stuck In Traffic, op. cit.*, p. 87; CARB, *The Land Use Air Quality Linkage*, 1994, p. 7; Frank and Pivo, *op. cit.*

64 Cervero notes the striking successes in suburban Bellevue, Washington, and Houston, Texas, in building workplaces with FARs of 7.5 and 5.0 respectively, and achieving substantial worker mode shares for transit and carpooling. Cervero, "Congestion Relief," *op. cit.*, pp. 122–23. In between his 1989 and 1997 books, Cervero revised downward (from 0.3–0.4 to 0.2–0.3) his description of floor-to-area ratios currently being built. See Bernick and Cervero, *op. cit.*, p. 74.

65 Newman and Kenworthy, *Cities and Automobile Dependence, op. cit.*, p. 62.

66 Kenworthy, *op. cit.*, p. 11.

67 See, *e.g.*, Ruth L Steiner, "Residential Density and Travel Patterns," in *Issues in Land Use and Transportation Planning, op. cit.*, pp. 37–43; California Air Resources Board (CARB), *Transportation-Related Land Use Strategies to Minimize Motor Vehicle Emissions*, June 1995, p. B-35 (citing 1994 work by Dunphy and Fisher). Professor Handy also faults the Holtzclaw research for attributing impacts to density without also examining the influence of neighborhood services and transit accessibility. See Handy, *op. cit.*, p. 21. This does not seem a glaring limitation, however, given that density, service, and transit are usually correlated in urban neighborhoods. In any event, the refinements in the most recent iterations of Hotlzclaw's research explicitly address some of these other factors. See, *e.g.*, Hotlzclaw, *et al.*, *Location Efficiency, op. cit.* Handy does

not dispute that the three factors together can produce changes in travel behavior, as discussed below in this section.

68 Holtzclaw, *op. cit.*

69 Kenworthy, *op. cit.*, p. 6.

70 Handy, *op. cit.*, pp. 7,3; Ewing, "Is Los Angeles-Style Sprawl Desirable?", *op. cit.*; Calthorpe, *op. cit.*, p. 48.

71 Bernick and Cervero, *op. cit.*, p. 74.

72 Cervero, "Jobs-Housing Balancing," *op. cit.*, pp. 136–137, 145.

73 Stephen C. Fehr, "Area Shoppers Find Search for a Parking Space Often Can Be a Maddening Mission," *The Washington Post*, September 1, 1996, p. B1.

74 George Abney, "The Statehouse," *Historic Preservation News*, vol. 34, December 1994/January 1995, p. 18.

75 Cervero, "Congestion Relief," *op. cit.*, pp. 123–24. Bernick and Cervero, *op. cit.*, pp. 85–91.

76 Calthorpe, *op. cit.*, p. 27.

77 See, e.g., Downs, *Stuck in Traffic*, pp. 98–99.

78 Reid H. Ewing, "Characteristics, Causes, and Effects of Sprawl: A Literature Review," *Environmental and Urban Issues*, Florida Atlantic University/Florida International University, 1994, p. 7. See also CARB, *Transportation-Related Land Use Strategies, op. cit.*, pp. B-37–38; Frank and Pivo, *op. cit.*.

79 Bernick and Cervero, *op. cit.*, pp. 90–91.

80 Cervero, "Congestion Relief," *op. cit.*, p. 124.

81 Downs, *Stuck in Traffic, op. cit.*, p. 100.

82 Arthur C. Nelson and James B. Duncan, *Growth Management Principles and Practices*, Chicago: American Planning Association, 1995, pp. 15–16 (referring to research by Reid Ewing).

83 CARB, *Transportation-Related Land Use Strategies, op. cit.*, pp. 3–16, B-66.

84 Handy, *op. cit.*

85 CARB, *Transportation-Related Land Use Strategies, op. cit.*, p. 3–14.

86 Oge, *op. cit.*, p. 2.

87 Cervero, "Congestion Relief," *op. cit.*, p. 122.

88 Equitable Real Estate Management, Inc., and Real Estate Research Corporation, *Emerging Trends in Real Estate: 1997*, Chicago: Real Estate Research Corporation, October 1996, p. 29.

89 CARB, *Transportation-Related Land Use Strategies, op. cit.*, pp. 3–16.

Chapter 2 (continued)

90 See *ibid.*, p. B-33 (citing research by Cheslow and Neels); Handy, *op. cit.*, p. 12. See also Pushkarev and Zupan, *op. cit.*

91 Downs, *Stuck in Traffic, op. cit.*, pp. 86–87.

92 Cervero, "Jobs-Housing Balancing and Regional Mobility," *op. cit.*, p. 121. Cervero's finding is consistent with international research from Denmark and Norway indicating that corporate relocation to the suburbs can double automobile commuting, even when workers' average commuting distance remains the same. OECD, *Urban Travel and Sustainable Development, op. cit.*, p. 42.

93 CARB, *The Land Use-Air Quality Linkage*, 1994, p. 8.

94 *Ibid.* p. 4. See also CARB, *Transportation and Land Use Strategies, op. cit.*, pp. 3-13–14, B-29–30; Downs, *Stuck in Traffic, op. cit.*, pp. 86–87.

95 The most visible proponents of this argument are Peter Gordon and Henry W. Richardson of the University of Southern California, who relentlessly defend dispersed land use. See, e.g., Peter Gordon and Henry W. Richardson, "Gasoline Consumption and Cities: A Reply," *Journal of the American Planning Association*, vol. 55, Summer 1989, pp. 342–46. Professor Handy, while noting limitations in their methodology, includes a number of publications by Gordon and Richardson in her comprehensive bibliography. See Handy, *op. cit.*, pp. 18–21.

96 See Handy, *op. cit.*, pp. 3–4; Ewing, "Is Los Angeles-Style Sprawl Desirable?", *op. cit.*

97 Peter W.G. Newman and Jeffrey R. Kenworthy, "Is There a Role for Physical Planners?" *Journal of the American Planning Association*, vol. 58, Summer 1992, pp. 3, 358–359.

98 See Calthorpe, *op. cit.*

99 Bernick and Cervero, *op. cit.*

100 Calthorpe, *op. cit.*, p. 35.

101 Bruce Friedman, *et al.*, "Effect of Neotraditional Neighborhood Design on Travel Characteristics," in *Issues in Land Use and Transportation Planning, op. cit.* See also Bernick and Cervero, *op. cit.*, pp. 103–111.

102 CARB, *Transportation-Related Land Use Strategies, op. cit.*, pp. 3–12. See also Bernick and Cervero, *op. cit.*, pp. 112–121.

103 Reid Ewing, *et al.*, "Getting Around a Traditional City, a Suburban Planned Unit Development, and Everything In Between," in *Issues in Land and Transportation Planning, op. cit.*, pp. 53–62.

104 L.D. Frank and G. Pivo, *op. cit.*

105 CARB, *The Land Use-Air Quality Linkage, op. cit.*, p. 10.

106 CARB, *Transportation-Related Land Use Strategies, op. cit.*, pp. B-54–55. Notwithstanding the mounting evidence, some critics speculate that better neighborhood design, by improving access to destinations, might actually increase driving trips, as well as walking. See, e.g., Randall Crane, "Cars and Drivers in New Suburbs," *Journal of the American Planning Association*, vol. 62, Winter 1996, pp. 51–65.

107 1000 Friends of Oregon, *Making The Connections, op. cit.*

108 1000 Friends of Oregon, *Analysis of Alternatives*, LUTRAQ, vol. 5, Portland OR: May 1997. In order to maximize transportation benefits, the LUTRAQ planners also reinforced neighborhood design features with market incentives, including modest parking surcharges for single-occupancy driving and subsidized transit passes. The analysis revealed that the LUTRAQ alternative, especially within the TOD neighborhoods, consistently outperformed conventional development both with and without the market incentives, but benefits were greatest with the incentives. *Id.*, Table 2-3 at 18.

109 1000 Friends of Oregon, *Making the Connections, op. cit.*

110 *Ibid.*

111 Easterbrook, *op. cit.*, pp. 304, 349, 354, 258.

112 Office of Air Quality Planning and Standards, U.S. Environmental Protection Agency, *National Air Quality and Emissions Trends Report*, 1966, at 3 (1998).

113 Oge, *op. cit.*, p. 1.

114 William Booth, "In L.A., a Clean Day is a Dream No Longer," *The Washington Post*, December 18, 1997, p. A1.

115 U.S. Environmental Protection Agency, Office of Mobile Sources, *Automobiles and Ozone*, Fact Sheet OMS-4, January 1993, p. 1.

116 CARB, *The Land Use-Air Quality Linkage, op. cit.* Easterbrook, the environmental optimist, goes further, claiming that today's new cars produce some 99 percent less pollution than cars built before 1970 and that today's cars in California produce only one-half of 1 percent of the pollution of that state's cars in 1970. See Easterbrook, *op. cit.*, pp. 186, 190.

117 Warren Brown and Martha M. Hamilton, "GM, Ford Prepare Clean-Air Cars," *The Washington Post*, December 18, 1997, p. A1.

118 National Vehicle and Fuel Emissions Laboratory, U.S. Environmental Protection Agency, *Annual*

Chapter 2 (continued)

Emissions and Fuel Consumption for an Average Vehicle, February 1995.

119 Energy Information Administration, *Annual Energy Outlook 1996,* DOE/EIA-0383 (96), January 1996, p. 48. Other recent sources have put the share as high as 72 percent. See Stacy C. Davis and Patricia S. Hu, Oak Ridge National Lab., *Transportation Energy Data Book,* 1991, p. 3-3.

120 *Annual Energy Outlook, op. cit.,* p. 74. In the *AEO,* energy uses are expressed in heat content, or British thermal units. In 1994, transportation uses accounted for 22.66 quadrillion BTUs ("quads") of petroleum consumption. The Energy Department's standard conversion factors are 5.8 million BTUs per barrel for crude oil consumption and 5.253 million BTUs per barrel for motor gasoline. *Id.* at 269 (Appendix I).

121 Office of Technology Assessment (OTA), *Saving Energy in U.S. Transportation,* Summary, 1994, pp. 7–8.

122 The U.S. produces 14.1 quads of crude oil domestically each year. Net imports amount to 17.25 quads annually. *Annual Energy Outlook, op. cit.,* p. 70. See also OTA, *op. cit.,* p. 2.

123 OTA, *op. cit.,* pp. 1, 10.

124 *Ibid.,* pp. 1–2; Environment and Energy Study Institute Fact Sheet, "Oil and Transportation," cited in *Getting There,* Washington, DC: The Advocacy Institute, 1996, pp. 14, 30.

125 *Annual Energy Outlook, op. cit.,* p. 23.

126 See D.L. Greene *et al.,* Transportation Energy to the Year 2020, in National Transportation Board, National Research Council, *A Look Ahead, Year 2020,* 1988.

127 Clay Chandler, "The 60 Watt Mind-Set," *The Washington Post,* November 14, 1997, p. A20.

128 Warren Brown, "Trucks Are Putting Cars Out of Commission," *The Washington Post,* October 7, 1998, p. C10.

129 Keith Bradsher, "Light Trucks Increase Profits But Foul Air More Than Cars," *The New York Times,* November 30, 1997, p. A1.

130 OTA, *op. cit.,* p. 9; *Annual Energy Outlook, op. cit.,* p. 24.

131 *Ibid.,* p. 23.

132 See, e.g., Pickrell, *op. cit.,* and additional discussion and references above in this chapter.

133 *Annual Energy Outlook, op. cit.,* pp. 118, 119.

134 IPCC, *Summary for Policymakers of the Contribution of Working Group I to the IPCC Second Assessment Report,* 1995.

135 *Ibid.*

136 Joby Warrick, "Earth at Its Warmest in Past 12 Centuries," *The Washington Post,* December 8, 1998, p. A3.

137 *Ibid.*

138 IPCC Working Group II, *Second Assessment Report, Summary for Policymakers* at SPM-10, 1995.

139 U.S. Climate Action Network, *Global Climate Change: U.S. Impacts and Solutions,* 1996.

140 IPCC (Working Group II), *op. cit.,* p. 6; U.S. Climate Action Network, *op. cit..*

141 *Ibid.*

142 *Ibid.*

143 U.S. Climate Action Network, *op. cit.*

144 IPCC (Working Group I), *op. cit.*

145 *Annual Energy Outlook, op. cit.,* p. 49.

146 *Ibid.,* pp. 70–71, 74–75.

147 Joseph J. Romm and Charles B. Curtis, "Mideast Oil Forever," in *The Atlantic Monthly,* April 1996, pp. 57–74, at 60.

148 *Ibid.*

149 Steve Nadis and James MacKenzie, *Car Trouble,* Boston: Beacon Press, 1993, p. 19.

150 D.L. Greene, *et al., The Outlook for U.S. Oil Dependence,* Oak Ridge National Laboratory, ORNL-6873, 1995, p. 3.

151 Romm and Curtis, *op. cit.,* p. 60.

152 *Annual Energy Outlook, op. cit.,* p. 50.

153 Romm and Curtis, *op. cit.,* p. 60.

154 Office of Mobile Sources, U.S. Environmental Protection Agency, *Motor Vehicles and the 1990 Clean Air Act,* Fact Sheet OMS-11, August 1994.

155 U.S. Department of Transportation, Federal Highway Administration, *Transportation Air Quality: Selected Facts and Figures,* FHWA-PD-96-006, 1996, pp. 20–22. See also Oge, *op. cit.*

156 National Vehicle and Fuel Emissions Laboratory, *op. cit.*

157 Office of Mobile Sources, U.S. Environmental Protection Agency, *Air Toxics from Motor Vehicles,* Fact Sheet OM5-2, August 1994. Office of Air Quality Planning and Standards, U.S. Environmental Protection Agency, *The Plain English Guide to the Clean Air Act,* 1996.

158 The particles are emitted both directly in significant quantities from diesel engines and indirectly from both cars and heavy vehicles as a by-product of nitrogen

Chapter 2 (continued)

oxide emissions. See, e.g., Office of Air and Radiation, U.S. Environmental Protection Agency, *1995 National Air Quality: Status and Trends, Six Principal Pollutants-Particulate Matter,* 1996; Office of Mobile Sources, U.S. Environmental Protection Agency, *Tighter Controls Evaluated for NOx, HC and PM Emissions From Heavy-Duty Engines* (Environmental Fact Sheet), September 1995.

159 *Ibid.*; CARB, *The Land Use-Air Quality Linkage, op. cit.,* p. 1

160 For example, over half the particulate pollution measured at street level in Manhattan comes from diesel vehicles. See New York State Department of Environmental Conservation, *New York State Implementation Plan: Inhalable Particulate (PM10),* September 1995, pp. 3, 9.

161 Office of Air and Radiation, U.S. Environmental Protection Agency, *Air Quality Trends—1994: Six Principal Pollutants,* 1995.

162 Office of Mobile Sources, *Automobiles and Ozone, op. cit.*; Chesapeake Bay Foundation, *A Dollars and Sense Partnership, op. cit.,* cited in Pelley, *op. cit.,* p. 6.

163 Office of Mobile Sources, *Automobiles and Ozone, op. cit.*

164 See U.S. Environmental Protection Agency, National Ambient Air Quality Standards for Ozone: Proposed Rule, *Federal Register,* vol. 61, December 13, 1996, pp. 65715–65750. Notwithstanding the scientific evidence, some participants in the debate over air standards have been particularly dismissive of ozone's adverse effects. According to Richard Klimisch, vice-president of the American Automobile Manufacturers Association, "What we're talking about is a temporary loss in lung function of 20 to 30 percent. That's not really a health effect." Joby Warrick, "Opponents Await Proposal To Limit Air Particulates," *The Washington Post,* November 27, 1996, pp. A1, 14.

165 Abt Associates, *Air Pollution-Related Social Costs of On-Highway Motor Vehicles, Part II: Physical and Economic Valuation Modeling,* June 25, 1998, p. 8, Exhibit 3. The estimate does not include values for changes in crop or timber yields due to ozone pollution.

166 Office of Mobile Sources, *Automobiles and Ozone, op. cit.*

167 Egan, "Urban Sprawl Strains Western States," *op. cit.*

168 "Vital Signs of the Golden State," *The Amicus Journal,* vol. 19, Summer 1997, pp. 36, 39. The article reports that air pollution in the Los Angeles area costs $7.4 billion per year.

169 Booth, *op. cit.*

170 "Air Quality Pact Follows Growing Concerns," *Asheville* (NC) *Citizen-Times,* December 27, 1998, p. B1.

171 See, *e.g.,* U.S. Department of Transportation, *Transportation Air Quality, op. cit.,* p. 13.

172 See Office of Air and Radiation, *1995 National Air Quality: Statistical Trends, op. cit.* Shprentz, *op. cit.,* p. 116.

173 Office of Air and Radiation, *1995 National Air Quality: Status and Trends, op. cit.* See also Deborah Sheiman Shprentz, *Breath-Taking: Premature Mortality Due to Particulate Air Pollution in 239 American Cities,* New York: Natural Resources Defense Council, 1996, pp. 9–40.

174 Abt Associates, *op. cit.* For particulate matter, the study does not attempt to value the substantial but hard-to-quantify effects of road dust. Nor does it estimate the considerable effects of other sources of particulate pollution, such as heavy industry and off-road diesel engines.

175 *Ibid.*

176 Office of Mobile Sources, *Automobiles and Ozone, op. cit.,* p. 4.

177 U.S. Department of Transportation, *Transportation Air Quality, op. cit.,* p. 19.

178 See, e.g., Office of Mobile Sources, *Tighter Controls Evaluated, op. cit.* OECD, *op. cit.,* p. 140.

179 Office of Air Quality Planning and Standards, *The Plain English Guide, op. cit.*

180 See, e.g., Peter W.G. Newman and Jeffrey R. Kenworthy, *Cities and Automobile Dependence, op. cit.,* and, by the same authors, "The Transport Energy Trade-Off: Fuel-Efficient Traffic Versus Fuel-Efficient Cites," *Transportation Research,* vol. 22A, 1988, pp. 163–174; "Gasoline Consumption and Cities: A Comparison of U.S. Cities with a Global Survey," *Journal of the American Planning Association,* vol. 55, Winter 1989, pp. 24–37; "Is There a Role for Physical Planners?" *op. cit.,* 1992; See also Jeff Kenworthy, *et al., Report for the World Bank, op. cit.*

181 Newman and Kenworthy, *Cities and Automobile Dependence, op. cit.,* p. 35; Kenworthy *et al., Report for the World Bank, op. cit.,* p. 24. The cities studied included, in the U.S.: Houston, Phoenix, Detroit, Denver, Los Angeles, San Francisco, Boston, Washington, Chicago, and New York; in Australia: Perth, Brisbane, Melbourne, Sydney, and Adelaide; in Canada: Toronto; in Russia: Moscow; in Europe: Hamburg, Frankfurt, Zurich, Stockholm, Brussels, Paris, London, Munich, Berlin, Copenhagen, Vienna, and Amsterdam; and in Asia: Tokyo, Singapore, and Hong Kong.

Chapter 2 (continued)

182 Newman and Kenworthy, *Cities and Automobile Dependence, op. cit.*, pp. 45–47; Newman and Kenworthy, "Gasoline Consumption and Cities," *op. cit.*, p. 29.

183 *Ibid.*, p. 27.

184 *Ibid.*, p. 29.

185 Newman and Kenworthy, "Gasoline Consumption and Cities," *op. cit.*, pp. 24–37.

186 Newman and Kenworthy, "The Transport Energy Trade-Off," *op. cit.*, pp. 167–68.

187 *Ibid.*, p. 166; Newman and Kenworthy, "Gasoline Consumption and Cities," *op. cit.*, p. 32.

188 *Ibid.*, p. 27–28.

189 *Ibid.*; Newman and Kenworthy, "The Transport Energy Trade-Off," *op. cit.*, p. 172. Notwithstanding the intuitive plausibility of Newman and Kenworthy's findings, they have met with criticism—sometimes vehement—in some quarters. In particular, Peter Gordon and Harry Richardson, cited above as defenders of dispersed land use, have been so disturbed by this research as to link the Australian scholars with "Maoist planning methods" and to suggest that they should "seek out another planet, preferably unpopulated," to implement their recommendations. Peter Gordon and Harry W. Richardson, "Gasoline Consumption and Cities: A Reply," *op. cit.*, pp. 342–346. Other critics, somewhat more reserved, have cited the problems inherent in working with such a large-scale international database, as we have noted above. Susan Handy, *How Land Patterns Affect Travel Patterns: A Bibliography*, Council of Planning Librarians, 1992, p. 24.

190 Richard Browning, "Impacts of Transportation on Household Energy Consumption," *World Transport Policy and Practice*, vol. 4, no.1, 1998.

191 CARB, *The Land Use-Air Quality Linkage, op. cit.*, p. 2.

192 CARB, *Transportation-Related Land Use Strategies, op. cit.*, pp. 1-3 through 1-7, 5-1 through 5-14.

193 Nitrogen oxides would decline by only three percent. 1000 Friends of Oregon, *Making the Connections, op. cit.*, p. 26.

194 *Ibid.*

195 CARB, *The Land Use-Air Quality Linkage*, p. 12; OECD, *op. cit.*, p. 94.

196 Overall vehicle usage could be cut by 5 to 9 percent under the San Diego scenario, reducing emissions between 1 and 2 percent. Ewing, "Characteristics, Causes, and Effects," *op. cit.*, p. 10.

197 The studies are reported in OECD, *op. cit.*, at 94–97.

198 Nelson and Duncan, *op. cit.*, pp. 13–15. See also CARB, *Transportation-Related Land Use Strategies, op. cit.*, p. B-50 (citing Australian research); V. Haines, "Energy and Urban Form: A Human Ecological Critique," *Urban Affairs Quarterly*, vol. 21, 1986, pp. 337–353.

199 James Howard Kuntsler, "Home from Nowhere," *The Atlantic Monthly*, vol. 278, September 1996, pp. 43–66.

200 Easterbrook, *op. cit.*, p. 386.

201 Rutherford H. Platt, *Land Use and Society*, Washington, DC: Island Press, 1996, p. 9–13.

202 See American Farmland Trust, *Current State Farmland Protection Activities*, Washington, DC: American Farmland Trust, 1991.

203 Easterbrook, *op. cit.*, pp. 562–566, 553–555.

204 A. Ann Sorensen, Richard P. Greene, and Karen Russ, *Farming on the Edge*, DeKalb, IL: American Farmland Trust, 1997, p. 18. If one includes all cropland, the amount lost each year approaches one million acres. Platt, *op. cit.*, p. 11; Nelson and Duncan, *op. cit.*, p. 38; "Farms in Our Future?", *American Farmland*, Fall 1995, p. 19.

205 "Farms in Our Future?" *op. cit.*, p. 20.

206 Ewing, "Characteristics, Causes, and Effects," *op. cit.*, p. 11.

207 Sorensen *et al.*, *op. cit.*, p. 18.

208 Nelson and Duncan, *op. cit.*, pp. 37–38.

209 American Farmland Trust, *Farming On The Edge: A New Look at the Importance and Vulnerability of Agriculture Near American Cities*, 1994. This publication was a predecessor to AFT's similarly titled 1997 publication, *Farming on the Edge*, cited herein as Sorensen *et al.*, *op. cit.*

210 Sorensen *et al.*, *op. cit.*, p. 18.

211 *Ibid.*, p. 4.

212 *Ibid.*, p. 8; Valerie Berton, "Harvest or Homes?" *American Farmland Trust*, Fall 1995, p.14; American Farmland Trust, *Alternatives for Future Urban Growth in California's Central Valley: The Bottom Line for Agriculture and Taxpayers*, Washington, DC, October 1995.

213 Berton, *op. cit.*, p. 14.

214 Sorensen *et al.*, *op. cit.*, p. 8. American Farmland Trust, *op. cit.*

215 *Ibid.*; Berton, *op. cit.*, p. 14. American Farmland Trust, *op. cit.*

Chapter 2 (continued)

216 Colorado is said to be losing 50,000 acres of agricultural land each year. Timothy Egan, "Portland's Hard Line on Managing Growth," *The New York Times*, December 30, 1996. In Carroll County, Maryland, the amount of farmland declined almost one-third, from 224,805 acres in 1960 to 157,505 in 1992, overwhelming the third-largest farmland preservation effort (22,652 acres) in the country. Pelley, *op. cit.*. In the Midwest, the Cleveland-Akron, Ohio, region has lost nearly one-fourth of its farmland in recent years. Sorensen *et al.*, *op. cit.*, p. 11.

217 Glenn Frankel and Peter Pae, "In Loudoun, Two Worlds Collide," *The Washington Post*, March 24, 1997, p. A10.

218 Dan Eggen, "A Growing Issue," *The Washington Post*, October 28, 1998, p. A3.

219 Nelson and Duncan, *op. cit.*, p. 38; Platt, *op. cit.*, pp. 10–13.

220 Nelson and Duncan, *op. cit.*, pp. 6–7, 40–44; Arendt, *op. cit.*, p. 292.

221 American Farmland Trust, *op. cit.*

222 Sorensen *et al.*, *op. cit.*, p. 9 and Table 9.

223 *Ibid.*, Tables 7 and 8.

224 *Ibid.*, Table 7.

225 *Ibid.*, Table 9.

226 Berton, *op. cit.*, p. 9.

227 Sorensen *et al.*, *op. cit.*, supplemental map.

228 Ewing, "Is Los Angeles-Style Sprawl Desirable?" *op. cit.*, p. 23; Michael E. Soulé, "Land Use Planning and Wildlife Maintenance," *Journal of the American Planning Association*, vol. 57, Summer 1991, pp. 313, 315.

229 Soulé, *op. cit.*, p. 313.

230 Reed F. Noss, Edward T. LaRoe III, and J. Michael Scott, "Endangered Ecosystems of the United States: A Preliminary Assessment of Loss and Degradation," Biological Resources Division, United States Geological Survey 4 (undated but available on the USGS web site, http:\\biology.usgs.gov, as of January 16, 1998).

231 *Ibid.*, pp. 58–60 (Appendix B).

232 "Endangered Species General Statistics," Division of Endangered Species, U.S. Fish and Wildlife Service, http://www.fws.gov, January 27, 1998.

233 *The 1997 Species Report Card: The State of U.S. Plants and Animals*, The Nature Conservancy, Summary, http:www.consci.tnc.org, January 8, 1998 (citing J.H. Lawton and R.M. May, *Extinction Rates*, Oxford: Oxford University Press, 1995).

234 "State of the Nation's Species," *The 1997 Species Report Card, op. cit.*

235 Although the literature on this subject is disappointingly scant, that could change as a result of two long-term ecological studies that have been launched by the National Science Foundation. The studies are centered on the Baltimore and Phoenix metropolitan regions.

236 See "Wetlands Loss Slows, Fish and Wildlife Series Study Shows," news release, U. S. Fish and Wildlife Service, September 17, 1997.

237 Noss, *et al.*, *op. cit.*, p. 14.

238 Northern Prairie Wildlife Research Center, United States Geological Survey, *Wetlands Losses in the United States* (undated but taken from the USGS web site at http:\\www.npwrc.usgs.gov, January 6, 1998).

239 See Brent Hulsey and Brent Koeller, *Floods, Deaths, and Wetlands Destruction*, Sierra Club, 1997.

240 "Wetlands Loss Slows," *op. cit.*

241 See Jocelyn Kaiser, "New Wetland Proposal Draws Flak," *Science*, vol. 279, February 13, 1998, p. 980; Joby Warrick, "New Wetlands Guidelines, New Openings," *The Washington Post*, January 31, 1998, p. A1.

242 Noss, *et al.*, *op. cit.*, p. 14.

243 *Ibid.*, pp. 11–12.

244 Scott Sunde, "Urban Sprawl Turns Green to Brown as Tree Cover Shrinks," *Seattle Post-Intelligencer*, July 15, 1998, p. A1.

245 Egan, "Urban Sprawl Strains Western States," *op. cit.*

246 Michael Jasny, *Leap of Faith*, New York: Natural Resources Defense Council, May 1997, p. 1-7.

247 *Ibid.*, pp. 1-7; Soulé, *op. cit.*, pp. 315–318.

248 Jasny, *op. cit.*

249 *Ibid.*, p. 1.

250 Soulé, *op. cit.*, pp. 318–321.

251 Todd Shields, "On Edge," *The Washington Post Magazine*, February 16, 1997, pp. 23, 24.

252 Ewing, "Is Los Angeles-Style Sprawl Desirable?" *op. cit.*, p.6.

253 The poll, conducted by the Biodiversity Project's Communications Consortium, is cited in Meg Maguire, *et al.*, "Beauty As Well As Bread," *Journal of the American Planning Association*, vol. 63, Summer 1997, pp. 317, 321.

254 Arendt, *op. cit.*, pp. 29–30.

255 *Ibid.*, p. 29.

Chapter 2 (continued)

256 A. Nelessen Associates, *Results of the Visual Preference Survey(tm) and Visions Implementation Workshop*, 1996; A. Nelessen Associates, *Fort Collins VPS Results Executive Summary*, undated (both documents provided courtesy of the Nelessen office).

257 Glenn Frankel and Stephen Fehr, "As the Economy Grows, the Trees Fall," *The Washington Post*, March 23, 1997, pp. A1, 20.

258 Andrew H. MacDonald, "Bay Watch: Safer, But Still Not Saved," *The Washington Post*, February 23, 1997, p. C3; Frankel and Fehr, *op. cit.*, p. A21.

259 Frankel and Pae, *op. cit.*, p. A10.

260 Frankel and Fehr, *op. cit.*, p. A21.

261 Maryland Office of Planning, *Maryland's Land 1973–1990: A Changing Resource*, 1991, cited in Pelley, *op. cit.*, at 7.

262 Frankel and Fehr, *op. cit.*, p. A20. The counties are Howard, Frederick, Calvert, and Charles, all between 15 and 60 miles from downtown Washington.

263 Tom Schueler, *Site Planning for Urban Stream Protection*, Center for Watershed Protection and the Metropolitan Washington Council of Governments, 1995, p. 73.

264 The research, intended to quantify the "non-farm" benefits of farmland, is being conducted by AFT's Center for Agriculture in the Environment in DeKalb, IL. It is expected to be published in the spring of 1999.

265 Tony Hiss, *The Experience of Place*, New York: Alfred A. Knopf, 1990, pp. 37–41.

266 Arendt, *op. cit.*, p. 5.

267 Hiss, *op. cit.*, p. 181.

268 Quoted in Frankel and Fehr, *op. cit.* Many Virginians are, in fact, concerned about development. A poll released in January 1999 by Virginia Commonwealth University indicates that a majority in the state would approve a tax increase to save open space and that large majorities rank traffic congestion and loss of open space as a serious problem. A large majority also favors growth management instead of building more roads as a means of addressing traffic congestion. See Dan Eggen, "Virginians Want Limits on Growth, Poll Shows," *The Washington Post*, January 7, 1999, B1.

269 See Roger S. Ulrich, Robert F. Simons, *et al.*, "Stress Recovery During Exposure to Natural and Urban Environments," *Journal of Environmental Psychology*, vol. 11, 1991, pp. 201–230. A series of reports by Ulrich and other researchers are cited in Meg Maguire, *et al.*, *op. cit.*, at 321; see also Hiss, *op. cit.*, p. 183.

270 J.B. Jackson, *Developing a Landscape Vernacular*, New York: Doubleday, 1991.

271 Randall Arendt *et al.*, *Rural By Design: Maintaining Small Town Character*, Chicago: American Planning Association, 1994, p. 281.

272 Walter Kulash, "Traditional Neighborhood Development: Will the Traffic Work?" paper presented at the Eleventh Annual Pedestrian Conference in Bellevue, Washington, October 1990 (based on hypothetical research). Other research indicates that many travelers will tolerate a longer travel time over a scenic route than they would through a route cluttered by suburban sprawl. Personal communication from Reid Ewing, December 22, 1998 (describing work by Roger Ulrich).

273 Arendt, *op. cit.*, pp. 283–286.

274 See discussion in Elizabeth Brabec and Kevin Kirby, *The Value of Nature and Scenery*, Scenic America Technical Information Series, vol. 1, no. 3, 1992.

275 Pelley, *op. cit.*, p. 9; Schueler, *op. cit.*, p. 65.

276 Downs, *New Visions*, *op. cit.*, pp. 151–152.

277 See "The Fourth Battle of Manassas," in Richard Moe and Carter Wilkie, *Changing Places: Rebuilding Community in the Age of Sprawl*, New York: Henry Holt and Company, 1997, pp. 3–35. Moe is the president of the National Trust for Historic Preservation.

278 See ten years' worth of endangered historic sites on the Trust's web site, *http://www.nthp.org*.

279 Scott Wilson, "Family Cemetery Is Threatened by Development," *The Washington Post*, October 16, 1997, D1.

280 Robert W. Burchell, *et al.*, *Impact Assessment of the New Jersey Interim State Development and Redevelopment Plan* (executive summary), 1992.

281 American Farmland Trust, *op. cit.*, p. 10; Berton, *op. cit.*, p. 14; see also Sorensen *et al.*, *op. cit.*, pp. 8–9.

282 The Clean Water Act is codified in the United States Code at 33 U.S.C. §§ 1251–1387.

283 Robert Griffin, Jr., "Introducing NPS Water Pollution," *EPA Journal*, November/December 1991, p. 6.

284 Easterbrook concedes, however, that the Cuyahoga River in Ohio and the Grand Calumet of Indiana remain severely polluted. See Easterbrook, *op. cit.*, pp. 627–630.

285 *Ibid.*

286 Griffin, *op. cit.*

287 Office of Wetlands, Oceans, and Watersheds (OWOW), U.S. Environmental Protection Agency, *Nonpoint Source Pollution: The Nation's Largest Water Quality Problem*, EPA 841-F-96-004A, 1996.

Chapter 2 (continued)

288 OWOW, *Nonpoint Source Pollution, op. cit.*; Chester L. Arnold, Jr, and C. James Gibbons, "Impervious Surface Coverage: The Emergence of a Key Environmental Indicator," *Journal of the American Planning Association*, vol. 62, Spring 1996, pp. 243, 245.

289 U.S. Environmental Protection Agency, *National Water Quality Inventory, 1996 Report to Congress*, April 1998, Figures 4-5 and 3-4.

290 Griffin, *op. cit.*, p. 7.

291 Arnold, *op. cit.*, pp. 244–246. See also Arendt, *op. cit.*, p. 281; City of Olympia and Washington State Department of Ecology, *Impervious Surface Reduction Study*, Final Report, May 1995, p. 1; Schueler, *op. cit.*, p. 10; Jonathan M. Harbor, "A Practical Method for Estimating the Impact of Land Use Change in Surface Runoff, Groundwater Recharge and Wetland Hydrology," *Journal of the American Planning Association*, vol. 60, 1994, p. 95; Richard D. Klein, "Urbanization and Stream Quality Impairment," *Water Resources Bulletin*, vol. 15, 1979, p. 949.

292 Schueler, *op. cit.*, pp. 21 and 19; Arnold, *op. cit.*, p. 244.

293 Schueler, *op. cit.*, p. 9.

294 *Ibid.*, pp. 21–22.

295 Arnold, *op. cit.*, p. 245.

296 Thompson, *op. cit.*, pp. 3–5.

297 Schueler, *op. cit.*, pp. 26, 161; Griffin, *op. cit.*, p. 7.

298 City of Olympia, *op. cit.*, pp. 1, 34–39; Schueler, *op. cit.*, pp. 24, 28, 37; Arnold, *op. cit.*, pp. 246–248.

299 Schueler, *op. cit.*, pp. 31.

300 Arnold, *op. cit.*, p. 246. Schueler agrees strongly but cautions that the research on imperviousness is still developing and needs to be standardized and applied to a variety of regions. Schueler, *op. cit.*, p. 50.

301 Arnold, *op. cit.*, pp. 247–248; City of Olympia, *op. cit.*, pp. 34–39.

302 Egan, "Urban Sprawl Strains Western States," *op. cit.*

303 Harbor, *op. cit.*, p. 101.

304 Richard Cohn-Lee and Diane Cameron, "Urban Stormwater Runoff Contamination of the Chesapeake Bay: Sources and Mitigation," *The Environmental Professional*, vol. 14, 1992, pp. 10-27.

305 Eric Lipton, "In Fairfax, Damaged Streams Stir Fears for the Future," *The Washington Post*, August 7, 1997, p. A1.

306 *Ibid.*

307 *Ibid.*

308 Kyle York Spencer, "Cary Considers Stop-Work Orders on Construction Sites," *The News and Observer* (Raleigh, North Carolina), August 20, 1997, p. B1.

309 Arendt, *op. cit.*, p. 281.

310 Arnold, *op. cit.*, pp. 248–49; City of Olympia, *op. cit.*, p. 38.

311 Schueler, *op. cit.*, pp. 26, 139, 161.

312 *Ibid.*, p. 23.

313 City of Olympia, *op. cit.*, p. 38.

314 Arnold, *op. cit.*, pp. 251–252; Schueler, *op. cit.*, pp. 170–71.

315 City of Olympia, *op. cit.*, pp. 46–55.

316 Robert D. Sykes, *Protecting Water Quality In Urban Areas*, 1989, pp. 3.1–3.18.

317 Schueler, *op. cit.*, p. 38.

318 *Ibid.*, pp. 20, 37–38.

319 See, e.g., South Carolina Coastal Conservation League, "Getting a Rein on Runoff: How Sprawl and the Traditional Town Compare," *South Carolina Coastal Conservation League Land Development Bulletin*, Number 7, Fall 1995. Arnold, *op. cit.*, p. 251; Jeff Gersh, "Subdivide and Conquer," *The Amicus Journal*, vol. 18, Fall 1996, pp. 14–20.

320 Michael McCabe, Administrator Region III, U.S. EPA, quoted in Karl Blankenship, "Chewing Up the Landscape," *Bay Journal*, Baltimore: Chesapeake Bay Foundation, December 1995, p. 1. See also Cohn-Lee and Cameron, *op. cit.*

321 "Cross-Media Pollution and the Chesapeake Bay," in *Resources* (Resources for the Future), vol. 124, Summer 1996, p. 20; MacDonald, *op. cit.*

322 City of Olympia, *op. cit.*, pp. 67–70. In its list of 19 total recommendations, growth management ranked behind only an administrative one, to "integrate impervious surface reduction into policies and regulations."

323 City of Olympia, *op. cit.*, pp. 71–112.

324 Newman and Kenworthy, *Cities and Automobile Dependence, op. cit.*, p. 87.

325 Egan, "Urban Sprawl Strains Western States," *op. cit.*

326 Schueler, *op. cit.*, pp. 38, 43, 75–76. See also Blankenship, *op. cit.*, pp. 1, 6.

Chapter 2 (continued)

327 Schueler, *op. cit.*, pp. 87–127; Arnold, *op. cit.*, p. 253; Anne Whiston Spirn, "Urban Nature and Human Design: Reviewing the Great Tradition," in Jay M. Stein, ed., *Classic Readings in Urban Planning*, New York: McGraw-Hill, 1995, pp. 475–495.

328 Schueler, *op. cit.*, pp. 172–181.

329 *Ibid.*, pp. 129–160.

330 *Ibid.*, p. 1.

331 Bernick and Cervero, *op. cit.*, p. 85.

332 Robert W. Burchell, *et al.*, *op. cit.*, pp. 13–14; Nelson, *op. cit.*, p. 17.

333 South Carolina Coastal Conservation League, *op. cit.*

Chapter 3

1 Henry L Diamond and Patrick F. Noonan, *Land Use in America*, Washington, DC: Island Press, 1996, p.5.

2 John Rebchook, "The Costs of Urban Sprawl Estimated in Billions: High Density 'Villages,' Added Light Rail Seen as Needed Measures," *Rocky Mountain News*, May 15, 1997, p. 2B.

3 Craig Timberg, "Budget Bust Follows Boom in Growth; "80s Suburban Sprawl Is Drain on Schools, Services in 1990s," *The Baltimore Sun*, February 24, 1997, p. 1B.

4 Anna Borgman, "As Exurbs Grow, So Does Burden of Borrowing," *The Washington Post*, February 26, 1995, p. B1.

5 William Presecky, "Regional Sprawl Linked to Higher Property Taxes," *Chicago Tribune*, January 30, 1995, p. 1N.

6 According to Henry Diamond and Patrick Noonan, we confront "a silent crisis, a quiet specter, but nonetheless a challenge that affects the well-being of virtually every American." Diamond and Noonan, *op. cit.*, p. 5.

7 Office of Policy, Planning and Evaluation, U.S. Environmental Protection Agency, *$mart Investments for City and County Managers: Energy, Environment, and Community Development*, Publication No. EPA-231-R-98-004, Washington, DC: U.S. Environmental Protection Agency, April 1998, p. 1-1.

8 Governor Parris Glendening, Remarks at the National Issues Forum on Forging Metropolitan Solutions to Urban and Regional Problems, Brookings Institution, May 28, 1997.

9 Peter Pochna and Clarke Canfield, "Growth Limits Clash with Landowner Rights; 'There Are No Easy Answers' as Southern Maine Municipalities Explore Various Strategies to Slow Growth and Its Costly Implications," *Portland Press Herald*, July 7, 1997, p. 1A.

10 Eric Lipton, "Once Rural Virginia Communities Pulled Into Northern Megalopolis," *The Washington Post*, January 23, 1998, p. B1.

11 Dan Eggen and Peter Pae, "Anti-Development Forces Massing," *The Washington Post*, December 14, 1997, p. A1.

12 Steve Stanek, "Some Fume As McHenry County Ups Its Gas Tax: Full Board Ignores Vote By Committee," *Chicago Tribune*, August 29, 1998; Mitch Martin, "McHenry Tax Bills Rise 3.3% On Average: County Homeowners' Charges to Arrive Late," *Chicago Tribune*, May 6, 1998.

13 By 1985, 30 states had adopted similar limitations. Gene Bunnell, "Fiscal Impact Studies as Advocacy and Storytelling," *Journal of Planning Literature*, vol. 12, November 1997, pp. 136–151.

14 Ted Gregory, "DuPage Tax Bills Increase by 5%: Average Rise is Biggest Since 1991," *Chicago Tribune*, March 28, 1998.

15 Dan Eggen, "Curbs on Development Proposed," *The Washington Post*, December 11, 1997, p. A1.

16 Eggen and Pae, *op. cit.*

17 Stephanie Banchero, "Students Feel the Squeeze: District 230 Seeks to Ease Crowding," *Chicago Tribune*, October 13, 1998.

18 Lola Smallwood, "Library Faces Threat of Red Ink," *Chicago Tribune*, July 8, 1998.

19 David Van Biema, reported by Elaine Lafferty, "A Social Emergency; In The Kind of Fiscal Crisis That May Soon Confront Others, Los Angeles County Considers Drastic Cuts," *Time*, July 3, 1995, p. 28.

20 Bond financing may represent a shift from "pay-as-you-go" financing of public infrastructure (by which governments gather resources before a project is undertaken) to "pay-as-you-use," which is increasingly being seen as more efficient and equitable between generations. Personal communication with Reid Ewing, December, 1998.

21 Timberg, *op. cit.*

22 Borgman, *op. cit.*

23 Chris Lester and Jeffrey Spivak, "Suburbs Can't Escape the Cost of Separation," *The Kansas City Star*, December 17, 1995.

24 Liz Willen, "Swollen City Debt Nears Limit/State Legislation Needed to Avoid Cap," *Newsday* (New York, NY), December 10, 1998, p. A6.

Chapter 3 (continued)

25 Southern California Association of Governments, *Preliminary Draft 97 Regional Transportation Plan,* Los Angeles: Southern California Association of Governments, 1997, p. 49.

26 *Ibid.* p. 51.

27 Chris Lester and Jeffrey Spivak, "Road System Puts Suburbs on the Map," *The Kansas City Star,* December 19, 1995.

28 Tom Horton, "A Fumbling Approach to Growth," *The Baltimore Sun,* December 8, 1995, p. 2C.

29 Robert W. Burchell and David Listokin, "Land, Infrastructure, Housing Costs, and Fiscal Impacts Associated with Growth." Paper prepared for the conference *Rail-Volution '96: Building Successful Communities with Rail,* Washington, DC, September 8, 1996.

30 *Ibid.*

31 *Ibid.*

32 Office of Technology Assessment, Congress of the United States, *The Technological Reshaping of Metropolitan America,* Publication No. OTA-ETI-643, Washington, DC: U.S. Government Printing Office, September 1995.

33 Burchell and Listokin, *op. cit.*

34 Office of Technology Assessment, *ap. cit.*

35 Real Estate Research Corporation, *The Costs of Sprawl: Environmental and Economic Costs of Alternative Residential Patterns at the Urban Fringe,* Washington, DC: U.S. Government Printing Office, 1974.

36 James E. Frank, *The Costs of Alternative Development Patterns: A Review of the Literature,* Washington, DC: The Urban Land Institute, 1989.

37 James Duncan *et al., The Search for Efficient Urban Growth Patterns,* Tallahassee, FL: Florida Department of Community Affairs, 1989, as found in: Office of Technology Assessment, *op. cit.;* Burchell and Listokin, *op. cit.*

38 Robert W. Burchell *et al., Impact Assessment of the New Jersey Interim State Development and Redevelopment Plan, Report II: Research Findings,* Trenton, NJ: New Jersey Office of State Planning, February 20, 1992. Some information from this report was derived from Burchell and Listokin, *op. cit.*

39 Office of Technology Assessment, *op. cit.*

40 Real Estate Research Corporation, *op. cit.*

41 For the RERC study, neighborhoods consisted of 1,000 dwelling units and communities consisted of 10,000 dwelling units with a combination of neighborhood types.

42 The study also included an analysis of environmental costs, natural resource consumption, and personal costs. The public and private services included: schools, streets, police and fire protection, sewers, storm drainage, water supply and distribution, gas, electricity, and telephone. Detailed information on the variety of impacts to specific services can be found in the original report by the RERC.

43 In reaching his conclusions, Frank made several modifications to the RERC results. For a discussion of these modifications, see Frank, *op. cit.,* p. 28.

44 Frank, *op. cit.,* p. 28–29.

45 *Ibid.* p. 30.

46 Duane Windsor, "A Critique of The Costs of Sprawl," *Journal of the American Planning Association,* vol. 45, 1979, pp. 279–92. As cited in Frank, *op. cit.,* p. 31.

47 Frank, *op. cit.*

48 *Ibid.* p. 39.

49 *Ibid.* p. 40.

50 *Ibid.* p. 40.

51 Duncan *op. cit.* As found in Office of Technology Assessment, *op. cit.*

52 In the Duncan study, costs for the following service categories were calculated: roadways, education, wastewater, potable water, solid waste, law enforcement, fire and emergency protection, and parks. The study did not include the costs of streets and water and sewer pipes needed within residential subdivisions (i.e., neighborhood costs) or on-site costs for sewer, water, gas, and electric utilities, because previous studies have shown that these vary with density and are usually paid by the owners.

53 Duncan, *op. cit.* As found in Office of Technology Assessment, *op. cit.*

54 Chesapeake Bay Program, U.S. Environmental Protection Agency, *Cost of Providing Government Services to Alternative Residential Patterns,* Washington, DC: U.S. Environmental Protection Agency, May 1993 , p. A-23.

55 Burchell *et al., op. cit.*

56 Burchell *et al., op. cit.,* as found in Burchell and Listokin, *op. cit.,* p. 16.

57 *Ibid.*

58 American Farmland Trust, *Alternatives for Future Urban Growth in California's Central Valley: The Bottom Line for Agriculture and Taxpayers,* Washington, DC: American Farmland Trust, October 1995.

59 *Ibid.* p. 40.

60 *Ibid.,* p. 7.

Chapter 3 (continued)

61 American Farmland Trust, *Density-Related Public Costs*, Washington, DC: American Farmland Trust, 1986.

62 *Ibid.*, p.4.

63 *Ibid.*, p. 24.

64 *Ibid.*, p. 4.

65 American Farmland Trust, *Living on the Edge: The Costs and Risks of Scatter Development*, DeKalb, IL: American Farmland Trust, 1998.

66 *Ibid.*

67 *Ibid.*

68 *Ibid.*

69 Michael Siegel, *Another Cost of Sprawl: The Effects of Land Use on Wastewater Utility Costs*, Washington, DC: Natural Resources Defense Council, 1998.

70 Specifically, variables measuring the density of the service area explained between 50 and 54 percent of O&M conveyance costs in multiple regression equations. The remainder of the variation was attributable to a combination of less influential factors, such as the age of the system, economies of scale, geographic and subsurface conditions, or historic maintenance policies. Additionally, variables for economies of scale (the number of service units and the volume of the system) produced significant results in single regression equations.

71 Siegel, *op. cit.*, p. 1.

72 These include services that are privately owned but publicly regulated.

73 R.W. Archer, "Land Speculation and Scattered Development; Failures in the Urban-Fringe Land Market," *Urban Studies*, vol. 10, 1973, pp. 367–372.

74 California Public Utilities Commission, *Staff Report Regarding Assembly Bill No. 4217 (Bronzan) Requiring An Investigation of the Methods of Cost Estimation, Revenue Allocation, and Rate Setting for California Electric Utilities*, Sacramento, CA: California Public Utilities Commission, January 1990. In this report, the dividing point between rural and urban is 35 customers per distribution mile of line. This translates to a dividing point of 150 feet between customers.

75 *Ibid.* pp. 10–11.

76 *Ibid.*, p. 2.

77 Office of Technology Assessment, *op. cit.*, p. 209.

78 See citations in Chapter Two, *op. cit.*

79 Peter Gordon and Harry Richardson, "Are Compact Cities a Desirable Planning Goal?" *Journal of the American Planning Association*, vol. 63, Winter 1997, p. 99.

80 Richard B. Peiser, "Does It Pay to Plan Suburban Growth?" *Journal of the American Planning Association*, vol. 50, Autumn 1984, pp. 419–433.

81 Richard B. Peiser, "Density and Urban Sprawl," *Land Economics*, vol. 65, August 1989, pp. 193–204.

82 Gordon and Richardson, "Are Compact Cities a Desirable Planning Goal?" *op. cit.*, p.99. See Helen F. Ladd, "Population Growth, Density, and the Costs of Providing Public Services," *Urban Studies*, Vol. 29, No. 2, 1992, pp. 273–295.

83 *Ibid.* p. 273.

84 Reid Ewing, "Is Los Angeles-Style Sprawl Desirable?" *Journal of the American Planning Association*, vol. 63, Winter 1997, pp. 115.

85 This is true also for environmental benefits related to vehicle use, including greenhouse emissions, energy consumption, and unhealthful air pollution. See discussion in chapter two, above.

86 American Farmland Trust, *Cost of Community Services Fact Sheet*, Washington, DC: American Farmland Trust, http://farm.fic.niu.edu/fic-ta/tafs-cocs.html, undated.

87 Other traditional sources include income and sales taxes, as well as federal and state grants. The mix of sources applied to pay for local services varies greatly from one jurisdiction to another.

88 American Farmland Trust, *Cost of Community Services Fact Sheet, op. cit.*

89 *Ibid.*

90 Duncan *et al.*, *op. cit.* As cited in Office of Technology Assessment,

91 Burchell *et al.*, *op. cit.*, p. 81.

92 *Ibid.* p. 81.

93 *Ibid.* p. 81.

94 Joseph Persky and Wim Wiewel, *Central City and Suburban Development: Who Pays and Who Benefits*, Chicago, IL: University of Illinois at Chicago, College of Urban Planning and Public Affairs, Great Cities Institute, 1996, as cited in David Bollier, *How Smart Growth Can Stop Sprawl: A Fledgling Citizen Movement Expands*, Washington, DC: Essential Books, 1998.

95 *Ibid.* p. 10.

96 American Planning Association, "Policy Guide On Impact Fees," Chicago IL: American Planning Association, undated. This document can be found at http://www.planning.org/govt/impact.html.

97 *Ibid.*

Chapter 3 (continued)

115 Alan A. Altshuler and Jose Gomez-Ibanez, *Regulation for Revenue. The Political Economy of Land Use Exactions*, Washington, DC and Cambridge, MA: Brookings Institution and Lincoln Institute of Land Policy, 1994.

116 William H. Oakland and William A. Testa, *Does Business Development Raise Taxes: An Empirical Appraisal*, Chicago, IL: Metropolitan Planning Council, 1995, p. 4.

117 Greg Sandoval, "Santa Clarita Makes Pitch to Lure Cruise Line to City," *Los Angeles Times*, April 23, 1997, p. B6.

118 Cynthia H. Craft, "Sacramento Throws in Kitchen Sink in Bid for Packard Bell Relocation," *Los Angeles Times*, October 4, 1994, p. D1.

119 Steve Liewer, "County Boosts Cash to Lure Businesses," *Sun-Sentinel* (Fort Lauderdale), October 26, 1994, p. 4B.

120 Rick Stouffer, "Incentive to Woo Business to Area Costs Taxpayers," *The Buffalo News*, November 12, 1995, p. 1A.

121 This point is elaborated also in chapters one and four of this book.

122 Deborah Stone, "Does Business Development Raise Taxes?: A Commentary," *Public Investment*, March 1995.

123 Burchell and Listokin, *op. cit.*, p. 18.

124 *Ibid.*, p. 18, citing Duncan, *op. cit.*

Chapter 4

1 Professors Peter Gordon and Harry Richardson of the University of Southern California, for example, argue that "Numerous consumer surveys have shown strong preferences for suburban living" and "the link between household preferences and preferred [low-density] spatial patterns is clear...." For a representative articulation of "pro-sprawl" arguments, see their article "Are Compact Cities a Desirable Planning Goal?" *Journal of the American Planning Association*, vol. 63, Winter 1997, pp. 95–106.

2 Press release from the National Association of Home Builders, Washington, DC (www.nahb.com:80/update/story5.html), September 9, 1998.

3 Boyce Thompson, "Growing Smart: Whether you call it smart growth or sprawl, it's an important issue that we all need to address," *Builder*, National Association of Home Builders, July 1998.

4 Olmsted's vision for urban planning was rooted in the belief that cities were great places that could be improved with the development of parklands, landscaping, significant architectural landmarks, and other design modifications—all of which formed the basis for Daniel Burnham's "City Beautiful" movement. Sennett essentially disliked cities and instead advocated "garden cities," which resemble today's low-density suburbs with single-family detached homes. For more discussion, see Mark Girouard, *Cities & People*, New Haven, CT: Yale University Press, 1985.

5 According to historian Henry Binford, however, the first American suburbs were communities founded on the outskirts of Boston in 1815. *See* his book, *The First Suburbs: Residential Communities on the Boston Periphery 1815–1860*, Chicago: University of Chicago Press, 1985.

6 Jane Jacobs, *The Death and Life of Great American Cities*, New York: Vintage Books, 1961, p. 310.

7 Robert Caro, *The Power Broker*, New York: Random House, 1974.

8 Jon C. Teaford, *The Twentieth-Century American City: Problem, Promise, and Reality*, Baltimore: Johns Hopkins University Press, 1986, p. 74.

9 Witold Rybczynski, *City Life*, New York: Touchstone Books, 1996.

10 Charles Bowden and Lew Kreinberg, *Street Signs Chicago: Neighborhood and Other Illusions of Big-City Life*, Chicago Review Press, 1981, p. 147.

11 William Frey and Elaine Fielding, *Changing Urban Populations, Regional Restructuring, Racial Polarization, and Poverty Concentration*, Population Studies Center, Ann Arbor: University of Michigan Press, February 1994.

12 James J. Flink, *The Automobile Age*, Cambridge, MA: Massachusetts Institute of Technology Press, 1988.

13 Hal Foust, "Elevated Drive Urged as Relief for Unemployed," *Chicago Tribune*, August 7, 1932.

14 David Hodge, "Social Impacts of Urban Transportation Decisions: Equity Issues," in *The Geography of Urban Transportation*, Susan Hanson, ed., New York: The Guilford Press, 1986, pp. 301–327.

15 DC Colony, "Residential Relocation: The Impact of Allowances and Procedures in Effect Since July 1, 1970," University of Toledo, for the Ohio Department of Transportation and the Federal Highway Administration, 1973; and Michael Perfater and Gary Allen, "Preliminary Findings of a Diachronic Analysis of Social and Economic Effects of Relocation due to Highways," Virginia Highway and Transportation Research Council, 1975.

Chapter 4 (continued)

98 Emil Malizia, Richard Norton, Craig Richardson, . and Michelle J. Zimet, "Reading, Writing, and Impact Fees: What's the Best Method For Calculating School Impact Fees?" *Planning*, vol. 63, September 1997, p. 17.

99 Marla Dresch and Steven M. Sheffrin, *Who Pays for Development Fees and Exactions?* San Francisco, CA: Public Policy Institute of California, 1997.

100 James E. Frank and Paul B. Downing, "Patterns of Impact Fee Use," in *Development Impact Fees: Policy Rationale, Practice, Theory, and Issues*, Arthur C. Nelson, ed., Chicago: Planners Press, 1998.

101 *Ibid.*, p. 13.

102 Frank, *op. cit.*, p. 42.

103 Frank and Downing, *op. cit.*, p. 13.

104 American Planning Association, *op. cit.*, p. 2.

105 Metropolitan Planning Council, *Issue Brief: The Debate Over Impact Fees*, Chicago, IL: Metropolitan Planning Council, 1993.

106 Douglas R. Porter, "Impact Fees Come to Anne Arundel County," *Urban Land*, July 1988, pp. 34–35. As cited in Urban Land Institute, *Project Infrastructure Development Handbook*, Washington, DC: Urban Land Institute, 1989, p. 127.

107 Thomas F. Luce, Barbara L. Lukermann, and Herbert Mohring, *Regional Sewer System Rate Structure Study*, Minneapolis, MN: Hubert H. Humphrey Institute of Public Affairs, University of Minnesota, December 7, 1992.

108 Myron Orfield, *Metropolitics: A Regional Agenda for Community and Stability*, Washington, DC and Cambridge, MA: The Brookings Institution and the Lincoln Institute of Land Policy, 1997, p. 71.

109 Siegel, *op. cit.*

110 Burchell and Listokin, *op. cit.*, p. 22.

111 Bunnell, *op. cit.*

112 Scott Wilson, "In Howard, Opposition Builds to Rouse's Mixed-Use Development Plan," *The Washington Post*, January 19, 1998, p. B1.

113 DuPage County Planning Department, *Impacts of Development On DuPage County Property Taxes*, DeKalb, IL: DuPage County Regional Planning Commission, 1992. As cited in Wim Wiewel, "The Fiscal Impact of Commercial Development," *Land Development*, vol. 6, no. 1, Spring-Summer 1993, pp. 10–13.

114 Michael J. Kinsley and Hunter Lovings, *Paying for Growth, Prospering From Development*, Snowmass, CO: Rocky Mountain Institute, 1995.

16 J. Buffington, D. Schafer, and C. Bullion, "Attitudes, Opinions, and Experiences of Business and Institutional Relocatees Displaced by Highways under the 1970 Relocation Assistance Program," Texas Transportation Institute, Texas A & M University.

17 In these cases, the freeways were the Cross-Bronx Expressway in New York City; I-40 in Nashville; Loop 1 ("Mo-Pac"), which runs through Clarkesville in Austin, TX; the Century Freeway in Los Angeles; and the Durham Freeway (a.k.a. East-West Expressway), in NC.

18 Caro, *op. cit.*

19 Ned Glascock, "The Street Paved with Pride," *The News and Observer* (Raleigh, NC), February 21, 1997, p. 7B.

20 J. Seley, "Spatial Bias: The Kink in Nashville's I-40," *Research on Conflict in Locational Decisions*, Philadelphia: Regional Science Department, University of Pennsylvania, 1970.

21 Private correspondence to Don Chen from Peggy Shepard and Cecil Corbin-Mark of WHEACT, Susanna Almanza and Raul Alvarez of PODER and Penn Loh of ACE, 1997–1998.

22 Robert Bullard and Glenn Johnson, eds., *Just Transportation: Dismantling Race & Class Barriers to Mobility*, Stony Creek, CT: New Society Publishers, 1997. See H.P. Hak, H. Abbey, and R.C. Talamo, "Prevalence of Asthma and Health Service Utilization of Asthmatic Children in an Inner City," *Journal of Allergy and Clinical Immunology*, No. 70, 1982, pp. 367–372; I.F. Goldstein and A.L. Weinstein, "Air Pollution and Asthma: Effects of Exposure to Short-Term Sulfur Dioxide Peaks," *Environmental Research*, No. 40, 1986, pp. 332–345; J. Schwartz, D. Gold, D.W. Dockey, *et. al.*, "Predictors of Asthma and Persistent Wheeze in a National Sample of Children in the United States," *American Review of Respiratory Disease*, No. 142, 1990, pp. 555–562; as cited in Robert Bullard, "Epilogue," in Robert Bullard and Glenn Johnson, *op. cit.*

23 Unfortunately, decades of rapid suburbanization passed before sociologists began to focus their attention on related urban social concerns. After all, the post-war decades were a prosperous time. U.S. poverty levels decreased from 39.5 million people in 1959 to 25.4 million in 1968, and from 22 percent of the U.S. population in 1959 to 12.8 percent in 1968. Attention to sprawl's impacts on urban areas was not significant until the mid-to-late 1960s, when researchers and political leaders began searching for explanations for declining conditions in urban African-American neighborhoods and for the race riots that began tearing through America's central cities. As Wilson writes in his landmark book, *The Truly Disadvantaged*, efforts like the Johnson Administration's War on Poverty spurred a boom in research and political interest in poverty and

Endnotes

Chapter 4 (continued)

urban studies beginning around 1965. See William Julius Wilson with Robert Aponte, "Appendix: Urban Poverty: A State-of-the-Art Review of the Literature," in *The Truly Disadvantaged: The Inner City, the Underclass, and Public Policy*, Chicago: University of Chicago Press, 1987.

24 For a more recent discussion on "concentration effects," see "Appendix A: Perspectives on Poverty Concentration" in Wilson's latest book, *When Work Disappears: The World of the New Urban Poor*, New York: Vintage Books, 1996.

25 Bishop Anthony M. Pilla, *The Church in the City*, Cleveland, OH: Diocese of Cleveland, November 19, 1993.

26 Parris Glendening, "Making Maryland the Best Place to Work, to Raise a Child and to Build a Family," presented in Annapolis, MD, 1997 State of the State Address, January 15, 1997.

27 *Current Population Survey*, U.S. Department of Commerce, Bureau of the Census, 1997.

28 Brian Burnes, "The Interstate Changed Our Lives," *The Kansas City Star*, September 3, 1996.

29 Constance E. Beaumont, *How Superstore Sprawl Can Harm Communities: And What Citizens Can Do About It*, Washington, DC: National Trust for Historic Preservation, 1994.

30 Kenneth E. Stone, "The Impact of Wal-Mart Stores on Other Businesses and Strategies for Co-Existing," Iowa State University, 1993, as cited in Beaumont, *op. cit.*

31 Beth Humstone, Jeff Squires, and Thomas Muller, "Fiscal and Economic Impact/Maple Tree Place Mall on Chittenden County Municipalities," July 1989.

32 Chernick Howard and Andrew Reschovsky, *Urban Fiscal Problems: Coordinating Actions Among Governments*, prepared for Metropolitan Assembly on Urban Problems: Linking Research to Action Conference, Chicago, IL: Center for Urban Affairs and Policy Research, Northwestern University, September 30–October 2, 1994.

33 Thomas Bier and the Ohio Housing Research Network, *Moving Up and Out: Government Policy and the Future of Ohio's Metropolitan Areas*, Cleveland, OH: The Urban University Program of the Ohio General Assembly and the Ohio Board of Regents, September 1994; Thomas Bier and The Ohio Housing Research Network, *The IRS Homeseller Capital Gain Provision: Contributor to Urban Decline*, Cleveland, OH: The Urban University Program of the Ohio General Assembly and the Ohio Board of Regents, January 1994; Roy Bahl, "Metropolitan Fiscal Disparities," *Cityscape: A Journal of Policy Development and Research*, Washington, DC: U.S. Department of Housing and Urban Development, vol. 1, August 1994, pp. 293–306.

34 Orfield, *op. cit.*; and David Rusk, *Cities Without Suburbs*, Washington, DC: The Woodrow Wilson Center Press, 1993.

35 Roberto Fernandez, *Spatial Mismatch: Housing, Transportation, and Employment in Regional Perspective*, prepared for Metropolitan Assembly on Urban Problems: Linking Research to Action Conference, Chicago, IL: Center for Urban Affairs and Policy Research, Northwestern University, September 30–October 2, 1994; Holzer, 1991. For a comprehensive analysis of three decades' worth of studies on spatial mismatch, see John F. Kain, "The Spatial Mismatch Hypothesis: Three Decades Later," *Housing Policy Debate*, vol. 3, pp. 371–459.

36 Mark Alan Hughes and Julie E. Sternberg, *The New Metropolitan Reality: Where the Rubber Meets the Road in Antipoverty Policy*, Washington, DC: The Urban Institute, 1992.

37 Robert Cervero, *Suburban Gridlock*, New Brunswick, NJ: Center for Urban Policy Research, 1986.

38 The comprehensive federal transportation law, the Transportation Equity Act for the 21st Century (TEA-21) includes up to $750 million over six years for transit-related "access to jobs" programs (Section 3037 of TEA-21).

39 Claudia Coulton, Nandita Verma, and Shanyang Guo, *Time Limited Welfare and the Employment Prospects of AFDC Recipients in Cuyahoga County*, Case Western Reserve University, Center on Urban Poverty and Social Change, Draft of October 11, 1996.

40 See Annalynn Lacombe, *Welfare Reform and Access to Jobs in Boston*, U.S. Department of Transportation, Bureau of Transportation Statistics, January 1998.

41 Michael Rich, "The Reality of Welfare Reform: Employment Prospects in Metropolitan Atlanta," *Georgia Academy Journal*, Summer 1997.

42 Brian Taylor, "Unjust Equity: An Examination of California's Transportation Development Act," *Transportation Research Record: Public Transit*, no. 1297, 1991, pp. 85–92.

43 David Hodge, "Social Impacts of Urban Transportation Decisions: Equity Issues," in *The Geography of Urban Transportation*, Susan Hanson, ed., New York: The Guilford Press, 1986, pp. 301–327. Also see Ira Hirschman, "Spatial Equity and Transportation Finance: A Case Study of the New York Metropolitan Region," Ph.D. Dissertation, New Brunswick, NJ: Department of Urban Planning and Policy Development, 1991.

Chapter 4 (continued)

44 The Los Angeles case, initiated by the Labor/Community Strategies Center and led by the NAACP Legal Defense Fund, was successful and forced the LA Metropolitan Transit Association to reinstate discount fares for bus service, as well as to reduce planned fare hikes. Don Chen, "LA Bus Riders Union Sues MTA," *Progress*, February 1995; and Bill Lann Lee, "Civil Rights and Legal Remedies: A Plan for Action," in Bullard and Johnson, eds., *op. cit.*

45 Paul B. Fischer, "Is Housing Mobility an Effective Anti-Poverty Strategy? An Examination of the Cincinnati Experience," Cincinnati, OH: Stephen H. Wilder Foundation, 1991.

46 Elliot Schlar and Walter Hook, "The Importance of Cities to the National Economy," in Henry Cisneros, ed. *Interwoven Destinies: Cities and the Nation*, New York: W.W. Norton & Co., 1993.

47 Michael B. Katz, "Reframing the 'Underclass Debate,'" in *The 'Underclass' Debate: Views from History*, Michael B. Katz, ed., Princeton, NJ: Princeton University Press, 1993.

48 Myron Orfield, *Metropolitics*, Washington, DC: The Brookings Institution, 1997. Despite the overwhelming evidence of this, supporters of sprawl still deny that it is a problem. For example, Peter Gordan and Harry Richardson explain the urban concentration of poverty and people of color as simply a matter of affordability: ". . . poor people are excluded from buying into expensive residential neighborhoods not because of exclusionary zoning but in exactly the way they are excluded from buying Mercedes, Lexus, Infiniti and BMW automobiles; they cannot afford them." Cited in "Striking at the Heart of 'Beyond Sprawl,'" *BIA News* vol. 19, no.1 (March 1996).

49 Naomi Wish and Stephen Eisdorfer, *The Impact of the Mount Laurel Initiatives: An Analysis of the Characteristics of Applicants and Occupants*, South Orange, NJ: Seton Hall University, 1996.

50 John Yinger, "Access Denied, Access Constrained: Results and Implications of the 1989 Housing Discrimination Study," in Michael Fix and Raymond J. Struyk, eds., *Clear and Convincing Evidence: Measurement of Discrimination in America*, Washington, DC: The Urban Institute Press, 1993.

51 John Yinger, *Housing Discrimination Study: Incidence and Severity of Unfavorable Treatment*, Washington, DC: U.S. Department of Housing and Urban Development, 1991; Alicia H. Munnell, Lynn E. Browne, James McEneaney, and Geoffrey M.B. Tootell, *Mortgage Lending in Boston: Interpreting HMDA Data*, Federal Reserve Bank of Boston, Working Paper 92-7, 1992.

52 Orfield, *op. cit.*

53 Orfield, *op. cit.*

54 Orfield, *op. cit.* at p. 162.

55 Richard Voith, "Central City Decline: Regional or Neighborhood Solutions," *Federal Reserve Bank of Philadelphia Business Review*, March/April 1996.

56 See, e.g., Thomas E. Bier, "Housing Dynamics of the Cleveland Area, 1950–2000," in *Cleveland: A Metropolitan Reader*, Kent State University, 1995, pp. 244, 255–257; Housing Policy Research Program, Cleveland State University, *Movement of Cuyahoga County Homesellers, 1987–1991*, Report to the Cuyahoga County Planning Commission, April 20, 1993; Ohio Housing Research Network, *Moving Up and Out: Government Policy and the Future of Ohio's Metropolitan Areas*, Report for the Ohio General Assembly, September 19, 1994.

57 Unfortunately, it took the academic community quite a long time to discover them. Initially, the mass exodus to the suburbs was greeted mainly with disinterest or mild approval. For example, in Bennett Berger's well known work, *Working Class Suburb*, he offers the equivalent of an academic yawn, finding that "the lives of the suburbanites I had been studying had not been profoundly affected in any statistically identifiable or sociologically interesting way." (Bennett Berger, *Working Class Suburb*, Berkeley: University of California Press, 1968.) In his history of the pioneer suburb, Levittown, New Jersey, Herbert Gans concludes that "Levittown permits most of its residents to be what they want to be," and that "whatever its imperfections, Levittown is a good place to live." (Herbert Gans, *The Levittowners*, New York: Vintage Books, 1967.) But, by 1979, sociologist David Popenoe countered that early survey research had tended to focus on heads of suburban households, which led him to call for new research on sprawl's impacts on everyone else, including women, the elderly, children, and people of color. (David Popenoe, "Urban Sprawl: Some Neglected Sociological Considerations," *Sociology and Social Research*, vol. 63, no. 2, January 1979.)

58 Numerous examples of the interconnections among social, environmental, and economic factors can be found in recent commentaries on civil society. See John Brehm and Wendy Rahn, "Individual Level Evidence for the Causes and Consequences of Social Capital," presented at a conference sponsored by the Pew Charitable Trust, the National Commission on Civic Renewal, and the Brookings Institution, November 25, 1996; Robert D. Putnam, "Bowling Alone: America's Declining Social Capital," *Journal of Democracy*, vol. 6, no. 1, January 1995; George Pettinico, "Civic Participation: Alive and Well in Today's Environmental Groups," *The Public Perspective*, June–July 1996.

Chapter 4 (continued)

59 Oleg Zinam, "Quality of Life, Quality of the Individual, Technology and Economic Development," *American Journal of Economics and Sociology*, vol. 48, 1989, pp. 55–68.

60 Stephen Cochrun, "Understanding and Enhancing Neighborhood Sense of Community," *Journal of Planning Literature*, vol. 9, 1994, pp. 92–99.

61 Robert Putnam, "Bowling Alone: America's Declining Social Capital," *Journal of Democracy*, September 1995.

62 See James Kunstler, *The Geography of Nowhere: The Rise and Decline of America's Man-Made Landscape*, New York: Simon & Schuster, 1993; and Andres Duany and Elizabeth Plater-Zyberk, "Neighborhoods and Suburbs," *Design Quarterly*, March 1995.

63 See Richard Sennett, *The Fall of Public Man*, New York: W.W. Norton, 1976.

64 Thomas Glynn, "Psychological Sense of Community Measurement and Application," *Human Relations*, vol. 34, 1981, pp. 789–818.

65 Jack Nasar and David Julian, "The Psychological Sense of Community in the Neighborhood," *Journal of the American Planning Association*, vol. 61, 1995, pp. 178–184.

66 William Shore, "Recentralization: The Single Answer to More Than a Dozen United States Problems and a Major Answer to Poverty," *Journal of the American Planning Association*, vol. 61, 1995, pp. 496–503.

67 Nicholas Lemann, "Stressed Out in Suburbia," *The Atlantic Monthly*, November 1989, pp. 34–48.

68 *Early Results Report*, 1995 Nationwide Personal Transportation Survey, U.S. Department of Transportation, Figure 11.

69 Intel Corporation spokeswoman Jeanne Forbis, as reported by the Associated Press regarding Intel's new "Internet car" initiative, January 7, 1998.

70 See Donald A. Redelmeier and Robert J. Tibshirani, "Association between Cellular-Telephone Calls and Motor Vehicle Collisions," *The New England Journal of Medicine*, vol. 336, no. 7, February 13, 1997.

71 "Using Car Phones Is as Dangerous as Driving Drunk," *Reuters/Fox* news report, February 13, 1997.

72 Francine D. Blau and Marianne A. Ferber, *The Economics of Women, Men, and Work*, Englewood Cliffs, NJ: Prentice-Hall, 1992; Joni Hersch and Leslie S. Stratton, "Housework, Wages, and the Division of Housework Time for Employed Spouses," *American Economic Review*, vol. 84, pp. 120–125, 1994; Arlie

Hochschild, *The Second Shift*, New York: Avon Books, 1989; John Robinson, "Who's Doing the Housework?" *American Demographics*, vol. 10, no. 12, 1988.

73 Susan Hanson and Ibipo Johnston, "Gender Differences in Work-Trip Length: Explanations and Implications," *Urban Geography*, vol. 6, 1995, pp. 193–219.

74 *Nationwide Personal Transportation Survey*, U.S. Department of Transportation, 1995.

75 Robert E. Griffiths, *1994 COG/TPB Household Travel Survey: Summary of Major Findings*, Washington, DC: Metropolitan Washington Council of Governments, January 1998.

76 Sandra Rosenbloom, "Travel by Women," in *1990 Nationwide Personal Transportation Survey: Demographic Special Reports*, Washington, DC: US Department of Transportation, Federal Highway Administration, February 1995, p. 2–9.

77 Raymond Novaco, Daniel Stokols, and Louis Milanesi, "Objective and Subjective Dimensions of Travel Impedance as Determinants of Commuting Stress," *American Journal of Community Psychology*, vol. 18, 1990, pp. 231–257; Raymond Novaco, Daniel Stokols, J. Campbell, and J. Stokols, "Transportation, Stress, and Community Psychology," *American Journal of Community Psychology*, no. 7, 1979, pp. 361–380; M. Schaeffer, S. Street, J. Singer and S. Baum, "Effects of Control on Stress Reactions of Commuters," *Journal of Applied Social Psychology*, vol.18, 1988, pp. 944–957; Daniel Stokols, Raymond Novaco, eds., *Transportation and Well-Being*, New York: Plenum Press, 1981; and Daniel Stokols, Raymond Novaco, J. Campbell and J. Stokols, "Traffic Congestion, Type-A Behavior, and Stress," *Journal of Applied Psychology*, vol. 63, 1978, pp. 467–480.

78 Meni Koslowsky and Moshe Krauz, "On the Relationship between Commuting, Stress Symptoms, and Attitudinal Measures: A LISREL Application," *Journal of Applied Behavioral Science*, vol. 29, 1994, pp. 485–492. The authors cite similar findings in E. Gaffuri and G. Costa, "Applied Aspects of Chronoergohygiene," *Chronobiologia*, no. 13, 1986, pp. 39–51; J. Seyfarth and W. Bost, "Teacher Turnover and the Quality of Worklife in Schools: An Empirical Study," *Journal of Research and Development in Education*, vol. 20, 1986, pp. 1–6; and P. Taylor and C. Pocock, "Commuter Travel and Sickness: Absence of London Office Workers," *British Journal of Preventive and Social Medicine*, no. 26, 1972, pp. 165–172.

79 NHTSA defines "aggressive driving" as "driving behavior that endangers or is likely to endanger people or property." It is different from "road rage," which refers to violent acts against fellow motorists. See "The Statement of the Honorable Ricardo Martinez, M.D.,

Chapter 4 (continued)

administrator, National Highway Traffic Safety Administration, before the Subcommittee on Surface Transportation, Committee on Transportation and Infrastructure, U.S. House of Representatives, July 17, 1997.

80 Stephen Sheppard, "The Qualitative Economics of Development Controls," *Journal of Urban Economics*, vol. 24, 1988, pp. 310–330.

81 *Ibid.*

82 The groups are the Natural Resources Defense Council, the Surface Transportation Policy Project, and the Center for Neighborhood Technology. See John Holtzclaw, *Using Residential Patterns and Transit to Decrease Auto Dependence and Costs*, San Francisco, CA: Natural Resources Defense Council, June 1994. As discussed in chapter five, a major implication of this research is that location-efficient households can apply their transportation savings to afford greater housing costs than households with comparable incomes in sprawling areas.

83 Kim Hoeveler, "Accessibility vs. Mobility: The Location Efficient Mortgage," *Public Investment* (Planners Advisory Service Memo, American Planning Association), September 1997.

84 American Automobile Association, Michigan Chapter, "Your Car Costs," 1997.

85 Research conducted by Don Chen at the Surface Transportation Policy Project based on the Consumer Expenditure Survey, U.S. Department of Commerce, 1998.

86 Todd Litman, *Autodependency as a Cost*, Victoria Transport Policy Institute, 1996.

87 *National Bicycling and Walking Study, Case Study 15*, Washington, DC: Federal Highway Administration, U.S. Department of Transportation, 1996.

88 "Implications of Emerging Travel Trends: April 20–21, 1994, Conference Proceedings," *1990 Nationwide Personal Transportation Survey*, Washington, DC: U.S. Department of Transportation, Federal Highway Administration, July 1994, p. 25.

89 Sandra Rosenbloom, "Travel by the Elderly," *1990 Nationwide Personal Transportation Survey: Demographic Special Reports*, Washington, DC: U.S. Department of Transportation, Federal Highway Administration, February 1995; see also Charles Lave and Richard Crepeau, "Travel by Households Without Vehicles," *1990 Nationwide Personal Transportation Survey: Travel Mode Special Reports*, Washington, DC: U.S. Department of Transportation, Federal Highway Administration, December 1994.

90 D. Hummon, Commonplaces: Community Ideology and Identity in American Culture, Binghamton, NY: SUNY Press, 1990.

91 Orfield, *op. cit.*, p. 24.

92 *Uniform Crime Report*, Federal Bureau of Investigation, Department of Justice, 1995.

93 Peter W.G. Newman and Jeffrey R. Kenworthy, *Cities and Automobile Dependence: A Sourcebook*, Aldershot, UK, and Brookfield, VT: Gower Publishing Co., 1989.

94 D. Sherrod and S. Cohen, "Density, Personal Control, and Design," in J. Aiello and A. Baum, eds., *Residential Crowding and Design*, New York: Plenum Press, 1979.

95 Orfield, *op. cit.*

96 Paul Klite, Robert A. Bardwell, Jason Setzman, "A Day in the Life of Local TV News in America," *Rocky Mountain Media Watch*, Content Analysis, no. 5, January 11, 1995, pp. 1–3.

97 Orfield, *op. cit.*, p. 22

98 *Id.*, p. 24.

99 Christy Fisher, "What We Love and Hate about Cities," *American Demographics*, October 1997.

100 Shore, *op. cit.*

101 William Julius Wilson, *When Work Disappears: The World of the New Urban Poor*, New York: Vintage Books, 1996.

102 *Ibid.*

Chapter 5

1 James Noonan and Peter McEntee, *The Potential for New Residential Development in Maryland* (Baltimore: Maryland Office of Planning), cited in Janet Pelley, *et al.*, *Sprawl Costs Us All*, Annapolis, MD: Sierra Club Foundation, 1997, p. 2.

2 Equitable Real Estate Management, Inc., and Real Estate Research Corporation, *Emerging Trends in Real Estate: 1997*, Chicago: Real Estate Research Corporation, October 1996, p. 28. The report contrasts "24-hour" cities with those that are abandoned during the evenings.

3 *Ibid.*, pp. 24–25. Lend Lease Real Estate Investments, *Emerging Trends in Real Estate 1999*, New York: Lend Lease Real Estate Investments, October 1998, pp. 23–29.

4 Haya E. Nasser, "New Approaches to Rebuilding Cities," *USA Today*, December 27, 1996, p. 2A.

Chapter 5 (continued)

5 *Ibid. See also* Roberto Suro, "Drop in Murder Rate Accelerates in Cities," *The Washington Post*, December 31, 1997, p. A1.

6 Cities that have begun to gain population in the 1990s after losing population in the 1980s include Denver, CO; Kansas City, MO; Atlanta, GA; Yonkers, NY; and Cedar Rapids, IA. Cleveland and Detroit are among the cities that have substantially slowed their population losses in the 1990s. See Judith Havemann, "'Civic Entrepreneurs' Boost Declining Cities," *The Washington Post*, December 9, 1997, p. A1.

7 Haya El Nasser, "Downtown Increasingly Becoming Hometown, " *USA Today*, September 25, 1998, p. 3A.

8 Lend Lease Real Estate Investments, *op. cit.*, p. 24. *See also* Michael Bernick and Robert Cervero, *Transit Villages in the 21st Century*, New York: McGraw-Hill, 1997, p. 138 ("In the San Francisco Bay Area, for instance, the share of population in the 25 to 34 and 65 and over age groups increased from 23.5 percent in 1980 to 30.8 percent in 1990.").

9 Robyn Meredith, "Demand for Single-Family Homes Helps Fuel Inner-City Resurgence," *The New York Times*, July 5, 1997, p. 1.

10 Jeff Kenworthy, Felix Laube, *et al.*, *Report for the World Bank*, Perth, Australia: Murdoch University, February 1997, p. 19.

11 Paul Span, "Auld Lang Syne on 42nd Street," *The Washington Post*, December 31, 1996, p. D1.

12 Surface Transportation Policy Project, *Transfer*, vol. 3, February 28, 1997, p.8.

13 23 U.S.C. §134 (October 1998), Transportation Equity Act for the 21st Century (TEA-21) (succeeding and continuing the features of the landmark Intermodal Surface Transportation Efficiency Act [ISTEA] of 1991). See Surface Transportation Policy Project, *TEA-21 User's Guide*, Washington, DC: Surface Transportation Policy Project, 1998, pp. 21–25.

14 See, e.g., Joe DiStefano and Matthew Raimi, *Five Years of Progress: 110 Communities Where ISTEA is Making a Difference*, Washington, DC: Surface Transportation Policy Project, 1996.

15 A comprehensive explication of the regional initiatives in force in the Twin Cities may be found in Myron Orfield, *Metropolitics: A Regional Agenda for Community and Stability*, Washington, DC: Brookings Institution Press, and Cambridge, MA: The Lincoln Institute of Land Policy, 1997.

16 Reid H. Ewing, "Is Los Angeles-Style Sprawl Desirable?" *Journal of the American Planning Association*, vol. 63, Winter 1997, pp. 107, 107–108.

17 See Randall Arendt, *et al.*, *Rural By Design: Maintaining Small Town Character*, Chicago: American Planning Association, 1994, pp. 173–74.

18 *Ibid.*, pp. 150–154.

19 Bernick and Cervero, *op. cit.*, p. 83 ("One doesn't need Hong Kong-like densities to sustain mass transit.").

20 Anthony Downs, *New Visions for Metropolitan America*, Washington, DC: The Brookings Institution; Cambridge, MA: Lincoln Institute of Land Policy, 1994, p. 146.

21 Peter W.G. Newman and Jeffrey R. Kenworthy, *Cities and Automobile Dependence: A Sourcebook*, Aldershot, UK, and Brookfield, VT: Gower Publishing Company, 1989, pp. 132–133.

22 Peter Calthorpe, *The Next American Metropolis*, New York: Princeton Architectural Press, 1993, p. 19.

23 *Ibid.*, pp. 41–43, 62–112.

24 *Ibid.*, pp. 27–28, 41–42.

25 Bernick and Cervero, *op. cit.*, pp. 6–11, 91–97. A well-articulated set of principles for compact neighborhood design has been presented also by Professor Ewing in his book, *Best Development Practices*, Tallahassee: Florida Department of Community Affairs, 1995, at pp. 17–49. Ewing's book is also available, in a separate format, from the American Planning Association in Chicago.

26 Bernick and Cervero, *op. cit.*, pp. 5, 15–33.

27 *Ibid.*, pp. 95–97, 86–87, 137, 351–371. The authors discuss examples of supportive zoning measures in Montgomery County, MD; Hillsboro, OR; Lynwood, WA; and San Diego.

28 See Kim Hoeveler, "Accessibility vs. Mobility: The Location Efficient Mortgage," *Public Investment* (Planners Advisory Service Memo), American Planning Association, September 1997. The LEM, being developed by the Natural Resources Defense Council, the Surface Transportation Policy Project, and the Center for Neighborhood Technology, was among the federal smart-growth policies featured in a speech delivered by Vice President Al Gore at the Brookings Institution on September 2, 1998.

29 See *Ibid.*, p. 32.

30 See, e.g., Ewing, "Is Los Angeles-Style Sprawl Desirable?" *op. cit.*, p. 114; California Air Resources Board (CARB), *Transportation-Related Land Use Strategies to Minimize Motor Vehicle Emissions*, June 1995, pp. B-63–64.

31 Calthorpe, *op. cit.*, p. 43.

32 Lend Lease Real Estate Investments, *op. cit.*, p. 24.

Chapter 5 (continued)

33 "Neighborhoods Ride the Rails: City, Suburbs Alike Revisit Village Hub Idea," *Chicago Sun-Times*, February 21, 1995.

34 Center for Neighborhood Technology, *Community Green Line Initiative*, p. 2 (undated).

35 Bernick and Cervero, *op. cit.*, pp. 187–269. The Berkeley researchers do caution, however, that "most visionary designs have been tempered or compromised by the sober realities of local market constraints, tax needs of local governments, and community politics. At the same time, these station areas still retain new urbanist features that make them alternative suburban communities and some of the first transit-based new urbanist communities actually being built in the United States." *Ibid.*, p. 187.

36 Equitable Real Estate Management, *op. cit.*, p.28.

37 Ewing, "Is Los Angeles-Style Sprawl Desirable?" *op. cit.*, p. 111. Bernick and Cervero, *op. cit.*, pp. 140–149.

38 Arendt, *Rural By Design*, supra, pp. 59, 237; see also J. Lacey and R. Arendt, *An Examination of Market Appreciation for Clustered Housing*, Amherst, MA: Center for Rural Massachusetts, 1990, cited in Pelley, *op. cit.*, at 10. J.D. Hunt, J.D.P. McMillan, and J.E. Abraham, "State Preference Investigation of Influences on Attractiveness of Residential Locations," in *Issues in Land Use and Transportation Planning, Models and Applications*, National Research Council: Transportation Research Record No. 1466, 1994, pp. 79–87.

39 Bernick and Cervero, *op. cit.*, pp. 156–164.

40 Robert Hanley, "A Fast-Growing Town Innovates in Curbing Suburban Sprawl," *New York Times*, December 29, 1996.

41 Dan Eggen, "A Growing Issue," *The Washington Post*, October 28, 1998, p. A3; State Resource Strategies, *1998 Elections: The Voters Speak Out on Resource Conservation, Community Quality, and Sprawl*, a report for the Sprawl Watch Clearinghouse, Washington, DC, November 4, 1998.

42 Le Ann Spencer, "Grayslake Project Sells Environment-Friendly Lifestyle," *Chicago Tribune*, Metro Lake Section, December 4, 1996.

43 See Bruce Friedman, *et al.*, "Effect of Neotraditional Neighborhood Design on Travel Characteristics," in *Issues in Land Use and Transportation Planning, op. cit.*, pp. 69–70.

44 Glenn Frankel and Stephen Fehr, "As the Economy Grows, the Trees Fall," *The Washington Post*, March 23, 1997, p. A21.

45 Stephen C. Fehr, "Montgomery's Line of Defense Against the suburban Invasion," *The Washington Post*, March 25, 1997, pp. A1, 10–11.

46 *Ibid.*

47 Timothy Egan, "Portland's Hard Line on Managing Growth," *The New York Times*, December 30, 1996.

48 Stephen C. Fehr, "Area Shoppers Find Search for a Parking Space Often Can Be a Maddening Mission," *The Washington Post*, September 1, 1996, p. B1.

49 A. Ann Sorensen, Richard P. Greene, and Karen Russ, *Farming On The Edge*, DeKalb, IL: American Farmland Trust, 1997, p. 18.

50 Sorensen, *et al.*, *op. cit.*, pp. 21–23.

51 Conservation organizations such as The Nature Conservancy, The National Trust for Historic Preservation, and Scenic America all recommend these sensible approaches. See, e.g., Scenic America, Principle for Conservation, www.scenic.org, December 17, 1998; Meg Maguire, *et al.*, "Beauty As Well As Bread," *Journal of the American Planning Association*, vol. 63, Summer 1997, pp. 317–328.

52 See, e.g., at the federal level, Endangered Species Act, 16 U.S.C. §§ 1631–1643; National Historic Preservation Act, 16 U.S.C. §§ 470 *et seq.*; National Environmental Policy Act, 42 U.S.C. §§ 4321 *et seq.*

53 See Randall G. Arendt, *Conservation Design for Subdivisions*, Washington, DC: Island Press, 1996; Reid Ewing, *Best Development Practices, op. cit.*, pp. 91–127. For a thorough discussion of some of the techniques available to conserve privately-owned land, see also Russell L. Brenneman and Sarah M. Bates, eds., *Land-Saving Action*, Covelo, CA: Island Press, 1984; Montana Land Reliance and Land Trust Exchange, *Private Options: Tools and Concepts for Land Conservation*, Covelo, CA: Island Press, 1982.

54 Constance E. Beaumont, *Better Models for Superstores*, Washington, DC: National Trust for Historic Preservation, 1997.

55 *Ibid.*

56 In 1998, the Pasadena store ranked among the chain's top ten producers in the country, according to its manager. Personal communication with Constance Beaumont, National Trust for Historic Preservation, January 5, 1999.

57 *Ibid.*

58 Frank Jossi, "Rewrapping the Big Box," *Planning*, vol. 64, August 1998, p. 16.

59 *See* Robert Cervero, *America's Suburban Centers: The Land Use-Transportation Link*, Boston: Unwin Hyman, 1989, generally and pp. 195–210.

Chapter 5 (continued)

60 For a full description of the Oregon law and its impacts, see Robert L. Liberty, "Oregon's Comprehensive Growth Management Program: An Implementation Review and Lessons for Other States," *Environmental Law Reporter News and Analysis*, vol. 22, June 1992, pp. 10367–9. See also Robert Liberty, "Planned Growth: The Oregon Model," *Natural Resources and Environment*, vol. 13, Summer 1998, p. 315; 1000 Friends of Oregon, *Questions and Answers About Oregon's Land Use Planning Program*, Portland, OR, 1997. Much of the discussion in this section is taken from these sources, supplemented where noted.

61 Michael J. Ybarra, "Putting City Sprawl On a Zoning Diet," *The New York Times*, June 16, 1996, section 1, page 1.

62 OECD, *op. cit.*, p. 94.

63 *Ibid.* Portland's success on these indicators may be contrasted with the relative failure of Hillsboro, some 20 miles to the west. Hillsboro adopted a less environmentally oriented approach to land use and transportation "and now has vast, low-density residential and industrial areas, congestion, air pollution, and a decaying city center, with 92 percent of trips being made by car." *Ibid.*, p. 217.

64 Egan, "Portland's Hard Line on Managing Growth," *op. cit.*, p. 2.

65 Equitable Real Estate Management, *et al.*, *op. cit.*, p. 33. Sprawling Charlotte, North Carolina was the other top-ranked region among the country's "smaller" real-estate markets.

66 Lincoln Institute of Land Policy, *Alternatives to Sprawl* (conference report), 1995, p. 16.

67 William Clairborne, "Cracks in Portland's 'Great Wall'," *The Washington Post*, September 29, 1997, pp. A1, 12.

68 Ybarra, *op. cit.*; Claiborne, *op. cit.*; Egan, "Portland's Hard Line on Managing Growth," *op. cit.*

69 CARB, *The Land Use-Air Quality Linkage, op. cit.*, pp. 13–14.

70 Claiborne, *op. cit.*

71 Terry M. Neal and Todd Shields, "Maryland Looks to Regulate the Promised Land," *The Washington Post*, February 23, 1997, p. A1.

72 Maryland Office of Planning, *Managing Maryland's Growth: What You Need to Know About Smart Growth and Neighborhood Conservation*, 1997.

73 Chesapeake Bay Foundation, *Summary of the Smart Growth Areas Bill*, 1997.

74 Maryland Office of Planning, *Managing Maryland's Growth, op. cit.*, pp. 9–10.

75 *Ibid.*, pp. 10–16.

76 As noted, undeveloped areas slated for future development must have a minimum average density of 3.5 dwellings per acre. Existing communities are essentially "grandfathered," being eligible with a minimum average density of only 2.0 dwellings per acre.

77 See, e.g., Peter S. Goodman, "Glendening vs. Suburban Sprawl," *The Washington Post*, October 6, 1998, p. B1.

78 See Mike Tidwell, "The Intercounty Connector . . . The Road to Ruin," *The Washington Post*, July 27, 1997, p. C3; Andrew MacDonald, "Chapman's Landing Idea Would Do Harm," *The Baltimore Sun*, November 6, 1996, p. 32A. As this report is being concluded, the highway project was being reconsidered, while the state had used resources in the Smart Growth Initiative to purchase and conserve as open space the watershed, known as Chapman's Landing, apparently ending the attempt to develop it.

79 Anthony Downs, "Contrasting Strategies For the Economic Development of Metropolitan Areas In the United States and Western Europe," Chapter Two in Paul Cheshire, Lanfranco Senn, Anita Summers, *et al.*, *Urban Change in the United States and Western Europe: Comparative Analysis and Policy*, 1993, p. 17.

80 U.S. Congress, Office of Technology Assessment (OTA), "Is the U.S. System Energy-Efficient? A Comparison with Europe," Chapter 3 in *Saving Energy in U.S. Transportation*, Washington, DC: U.S. Government Printing Office, July 1994, p. 78.

81 Downs, "Contrasting Strategies," *op. cit.*, pp. 16–17.

82 Leo H. Klaassen and Paul C. Cheshire, "Urban Analysis Across The Atlantic Divide," chapter twenty in Cheshire, Senn, Summers, *et al.*, *op. cit.*, p. 591.

83 See, e.g., Jay Hawkins, "Notes From the U.K." (interview with British planning expert Barry Cullingworth), *Planning*, vol. 64, August 1998, p. 14.

84 Downs, "Contrasting Strategies," *op. cit.*, p. 17.

85 United Kingdom, Department of the Environment and Department of Transport, *Planning Policy Guidance: Transport* (PPG 13), cited in Keith Bartholomew, *Policies & Places: Land Use and Transport In The Netherlands and the United Kingdom*, 1000 Friends of Oregon, 1995, at p. 11.

86 Bartholomew, *op. cit.*, p. 11.

87 John Tagliabue, "Europeans Agonize Over the Mall," *The New York Times*, September 10, 1996, p. D1.

88 OECD, *op. cit.*, pp. 92–93.

Chapter 5 (continued)

89 See also John Pucher, "Urban Travel Behavior as the Outcome of Public Policy: The Example of Modal-Split in Western Europe and North America," *Journal of the American Planning Association*, vol. 54, 1988, pp. 509–520; and John Pucher, "Urban Passenger Transport in the United States and Europe: A Comparative Analysis of Public Policies," *Transport Reviews*, vol. 15, 1995, pp. 211–227.

90 "Estimate of Green Belt Land Revised," *The Financial Times*, August 18, 1990, p. 14.

91 Federal Ministry for Regional Planning, Building and Urban Development, *Habitat II, Global Best Practices Initiative in Improving the Living Environment, German Best Practices*, Bonn: Druck- und Werbegesellschaft mGH, 1996, p. 16.

92 See, e.g., Downs, "Contrasting Strategies," *op. cit.*, p. 30; articles by Pucher, *op. cit.*

93 Bernick and Cervero, *op. cit.*, p. 289.

94 *Ibid.* pp. 11–12. *See also Ibid.* pp. 289-305. The authors observe that Stockholm's success in avoiding automobile dependence is attributable not only to deliberate land-use planning but also to complementary policies such as low transit fares and relatively high costs for parking and vehicle taxes.

95 Michael Simmons, "Rural England Lost In Concrete: Environmentalists fire warning shot at the Government as urban sprawl threatens to gobble up more and more of countryside," *The Guardian*, July 29, 1993, p. 3.

96 Alex Marshall, "Eurosprawl," *Metropolis*, January/February 1995, p. 77.

97 *Ibid.*, *op. cit.*, pp. 79,81.

98 *Ibid.*, p. 77.

Epilogue

1 Organization for Economic Cooperation and Development and European Conference of Ministers of Transport, *Urban Travel and Sustainable Development*, 1995, pp. 97–98.

Bibliography

Books and Reports

Abt Associates. *Air Pollution-Related Social Costs of On-Highway Motor Vehicles, Part II: Physical and Economic Valuation Modeling,* June 25, 1998.

Altshuler, Alan A. and Jose Gomez-Ibanez with Arnold M. Howitt. *Regulation for Revenue: The Political Economy of Land Use Exactions.* Washington, DC: Brookings Institution; and Cambridge, MA: Lincoln Institute of Land Policy, 1994.

American Automobile Association, Michigan Chapter. *Your Car Costs,* 1997.

American Farmland Trust. *Alternatives for Future Urban Growth in California's Central Valley: The Bottom Line for Agriculture and Taxpayers.* Washington, DC: American Farmland Trust, October 1995.

American Farmland Trust. *Cost of Community Services Fact Sheet.* Washington, DC: American Farmland Trust, http://farm.fic.niu.edu/fic-ta/tafs-cocs.html.

American Farmland Trust. *Current State Farmland Protection Activities.* Washington, DC: American Farmland Trust, 1991.

American Farmland Trust. *Density-Related Public Costs.* Washington, DC: American Farmland Trust, 1986.

American Farmland Trust. *Farming On The Edge: A New Look at the Importance and Vulnerability of Agriculture Near American Cities.* Washington, DC: American Farmland Trust, 1994.

American Planning Association. *Policy Guide on Impact Fees.* Chicago, IL: American Planning Association, undated, found at http://www.planning.org/govt/impact.html, January 1999.

Arendt, Randall G. *Conservation Design for Subdivisions.* Washington, DC: Island Press, 1996.

Arendt, Randall *et al. Rural By Design: Maintaining Small Town Character.* Chicago, IL: American Planning Association, 1994.

Bartholemew, Keith. *Policies & Places: Land Use and Transport In The Netherlands and the United Kingdom.* Portland, OR: 1000 Friends of Oregon, 1995.

Beaumont, Constance E. *Better Models for Superstores.* Washington, DC: National Trust for Historic Preservation, 1997.

Beaumont, Constance E. *How Superstore Sprawl Can Harm Communities and What Citizens Can Do About It.* Washington, DC: National Trust for Historic Preservation, 1994.

Berger, Bennett. *Working Class Suburb.* Berkeley, CA: University of California Press, 1968.

Bernick, Michael and Robert Cervero. *Transit Villages In the 21st Century.* New York: McGraw-Hill, 1997.

191

Books and Reports (continued)

Bier, Thomas and the Ohio Housing Research Network. *Moving Up and Out: Government Policy and the Future of Ohio's Metropolitan Areas.* Cleveland, OH: The Urban University Program of the Ohio General Assembly and the Ohio Board of Regents, September 1994.

Bier, Thomas and The Ohio Housing Research Network. *The IRS Homeseller Capital Gain Provision: Contributor to Urban Decline.* Cleveland, OH: The Urban University Program of the Ohio General Assembly and the Ohio Board of Regents, January 1994.

Binford, Henry. *The First Suburbs: Residential Communities on the Boston Periphery 1815–1860.* Chicago, IL: University of Chicago Press, 1985.

Blau, Francine D. and Marianne A. Ferber. *The Economics of Women, Men, and Work.* Englewood Cliffs, NJ: Prentice-Hall, 1992.

Bollier, David. *How Smart Growth Can Stop Sprawl: A Fledgling Citizen Movement Expands.* Washington, DC: Essential Books, 1998.

Bowden, Charles and Lew Kreinberg. *Street Signs Chicago: Neighborhood and Other Illusions of Big-City Life.* Chicago, IL: Chicago Review Press, 1981.

Brabec, Elizabeth and Kevin Kirby. *The Value of Nature and Scenery.* Washington, DC: Scenic America Technical Information Series, vol. 1, no. 3, 1992.

Brehm, John and Wendy Rahn. *Individual Level Evidence for the Causes and Consequences of Social Capital.* Presented at a conference sponsored by the Pew Charitable Trust, the National Commission on Civic Renewal, and the Brookings Institution, November 25, 1996.

Brenneman, Russell L. and Sarah M. Bates, eds. *Land-Saving Action.* Covelo, CA: Island Press, 1984.

Buffington, J. D. Schafer and C. Bullion. *Attitudes, Opinions, and Experiences of Business and Institutional Relocates Displaced by Highways under the 1970 Relocation Assistance Program.* Texas Transportation Institute, Texas A&M University.

Bullard, Robert and Glenn Johnson, eds. *Just Transportation: Dismantling Race & Class Barriers to Mobility.* Stony Creek, CT: New Society Publishers, 1997.

Burchell, Robert W. and David Listokin. "Land, Infrastructure, Housing Costs, and Fiscal Impacts Associated with Growth: The Literature on the Impacts of Sprawl versus Managed Growth." Presented at the conference *Rail-Volution '96: Building Successful Communities with Rail,* Washington, DC, September 8, 1996.

Burchell, Robert W. *et al. Impact Assessment of the New Jersey Interim State Development and Redevelopment Plan, Report II: Research Findings.* Trenton, NJ: New Jersey Office of State Planning, February 20, 1992.

California Air Resources Board. *The Land Use-Air Quality Linkage.* Sacramento, CA: California Air Resources Board, 1994.

California Air Resources Board. *Transportation-Related Land Use Strategies to Minimize Motor Vehicle Emissions.* Sacramento, CA: California Air Resources Board, June 1995.

Books and Reports (continued)

California Public Utilities Commission. *Staff Report Regarding Assembly Bill No. 4217 (Bronzan) Requiring An Investigation of the Methods of Cost Estimation, Revenue Allocation, and Rate Setting for California Electric Utilities.* Sacramento, CA: California Public Utilities Commission, 1990.

Calthorpe, Peter. *The Next American Metropolis.* New York: Princeton Architectural Press, 1993.

Caro, Robert. *The Power Broker.* New York: Random House, 1974.

Carroll County (MD) Bureau of Planning. *Managing Growth.* Issue no. 1, March 1996.

Center for Neighborhood Technology. *Community Green Line Initiative: Land Use Planning, Community Development and Public Transit-the Pulaski Station Project.* Chicago, IL: Center for Neighborhood Technology, undated.

Cervero, Robert. *America's Suburban Centers—The Land Use-Transportation Link.* Boston, MA: Unwin Hyman, 1989.

Cervero, Robert. *Suburban Gridlock.* New Brunswick, NJ: Center for Urban Policy Research, 1986.

Chesapeake Bay Foundation. *A Dollars and Sense Partnership: Economic Development and Environmental Protection.* Annapolis, MD: Chesapeake Bay Foundation, 1996.

Chesapeake Bay Foundation. *Summary of the Smart Growth Areas Bill,* 1997.

Chesapeake Bay Program. *Cost of Providing Government Services to Alternative Residential Patterns.* Prepared for the Chesapeake Bay Program's Subcommittee on Population Growth and Development, produced under contract no. 68-WI-0043 for the Environmental Protection Agency. Annapolis, MD: Chesapeake Bay Program, May 1993.

City of Olympia and Washington State Department of Ecology, *Impervious Surface Reduction Study.* Final Report, May 1995.

Cox, Wendell. *Demographic Briefs: U.S. Urbanized Area Population and Density Trends: 1950-1990.* Belleville, IL: Wendell Cox Consultancy, 1996.

DC Colony. *Residential Relocation: The Impact of Allowances and Procedures in Effect Since July 1, 1970.* University of Toledo, for the Ohio Department of Transportation and the Federal Highway Administration, 1973.

Davis, Stacy C. and Patricia S. Hu. *Transportation Energy Data Book.* Oak Ridge, TN: Oak Ridge National Laboratory, 1991.

Diamond, Henry L. and Patrick F. Noonon. *Land Use in America.* Washington, DC: Island Press, 1996.

DiStefano, Joe and Matthew Raimi. *Five Years of Progress: 110 Communities Where ISTEA is Making a Difference.* Washington, DC: Surface Transportation Policy Project, 1996.

Downs, Anthony. *New Visions for Metropolitan America.* Washington, DC: The Brookings Institution; and Cambridge, MA: The Lincoln Institute of Land Policy, 1994.

Downs, Anthony. *Stuck in Traffic.* Washington, DC: The Brookings Institution; and Cambridge, MA: The Lincoln Institute of Land Policy, 1992.

Books and Reports (continued)

Dresch, Marla and Steven M. Sheffrin. *Who Pays for Development Fees and Exactions?* San Francisco, CA: Public Policy Institute of California, 1997.

Duncan, James *et al. The Search for Efficient Urban Growth Patterns: A Study of the Fiscal Impacts of Development in Florida.* Tallahassee, FL: Florida Department of Community Affairs, July 1989.

Dunphy, Robert and Kimberly Fisher. "Transportation, Congestion, and Density: New Insights." *Transportation Research Record No. 1552.* Washington, DC: Transportation Research Board, 1996.

DuPage County Regional Planning Commission. *Impacts of Development on DuPage County Property Taxes.* Wheaton, IL: DuPage County Regional Planning Commission, 1992.

Easterbrook, Gregg. *A Moment on the Earth: The Coming Age of Environmental Optimism.* New York: Penguin Books USA, 1996.

Economic and Statistics Administration, U.S. Census Bureau, U.S. Department of Commerce. *Geophysical Mobility: March 1995 to March 1996.* P20-497, December 3, 1997.

Environment and Energy Study Institute Fact Sheet. "Oil and Transportation," cited in *Getting There.* Washington, DC: The Advocacy Institute, 1996, pp. 14, 30.

Environmental Law and Policy Center of the Midwest. *Portrait of Sprawl: Northeastern Illinois Population Change.* Map. Chicago, IL: Environmental Law and Policy Center of the Midwest, undated.

Equitable Real Estate Management, Inc., and Real Estate Research Corporation. *Emerging Trends in Real Estate: 1997.* Chicago, IL: Real Estate Research Corporation, October 1996.

Ewing, Reid. *Best Development Practices.* Tallahassee, FL: Florida Department of Community Affairs, 1995.

Federal Bureau of Investigation, Department of Justice. *Uniform Crime Report,* 1995.

Federal Ministry for Regional Planning, Building and Urban Development. *Habitat II, Global Best Practices Initiative in Improving the Living Environment, German Best Practices.* Bonn: Druck- und Werbegesellschaft mGH, 1996.

Fernandez, Roberto. *Spatial Mismatch: Housing, Transportation, and Employment in Regional Perspective.* Prepared for the "Metropolitan Assembly on Urban Problems: Linking Research to Action" conference. Chicago, IL: Center for Urban Affairs and Policy Research, Northwestern University, September 30-October 2, 1994.

Fischer, Paul B. *Is Housing Mobility an Effective Anti-Poverty Strategy? An Examination of the Cincinnati Experience.* Cincinnati, OH: Stephen H. Wilder Foundation, 1991.

Fisher, Ronald L. *State and Local Public Finance.* Chicago, IL: Irwin, 1996.

Flink, James J. *The Automobile Age.* Cambridge, MA: Massachusetts Institute of Technology Press, 1988.

Frank, James E. *The Costs of Alternative Development Patterns: A Review of the Literature.* Washington, DC: The Urban Land Institute, 1989.

Books and Reports (continued)

Frey, William and Elaine Fielding. *Changing Urban Populations, Regional Restructuring, Racial Polarization, and Poverty Concentration.* Population Studies Center, Ann Arbor, MI: University of Michigan Press, February 1994.

Gans, Herbert. *The Levittowners.* New York: Vintage Books, 1967.

Girouard, Mark. *Cities & People.* New Haven, CT: Yale University Press, 1985.

Glendening, Governor Parris. *Making Maryland the Best Place to Work, to Raise a Child and to Build a Family.* Presented in Annapolis, MD, 1997 State of the State Address, January 15, 1997.

Glendening, Governor Parris. *Remarks at the National Issues Forum on Forging Metropolitan Solutions to Urban and Regional Problems,* Brookings Institution, May 28, 1997.

Greene, D.L. *et al.* "Transportation Energy to the Year 2020." In *A Look Ahead, Year 2020.* Washington, DC: National Transportation Board, National Research Council, 1988.

Greene, D.L. *et al. The Outlook for U.S. Oil Dependence.* Oak Ridge, TN: Oak Ridge National Laboratory, ORNL-6873, 1995.

Griffiths, Robert E. *1994 COG/TPB Household Travel Survey: Summary of Major Findings.* Washington, DC: Metropolitan Washington Council of Governments, January 1998.

Handy, Susan. *How Land Use Patterns Affect Travel Patterns: A Bibliography.* Council of Planning Librarians, 1992.

Harvey, Greig. *Relation of Residential Density to VMT Per Resident.* Oakland, CA: Metropolitan Planning Commission, 1990.

Hill, Edward W. and John Brennan. *Where Is the Renaissance? Employment Specialization Within Ohio's Metropolitan Areas.* Presented at the Conference on Interdependence of Central Cities and Suburbs, sponsored by the Brookings Institution, the Lincoln Land Institute, and the University of Illinois at Chicago, September 24, 1998.

Hirschman, Ira. "Spatial Equity and Transportation Finance: A Case Study of the New York Metropolitan Region." Ph.D. Dissertation, New Brunswick, NJ: Department of Urban Planning and Policy Development, 1991.

Hiss, Tony. *The Experience of Place.* New York: Alfred A. Knopf, 1990.

Hochschild, Arlie. *The Second Shift.* New York: Avon Books, 1989.

Holtzclaw, John. *Explaining Urban Density and Transit Impacts on Auto Use.* Presented to the California State Energy Resources Conservation and Development Commission, 1990.

Holtzclaw, John. *Using Residential Patterns and Transit to Decrease Auto Dependence and Costs.* San Francisco, CA: Natural Resources Defense Council; and Costa Mesa, CA: California Home Energy Efficiency Rating Systems, 1994.

Holtzclaw, John *et al. Location Efficiency: Neighborhood and Socio-Economic Characteristics Determine Auto Ownership and Driving: Studies in Chicago, Los Angeles, and San Francisco.* Monograph, publication pending.

Books and Reports (continued)

Housing Policy Research Program, Cleveland State University. *Movement of Cuyahoga County Homesellers, 1987-1991.* Report to the Cuyahoga County (Ohio) Planning Commission, April 20, 1993

Howard, Chernick and Andrew Reschovsky. *Urban Fiscal Problems: Coordinating Actions Among Governments,* prepared for the "Metropolitan Assembly on Urban Problems: Linking Research to Action" conference. Chicago, IL: Center for Urban Affairs and Policy Research, Northwestern University, September 30-October 2, 1994.

Hughes, Mark Alan and Julie E. Sternberg. *The New Metropolitan Reality: Where the Rubber Meets the Road in Antipoverty Policy.* Washington, DC: The Urban Institute, 1992.

Hulsey, Brent and Brent Koeller. *Floods, Deaths, and Wetlands Destruction.* Sierra Club, 1997.

Hummon, D. *Commonplaces: Community Ideology and Identity in American Culture,* Binghamton, NY: SUNY Press, 1990.

Humstone, Beth, Jeff Squires and Thomas Muller. *Fiscal and Economic Impact/Maple Tree Place Mall on Chittenden County Municipalities,* July 1989.

International Panel on Climate Change (IPCC) Working Group II. *Second Assessment Report, Summary for Policymakers.* SPM-10, 1995.

International Panel on Climate Change. *Summary for Policymakers of the Contribution of Working Group I to the IPCC Second Assessment Report,* 1995.

Jackson, J.B. *Developing a Landscape Vernacular.* New York: Doubleday, 1991.

Jacobs, Jane. *The Death and Life of Great American Cities.* New York: Vintage Books, 1961.

Jasny, Michael. *Leap of Faith.* New York: Natural Resources Defense Council, May 1997.

Kenworthy, Jeff and Felix Laube *et al. Report for the World Bank.* Perth, Australia: Murdoch University, February 1997.

Kinsley, Michael J. and Hunter Lovings. *Paying for Growth, Prospering From Development.* Snowmass, CO: Rocky Mountain Institute, 1995.

Kulash, Walter. *Traditional Neighborhood Development: Will the Traffic Work?* Presented at the Eleventh Annual Pedestrian Conference in Bellevue, Washington, October 1990.

Kunstler, James. *The Geography of Nowhere: The Rise and Decline of America's Man-Made Landscape.* New York: Simon & Schuster, 1993.

Lacey, J. and R. Arendt. *An Examination of Market Appreciation for Clustered Housing.* Amherst, MA: Center for Rural Massachusetts, 1990.

Lawton, J.H. and R.M. Macy. *Extinction Rates.* Oxford: Oxford University Press, 1995.

Lend Lease Real Estate Investments and PricewaterhouseCoopers. *Emerging Trends in Real Estate 1999.* New York: Lend Lease Real Estate Investments, October 1998.

Lincoln Institute of Land Policy. *Alternatives to Sprawl.* Policy report based on the conference "Alternatives to Sprawl," sponsored by the Lincoln Institute of Land Policy, The Brookings Institution, and the National Trust for Historic Preservation, Washington, DC, March 1995. Cambridge, MA: Lincoln Institute of Land Policy, 1995.

Books and Reports (continued)

Litman, Todd. *Autodependency as a Cost*. Victoria Transport Policy Institute, 1996.

Luce, Jr., Thomas F., Barbara L. Lukermann, and Herbert Mohring. *Regional Sewer System Rate Structure Study*. Minneapolis, MN: Hubert H. Humphrey Institute of Public Affairs, University of Minnesota, December 7, 1992.

Martinez, Ricardo, M.D., Administrator, National Highway Traffic Safety Administration. *Statement before the Subcommittee on Surface Transportation, Committee on Transportation and Infrastructure*, U.S. House of Representatives, July 17, 1997.

Maryland Office of Planning. *Managing Maryland's Growth: What You Need to Know About Smart Growth and Neighborhood Conservation*. Annapolis, MD: Maryland Office of Planning, 1997.

Maryland Office of Planning. *Maryland's Land 1973-1990: A Changing Resource*. Annapolis, MD: Maryland Office of Planning, 1991.

McCublin, D.R. and M.A. Delucchi. *The Social Cost of the Health Effects of Motor Vehicle Air Pollution*. Report 11 in *The Annualized Social Cost of Motor Vehicle Use in the U.S.* University of California Institute of Transportation Studies, 1966.

Metropolitan Planning Council. *Issue Brief: The Debate Over Impact Fees*. Chicago, IL: Metropolitan Planning Council, 1993.

Moe, Richard and Carter Wilkie. *Changing Places: Rebuilding Community in the Age of Sprawl*. New York: Henry Holt and Company, 1997.

Montana Land Reliance and Land Trust Exchange. *Private Options: Tools and Concepts for Land Conservation*. Covelo, CA: Island Press, 1982.

Moore, Terry and Paul Thorsnes. *The Transportation/Land Use Connection*. Chicago: American Planning Association, Planners Advisory Service Report no. 448/449, 1994.

Munnell, Alicia H., Lynn E. Browne, James McEneaney, and Geoffrey M.B. Tootell. *Mortgage Lending in Boston: Interpreting HMDA Data*. Federal Reserve Bank of Boston, Working Paper 92-7, 1992.

Nadis, Steve and James MacKenzie. *Car Trouble*. Boston, MA: Beacon Press, 1993.

National Vehicle and Fuel Emissions Laboratory, U.S. Environmental Protection Agency. *Annual Emissions and Fuel Consumption for an Average Vehicle*. February 1995.

The Nature Conservancy. *The 1997 Species Report Card: The State of U.S. Plants and Animals*, Summary. http:www.consci.tnc.org, January 8, 1998.

A. Nelessen Associates. *Results of the Visual Preference Survey(tm) and Visions Implementation Workshop (Aurora, CO)*, 1996.

A. Nelesson Associates and the City of Fort Collins. *Fort Collins VPS Results*. Executive Summary, undated.

Nelson, Arthur C. and James B. Duncan. *Growth Management Principles and Practices*. Chicago, IL: American Planning Association, 1995.

Nelson, Arthur C., editor. *Development Impact Fees: Policy Rationale, Practice, Theory, and Issues*. Chicago, IL: American Planning Association, 1988.

Books and Reports (continued)

New York State Department of Environmental Conservation. *New York State Implementation Plan: Inhalable Particulate (PM10)*. September 1995.

Newman, Peter W.G. and Jeffrey R. Kenworthy. *Cities and Automobile Dependence: A Sourcebook*. Aldershot, UK, and Brookfield, VT: Gower Publishing Co., 1989.

Noonan, James and Peter McEntee. *The Potential for New Residential Development in Maryland*. Baltimore, MD: Maryland Office of Planning.

Northeastern Illinois Planning Commission. *Strategic Plan for Land Resource Management*, 1992.

Oakland, William H. and William A. Testa. *Does Business Development Raise Taxes: An Empirical Appraisal*. Chicago, IL: Metropolitan Planning Council and the Federal Reserve Bank of Chicago, 1995.

Office of Technology Assessment, Congress of the United States. *The Technological Reshaping of Metropolitan America*. Publication No. OTA-ETI-643, Washington, DC: U.S. Government Printing Office, September 1995.

Office of Technology Assessment, *Saving Energy in U.S. Transportation*. Summary . Washington, DC: U.S. Government Printing Office, 1994.

Oge, Margo, Director, Office of Mobile Sources, U.S. Environmental Protection Agency. *Automotive Emissions: Progress and Challenges*. Presentation to Automotive Management Briefing Session, Traverse City, MI, August 9, 1995 (http://www.epa.gov/omswww/speech.htm, October 21, 1996).

Ohio Housing Research Network. *Moving Up and Out: Government Policy and the Future of Ohio's Metropolitan Areas*. Report for the Ohio General Assembly, September 19, 1994.

1000 Friends of Oregon. *Analysis of Alternatives* (LUTRAQ Volume 5). Portland, OR: 1000 Friends, May 1997.

1000 Friends of Oregon. *Making the Connections: A Summary of the LUTRAQ Project*, prepared by Parsons Brinckerhoff. Portland, OR: 1000 Friends of Oregon, February 1997.

1000 Friends of Oregon. *Questions and Answers About Oregon's Land Use Planning Program*. Portland, OR: 1000 Friends of Oregon, 1997.

Orfield, Myron. *Metropolitics: A Regional Agenda for Community and Stability*. Washington, DC: Brookings Institution Press; and Cambridge, MA: The Lincoln Institute of Land Policy, 1997.

Organization for Economic Cooperation and Development and European Conference of Ministers of Transport. *Urban Travel and Sustainable Development*. Paris: Organization for Economic Cooperation and Development, 1995.

Pelley, Janet *et al. Sprawl Costs Us All*. Annapolis, MD: Sierra Club Foundation, 1997.

Perfater, Michael and Gary Allen. *Preliminary Findings of a Diachronic Analysis of Social and Economic Effects of Relocation Due to Highways*. Virginia Highway and Transportation Research Council, 1975.

Books and Reports (continued)

Persky, Joseph and Wim Wiewel. *Central City and Suburban Development: Who Pays and Who Benefits.* Chicago, IL: University of Illinois at Chicago, College of Urban Planning and Public Affairs, Great Cities Institute, 1996.

Pickrell, Don. *Description of VMT Forecasting Procedure for "Car Talk" Baseline Forecasts.* Volpe Center, U.S. Department of Transportation, undated.

Pilla, Bishop Anthony M. *The Church in the City.* Cleveland, OH: Diocese of Cleveland, November 19, 1993.

Pisarski, Alan. *New Perspectives in Commuting.* Washington, DC: Federal Highway Administration Office of Highway Information Management, July 1992.

Platt, Rutherford H. *Land Use and Society.* Washington, DC: Island Press, 1996.

Puget Sound Council of Governments. *Vision 2020: Growth and Transportation Strategy for the Central Puget Sound Region.* October 1990.

Pushkarev, Boris and Jeffrey Zupan, *Public Transport and Land Use Policy.* Bloomington, IN: Indiana University Press, 1977.

Quade, Parsons Brinckerhoff and Douglas. *Commuter and Light Rail Transit Corridors: The Land Use Connection,* 1996.

Ravitch, Diane. *A New Era in Urban Education?* Washington, DC: The Brookings Institution, Policy Brief #35, August 1998.

Real Estate Research Corporation. *The Costs of Sprawl: Environmental and Economic Costs of Alternative Residential Patterns at the Urban Fringe.* Washington, DC: U.S. Government Printing Office, 1974.

Rubin, Mark and Margery Austin Turner. *Patterns of Employment Growth in the Washington Metropolitan Area.* Publication pending.

Rusk, David. *Cities Without Suburbs.* Washington, DC: The Woodrow Wilson Center Press, 1993.

Rybczynski, Witold. *City Life.* New York: Touchstone Books, 1996.

Schueler, Tom. *Site Planning for Urban Stream Protection.* Washington, DC: Metropolitan Council of Governments, Environmental Land Planning Series, 1995.

Sennett, Richard. *The Fall of Public Man.* New York: W.W. Norton, 1976.

Shprentz, Deborah Sheiman. *Breath-Taking: Premature Mortality Due to Particulate Air Pollution in 239 American Cities.* New York: Natural Resources Defense Council, 1996.

Siegel, Michael. *Another Cost of Sprawl: The Effects of Land Use on Wastewater Utility Costs.* Washington, DC: Natural Resources Defense Council, 1998.

Sorensen, A. Ann and J. Dixon Esseks. *Living on the Edge: The Costs and Risks of Scatter Development.* DeKalb, IL: American Farmland Trust and Northern Illinois University, March 1998.

Sorensen, A. Ann, Richard P. Greene, and Karen Russ, *Farming On The Edge.* DeKalb, IL: American Farmland Trust, 1997.

Books and Reports (continued)

Southern California Association of Governments. *Preliminary Draft '97 Regional Transportation Plan*. Los Angeles: Southern California Association of Governments, 1997.

State Resource Strategies. *1998 Elections: The Voters Speak Out on Resource Conservation, Community Quality, and Sprawl*. A report for the Sprawl Watch Clearinghouse, Washington, DC, November 4, 1998.

Stokols, Daniel and Raymond Novaco, eds. *Transportation and Well-Being*. New York: Plenum Press, 1981.

Stone, Kenneth E. *The Impact of Wal-Mart Stores on Other Businesses and Strategies for Co-Existing*. Iowa State University, 1993.

Surface Transportation Policy Project. *An Analysis of the Relationship Between Highway Expansion and Congestion in Metropolitan Areas: Lessons from the 15-Year Texas Transportation Institute Study*. Washington, DC: Surface Transportation Policy Project, November 1998.

Surface Transportation Policy Project. *TEA-21 User's Guide*. Washington, DC: Surface Transportation Policy Project, 1998.

Sykes, Robert D. *Protecting Water Quality In Urban Areas*, 1989.

Teaford, Jon C. *The Twentieth-Century American City: Problem, Promise, and Reality*. Baltimore, MD: Johns Hopkins University Press, 1986.

Thompson, Paul. *Poison Runoff: A Guide to State and Local Control of Nonpoint Source Water Pollution*. New York: Natural Resources Defense Council, 1989.

Transportation Research Board, National Research Council. *Special Report 245: Expanding Metropolitan Highways*. Washington, DC: 1995.

U.S. Climate Action Network. *Global Climate Change: U.S. Impacts and Solutions*. Washington, DC: 1996.

U.S. Congress, Office of Technology Assessment. *Saving Energy in U.S. Transportation* (Summary). Washington, DC: 1994.

U.S. Department of Commerce, Bureau of the Census. *Current Population Survey*. Washington, DC: 1997.

U.S Department of Commerce, Bureau of the Census. *Estimates of the Population of Metropolitan Areas*. MA-96-9. Washington, DC: December 1997.

U.S. Department of Energy, Energy Information Administration, *Annual Energy Outlook 1996*. DOE/EIA-0383(96). Washington, DC: January 1996.

U.S. Department of Transportation. *Our Nation's Travel: 1995 NPTS Early Results Report*. Washington, DC: September 1997.

U.S. Department of Transportation, Federal Highway Administration. *Highway Statistics 1989*. Washington, DC: 1990.

U.S. Department of Transportation, Federal Highway Administration. *Highway Statistics 1994*. Washington, DC: 1995.

Books and Reports (continued)

U.S. Department of Transportation, Federal Highway Administration. *National Bicycling and Walking Study, Case Study 15.* Washington, DC: 1996.

U.S. Department of Transportation, Federal Highway Administration. *Transportation Air Quality: Selected Facts and Figures.* Publication No. FHWA-PD-96-006. Washington, DC: 1996.

U.S. Department of Transportation. *Travel Behavior Issues In the 90s,* 1990 National Personal Transportation Survey. Washington, DC: 1992.

U.S. Environmental Protection Agency. *National Water Quality Inventory, 1996 Report to Congress.* Washington, DC: April 1998.

U.S. Environmental Protection Agency, Office of Air and Radiation. *Air Quality Trends— 1994: Six Principal Pollutants.* Washington, DC: 1995.

U.S. Environmental Protection Agency, Office of Air and Radiation. *1995 National Air Quality: Status and Trends, Six Principal Pollutants - Particulate Matter.* Washington, DC: 1996.

U.S. Environmental Protection Agency, Office of Air Quality Planning and Standards. *The Plain English Guide to the Clean Air Act.* Washington, DC: 1996.

U.S. Environmental Protection Agency, Office of Mobile Sources. *Air Toxics from Motor Vehicles.* Fact Sheet OM5-2. Washington, DC: August 1994.

U.S. Environmental Protection Agency, Office of Mobile Sources. *Automobiles and Ozone.* Fact Sheet OMS-4. Washington, DC: January 1993 (http://www.epa.gov/omswww/04-ozone.htm, October 21, 1996).

U.S. Environmental Protection Agency, Office of Mobile Sources. *Motor Vehicles and the 1990 Clean Air Act.* Fact Sheet OMS-11. Washington, DC: August 1994.

U.S. Environmental Protection Agency, Office of Mobile Sources. *Tighter Controls Evaluated for NOx, HC and PM Emissions From Heavy-Duty Engines.* Environmental Fact Sheet. Washington, DC: September 1995.

U.S. Environmental Protection Agency, Office of Policy, Planning and Evaluation. *$mart Investments for City and County Managers: Energy, Environment, and Community Development.* Publication No. EPA-231-R-98-004. Washington, DC: April 1998.

U.S. Environmental Protection Agency, Office of Wetlands, Oceans and Watersheds. *Managing Urban Runoff.* EPA 841-F-96-004G. Washington, DC: 1996.

U.S. Environmental Protection Agency, Office of Wetlands, Oceans and Watersheds. *Non-point Source Pollution: The Nation's Largest Water Quality Problem.* EPA 841-F-96-004A. Washington, DC: 1996.

U.S. Fish and Wildlife Service. "Wetlands Loss Slows, Fish and Wildlife Series Study Shows." News release. Washington, DC: September 17, 1997.

U.S. Fish and Wildlife Service, Division of Endangered Species. "Endangered Species General Statistics." http://www.fws.gov. Washington, DC: January 27, 1998.

Books and Reports (continued)

U.S. Geological Survey, Northern Prairie Wildlife Research Center. *Wetlands Losses in the United States*. Undated but taken from the USGS web site at http:\\www.npwrc.usgs.gov, January 6, 1998.

United Kingdom, Department of the Environment and Department of Transport. *Planning Policy Guidance: Transport* (PPG 13).

Urban Land Institute. *Project Infrastructure Development Handbook*. Washington, DC: Urban Land Institute, 1989.

Village of Schaumburg. Information from the Roosevelt University web site, http://www.roosevelt.edu/metro/vschaumb.htm, January 6, 1999.

Wilson, William Julius. *When Work Disappears: The World of the New Urban Poor*. New York: Vintage Books, 1996.

Wish, Naomi and Stephen Eisdorfer. *The Impact of the Mount Laurel Initiatives: An Analysis of the Characteristics of Applicants and Occupants*. South Orange, NJ: Seton Hall University, 1996.

Yinger, John. *Housing Discrimination Study: Incidence and Severity of Unfavorable Treatment*. Washington, DC: U.S. Department of Housing and Urban Development, 1991.

Articles

Abney, George. "The Statehouse." *Historic Preservation News*, vol. 34, December 1994/January 1995, p. 18.

"Air Quality Pact Follows Growing Concerns." *Asheville Citizen-Times*, December 27, 1998, p. B1.

American Farmland Trust. "Farms In Our Future?" *American Farmland*, Fall 1995.

Archer, R.W. "Land Speculation and Scattered Development; Failures in the Urban-Fringe Land Market." *Urban Studies*, vol. 10, 1973, pp. 367-372.

Arnold, Jr., Chester L. and C. James Gibbons. "Impervious Surface Coverage: The Emergence of a Key Environmental Indicator." *Journal of the American Planning Association*, vol. 62, Spring 1996, pp. 243-258.

Bahl, Roy. "Metropolitan Fiscal Disparities." *Cityscape: A Journal of Policy Development and Research*, Washington, DC: U.S. Department of Housing and Urban Development, vol. 1, August 1994, pp. 293-306.

Banchero, Stephanie. "Students Feel the Squeeze: District 230 Seeks to Ease Crowding." *Chicago Tribune*, October 13, 1998.

Behr, Peter. "Northern Virginia Is Still Where The Jobs Are." *The Washington Post*, August 31, 1996, p. F1.

Berton, Valerie. "Growing Pains." *American Farmland*, vol. 16, Fall 1995, p. 8.

Berton, Valerie. "Harvest or Homes?" *American Farmland*, Fall 1995, p.14.

Articles (continued)

Bier, Thomas E. "Housing Dynamics of the Cleveland Area, 1950-2000," *Cleveland: A Metropolitan Reader.* Kent State University Press, 1995, p. 244-259.

Blankenship, Karl. "Chewing Up the Landscape." *Bay Journal.* Baltimore, MD: Chesapeake Bay Foundation, December 1995, p. 6.

Booth, William. "In L.A., a Clean Day is a Dream No Longer." *The Washington Post,* December 18, 1997, p. A1.

Borckman, Phil. "Motorola On Board Elgin's Revival." *Chicago Tribune,* Metro Northwest Section, August 15, 1996.

Borgman, Anna. "As Exurbs Grow, So Does Burden of Borrowing." *The Washington Post,* February 26, 1995, p. B1.

Bradsher, Keith. "Light Trucks Increase Profits But Foul Air More Than Cars." *The New York Times,* November 30, 1997, p. A1.

Brown, Warren. "Trucks Are Putting Cars Out of Commission." *The Washington Post,* October 7, 1998, p. C10.

Brown, Warren and Martha M. Hamilton. "GM, Ford Prepare Clean-Air Cars." *The Washington Post,* December 18, 1997, p. A1.

Browning, Richard. "Impacts of Transportation on Household Energy Consumption." *World Transport Policy and Practice,* vol. 4, no. 1, 1998.

Bunnell, Gene. "Fiscal Impact Studies as Advocacy and Storytelling," *Journal of Planning Literature,* vol. 12, November 1997, pp. 136-151.

Burnes, Brian. "The Interstate Changed Our Lives." *The Kansas City Star,* September 3, 1996.

Cannon, Lou. "New Fiscal Crisis in California May Slash Local Services." *The Washington Post,* May 23, 1993, p. A6.

Cervero, Robert. "Congestion Relief: The Land Use Alternative." *Journal of Planning Education and Research,* vol. 10, 1991, pp. 119-129.

Cervero, Robert. "Jobs-Housing Balancing and Regional Mobility." *Journal of the American Planning Association,* vol. 55, Spring 1989, pp. 136-150.

Chandler, Clay. "The 60 Watt Mind-Set." *The Washington Post,* November 14, 1997, p. A20.

Chen, Don. "LA Bus Riders Union Sues MTA." *Progress,* February 1995

Christian, Sue Ellen. "Growth Without Pain: McHenry Seeks An Elusive Mix." *Chicago Tribune,* McHenry County edition, April 11, 1995.

Clairborne, William. "Cracks in Portland's 'Great Wall'." *The Washington Post,* September 29, 1997, pp. A1, 12.

Cochrun, Stephen. "Understanding and Enhancing Neighborhood Sense of Community." *Journal of Planning Literature,* vol. 9, 1994, pp. 92-99.

Cohn, D'Vera. "DC Population Still Declining In Latest Count." *The Washington Post,* December 31, 1996, pp. A1, 10.

Articles (continued)

Cohn, D'Vera. "Numerical Order." *The Washington Post Magazine*, February 16, 1997, p. 12.

Cohn-Lee, Richard and Diane Cameron. "Urban Stormwater Runoff Contamination of the Chesapeake Bay: Sources and Mitigation." *The Environmental Professional*, vol. 14, 1992, pp. 10-27.

Coulton, Claudia, Nandita Verma, and Shanyang Guo. *Time Limited Welfare and the Employment Prospects of AFDC Recipients in Cuyahoga County.* Case Western Reserve University, Center on Urban Poverty and Social Change, Draft of October 11, 1996.

Craft, Cynthia H. "Sacramento Throws in Kitchen Sink in Bid for Packard Bell Relocation." *Los Angeles Times*, October 4, 1994, p. D1.

Crane, Randall. "Cars and Drivers in New Suburbs." *Journal of the American Planning Association*, vol. 62, Winter 1996, pp. 51-65.

Davis, Judy S., Arthur C. Nelson, and Kenneth J. Ducker. "The New 'Burbs: The Exurbs and Their Implications for Planning Policy." *Journal of the American Planning Association*, vol. 60, Winter 1994, pp. 45-59.

Dendoff, Julie. "Harvey's Hope Could Rise From Mall's Rubble." *Chicago Tribune*, Metro Chicago edition, August 22, 1996.

Downs, Anthony. "Contrasting Strategies For the Economic Development of Metropolitan Areas In the United States and Western Europe." Chapter Two in Paul Cheshire, Lanfranco Senn, Anita Summers, *et al., Urban Change in the United States and Western Europe: Comparative Analysis and Policy*, 1993.

Duany, Andres and Elizabeth Plater-Zyberk. "Neighborhoods and Suburbs." *Design Quarterly*, March 1995.

Eco City Cleveland, "Sprawl Without Growth." *Moving to Corn Fields: A Reader on Urban Sprawl and the Regional Future of Northeast Ohio*, 1996, pp. 9-11.

Egan, Timothy. "Portland's Hard Line on Managing Growth." *The New York Times*, December 30, 1996.

Egan, Timothy. "Urban Sprawl Strains Western States." *The New York Times*, December 29, 1996.

Eggen, Dan. "A Growing Issue." *The Washington Post*, October 28, 1998, p. A3.

Eggen, Dan. "Virginians Want Limits on Growth, Poll Shows." *The Washington Post*, January 7, 1999, B1.

Eggen, Dan and Justin Blum. "Va. Counties Look to Fees to Ease Growing Pains." *The Washington Post*, March 15, 1998, p. B1.

Eggen, Dan and Peter Pae. "Anti-Development Forces Massing." *The Washington Post*, December 14, 1997, p. A1.

El Nasser, Haya. "Downtown Increasingly Becoming Hometown." *USA Today*, September 25, 1998, p. 3A.

Articles (continued)

El Nasser, Haya. "New Approaches to Rebuilding Cities." *USA Today*, December 27, 1996, p. 2A.

Environmental Law and Policy Center of the Midwest. "Anti-Sprawl Groups Respond to UIC/Tollway Study on Highways and Sprawl." Press release, November 9, 1998.

Epstein, Lee R. "Where Yards Are Wide: Have Land Use Planning and Law Gone Astray?" *William and Mary Environmental Law and Policy Review*, vol. 21, 1997, pp. 345-379.

"Estimate of Green Belt Land Revised." *The Financial Times*, August 18, 1990, p. I4.

Evans, Judith. "Home Buyers Favor Suburbs Over Cities." *The Washington Post*, June 29, 1996, p. E1.

Ewing, Reid H. "Characteristics, Causes, and Effects of Sprawl: A Literature Review." *Environmental and Urban Issues.* Florida Atlantic University/Florida International University, 1994, pp. 1-15.

Ewing, Reid H. "Is Los Angeles-Style Sprawl Desirable? *Journal of the American Planning Association*, vol. 63, Winter 1997, pp. 107-126.

Ewing, Reid *et al.* "Getting Around a Traditional City, a Suburban Planned Unit Development, and Everything In Between," *Issues in Land Use and Transportation Planning, Models and Applications.* Washington, DC: Transportation Research Record No. 1466, 1994, pp. 53-62.

Fehr, Stephen C. "Area Shoppers Find Search for a Parking Space Often Can Be a Maddening Mission." *The Washington Post*, September 1, 1996, p. B1.

Fehr, Stephen C. "Montgomery's Line of Defense Against the Suburban Invasion." *The Washington Post*, March 25, 1997, pp. A1, 10-11.

Fisher, Christy. "What We Love and Hate about Cities." *American Demographics*, October 1997.

Foust, Hal. "Elevated Drive Urged as Relief for Unemployed." *Chicago Tribune*, August 7, 1932.

Frank, James E. and Paul B. Downing. "Patterns of Impact Fee Use." *Development Impact Fees: Policy Rationale, Practice, Theory, and Issues*, Arthur C. Nelson, ed. Chicago, IL: Planners Press, 1998.

Frank, L.D. and G. Pivo. "Impacts of Mixed Use and Density on Three Modes of Travel." *Issues in Land Use and Transportation Planning, Models and Applications.* Washington, DC: Transportation Research Record No. 1466, 1994, pp. 44-52.

Frankel, Glenn and Stephen Fehr. "As the Economy Grows, the Trees Fall." *The Washington Post*, March 23, 1997, pp. A1, 20-21.

Frankel, Glenn and Peter Pae. "In Loudoun, Two Worlds Collide." *The Washington Post*, March 24, 1997, pp. A1, 10-11.

Friedman, Bruce *et al.*, "Effect of Neotraditional Neighborhood Design on Travel Characteristics." *Issues in Land Use and Transportation Planning, Models and Applications.* National Research Council: Transportation Research Record No. 1466, 1994.

Articles (continued)

Gaffuri, E. and G. Costa. "Applied Aspects of Chronoergohygiene." *Chronobiologia*, no. 13, 1986, pp. 39-51

Gersh, Jeff. "Subdivide and Conquer." *The Amicus Journal*, vol. 18, Fall 1996, pp. 14-20.

Gillis, Michael. "Judge Stalls Tollway." *Chicago-Sun Times*, January 17, 1997, p. 1.

Glynn, Thomas. "Psychological Sense of Community Measurement and Application." *Human Relations*, vol. 34, 1981, pp. 789-818.

Glascock, Ned. "The Street Paved with Pride." *The News and Observer* (Raleigh, NC), February 21, 1997, p. 7B.

Goldstein, I.F. and A.L. Weinstein. "Air Pollution and Asthma: Effects of Exposure to Short-Term Sulfur Dioxide Peaks." *Environmental Research*, no. 40, 1986, pp. 332-345.

Goodman, Peter S. "Glendening vs. Suburban Sprawl." *The Washington Post*, October 6, 1998, p. B1.

Gordon, Peter and Harry Richardson. "Are Compact Cities a Desirable Planning Goal?" *Journal of the American Planning Association*, vol. 63, Winter 1997, pp. 95-106.

Gordon, Peter and Henry W. Richardson. "Gasoline Consumption and Cities: A Reply." *Journal of the American Planning Association*, vol. 55, Summer 1989, pp. 342-46.

Grady, William. "Growth Shows Another Side." *Chicago Tribune*, Metro DuPage section, December 17, 1996.

Gregory, Ted. "DuPage Tax Bills Increase by 5%: Average Rise Is Biggest Since 1991." *Chicago Tribune*, March 28, 1998.

Griffin, Robert Jr. "Introducing NPS Water Pollution." *EPA Journal*, November/December 1991, p. 6.

Haines, V. "Energy and Urban Form: An Human Ecological Critique." *Urban Affairs Quarterly*, vol. 21, 1986, pp. 337-353.

Hak, H.P., H. Abbey, and R.C. Talamo. "Prevalence of Asthma and Health Service Utilization of Asthmatic Children in an Inner City." *Journal of Allergy and Clinical Immunology*, no. 70, 1982, pp. 367-372.

Hanley, Robert. "A Fast-Growing Town Innovates in Curbing Suburban Sprawl." *The New York Times*, December 29, 1996.

Hanson, Susan and Ibipo Johnston. "Gender Differences in Work-Trip Length: Explanations and Implications." *Urban Geography*, vol. 6, 1995, pp. 193-219.

Harbor, Jonathan M. "A Practical Method for Estimating the Impact of Land Use Change in Surface Runoff, Groundwater Recharge and Wetland Hydrology." *Journal of the American Planning Association*, vol. 60, 1994, pp. 95-108.

Havemann, Judith. "'Civic Entrepreneurs' Boost Declining Cities." *The Washington Post*, December 9, 1997, p. A1.

Hawkins, Jay. "Notes From the U.K." (interview with British planning expert Barry Cullingworth). *Planning*, vol. 64, August 1998, p. 14-15.

Articles (continued)

Hersch, Joni and Leslie S. Stratton. "Housework, Wages, and the Division of Housework Time for Employed Spouse." *American Economic Review*, vol. 84, pp. 120-125, 1994.

Hodge, David. "Social Impacts of Urban Transportation Decisions: Equity Issues." *The Geography of Urban Transportation*, Susan Hanson, ed. New York: The Guilford Press, 1986, pp. 301-327.

Hoeveler, Kim. "Accessibility vs. Mobility: The Location Efficient Mortgage." *Public Investment*, Planners Advisory Service Memo, American Planning Association, September 1997.

Horton, Tom. "A Fumbling Approach to Growth." *The Baltimore Sun*, December 8, 1995, p. 2C.

Hunt, J.D., J.D.P. McMillan, and J.E. Abraham. "State Preference Investigation of Influences on Attractiveness of Residential Locations." *Issues in Land Use and Transportation Planning, Models and Applications*. National Research Council: Transportation Research Record No. 1466, 1994, pp. 79-87.

"Implications of Emerging Travel Trends: April 20-21, 1994, Conference Proceedings." *1990 Nationwide Personal Transportation Survey*. Washington, DC: U.S. Department of Transportation, Federal Highway Administration, July 1994.

Jossi, Frank "Rewrapping the Big Box." *Planning*, vol. 64, August 1998, p. 16-18.

Kain, John F. "The Spatial Mismatch Hypothesis: Three Decades Later." *Housing Policy Debate*, vol. 3, pp. 371-459.

Kaiser, Jocelyn. "New Wetland Proposal Draws Flak." *Science*, vol. 279, February 13, 1998, p. 980.

Katsuyama, Byron. "Privatization? We Do That." *Municipal Research News*, March 1995.

Katz, Michael B. "Reframing the 'Underclass' Debate." *The 'Underclass' Debate: Views from History*, Michael B. Katz, ed. Princeton, NJ: Princeton University Press, 1993.

Klaassen, Leo H. and Paul C. Cheshire. "Urban Analysis Across The Atlantic Divide." Chapter Twenty in Paul Cheshire, Lanfranco Senn, Anita Summers, *et al.*, *Urban Change in the United States and Western Europe: Comparative Analysis and Policy*, 1993.

Klein, Richard D. "Urbanization and Stream Quality Impairment." *Water Resources Bulletin*, vol. 15, 1979.

Klite, Paul, Robert A. Bardwell and Jason Setzman. "A Day in the Life of Local TV News in America." *Rocky Mountain Media Watch, Content Analysis*, no. 5, January 11, 1995, pp. 1-3.

Koslowsky, Meni and Moshe Krauz. "On the Relationship between Commuting, Stress Symptoms, and Attitudinal Measures: A LISREL Application." *Journal of Applied Behavioral Science*, vol. 29, 1994, pp. 485-492.

Kotkin, Joel. "White Flight to the Fringes." *The Washington Post*, March 10, 1996, pp. C1.

Kuntsler, James Howard. "Home from Nowhere." *The Atlantic Monthly*, vol. 278, September 1996, pp. 43-66.

Articles (continued)

Lacombe, Annalynn. *Welfare Reform and Access to Jobs in Boston.* US Department of Transportation, Bureau of Transportation Statistics, January 1998.

Ladd, Helen F. "Population Growth, Density, and the Costs of Providing Public Services." *Urban Studies*, vol. 29, no. 2, 1992, pp. 273-295.

Lave, Charles and Richard Crepeau. "Travel by Households Without Vehicles." *1990 Nationwide Personal Transportation Survey: Travel Mode Special Reports.* Washington, DC: U.S. Department of Transportation, Federal Highway Administration, December 1994.

Lee, Bill Lann. "Civil Rights and Legal Remedies: A Plan for Action." *Just Transportation: Dismantling Race & Class Barriers to Mobility*, Bullard and Johnson, eds. Stony Creek, CT: New Society Publishers, 1997.

Leinberger, Christopher B. "The Metropolis Observed." *Urban Land*, vol. 57, October 1998, pp. 28-33.

Lemann, Nicholas. "Stressed Out in Suburbia." *The Atlantic Monthly*, November 1989, pp. 34-48.

Lester, Chris and Jeffrey Spivak. "Road System Puts Suburbs on the Map." *The Kansas City Star*, December 19, 1995.

Lester, Chris and Jeffrey Spivak. "Suburbs Can't Escape the Cost of Separation." *The Kansas City Star*, December 17, 1995.

Lester, Chris, Jeffrey Spivack, Gregory Reeves, Steve Nicely. "Divided We Sprawl." *The Kansas City Star*, December 17-22, 1995, reprint, pp. 1-20.

Lewis, Roger K. "Future Shock: A Bold Vision For Aging Cities." *The Washington Post*, July 20, 1996, pp. E1, 20.

Liberty, Robert L. "Oregon's Comprehensive Growth Management Program: An Implementation Review and Lessons for Other States." *Environmental Law Reporter News and Analysis*, vol. 22, June 1992, pp. 10367-9.

Liberty, Robert. "Planned Growth: The Oregon Model." *Natural Resources and Environment*, vol. 13, Summer 1998.

Liewer, Steve. "County Boosts Cash to Lure Businesses." *Sun-Sentinel* (Fort Lauderdale), October 26, 1994, p. 4B.

Lipton, Eric. "In Fairfax, Damaged Streams Stir Fears for the Future." *The Washington Post*, August 7, 1997, p. A1.

Lipton, Eric. "Once Rural Virginia Communities Pulled Into Northern Megalopolis." *The Washington Post*, January 23, 1998, p. B1.

Lynch, Kevin. "What Is the Form of a City, and How Is It Made?" *Classic Readings in Urban Planning*, Jay M. Stein, ed. New York: McGraw-Hill, 1995, pp. 179-187.

MacDonald, Andrew H. "Bay Watch: Safer, But Still Not Saved." *The Washington Post*, February 23, 1997, p. C3.

Articles (continued)

MacDonald, Andrew. "Chapman's Landing Idea Would Do Harm." *The Baltimore Sun*, November 6, 1996, p. 32A.

Maguire, Meg *et al.* "Beauty As Well As Bread." *Journal of the American Planning Association*, vol. 63, Summer 1997, pp. 317-328.

Malizia, Emil, Richard Norton, Craig Richardson, and Michelle J. Zimet. "Reading, Writing, and Impact Fees: What's the Best Method For Calculating School Impact Fees?" *Planning*, vol. 63, September 1997, p. 17.

Marshall, Alex. "Eurosprawl." *Metropolis*, January/February 1995, p. 77.

Martin, Mitch. "McHenry Tax Bills Rise 3.3% On Average: County Homeowners' Charges to Arrive Late." *Chicago Tribune*, May 6, 1998.

Meredith, Robyn. "Demand for Single-Family Homes Helps Fuel Inner-City Resurgence." *The New York Times*, July 5, 1997, p. 1.

Messenger, T. and R. Ewing. "Transit-Oriented Development in the Sunbelt." *Transportation Research Record No. 1552.* 1996, pp. 145-152.

Nasar, Jack and David Julian. "The Psychological Sense of Community in the Neighborhood." *Journal of the American Planning Association*, vol. 61, 1995, pp.178-184.

National Association of Home Builders. Press release. Washington, DC, www.nahb.com:80/update/story5.html, September 9, 1998.

National Municipal Research. "Why Infrastructure Will Be Getting Short Shrift." *Fiscal Stress Monitor*, November 1995.

Natural Resources Defense Council. "Vital Signs of the Golden State." *The Amicus Journal*, vol. 19, Summer 1997, pp. 36-39.

Neal, Terry M. and Todd Shields. "Maryland Looks to Regulate the Promised Land." *The Washington Post*, February 23, 1997, p. A1.

"Neighborhoods Ride the Rails: City, Suburbs Alike Revisit Village Hub Idea." *Chicago Sun-Times*, February 21, 1995.

Nelson Nygard Consulting Associates. "Land Use and Transit Demand: The Transit Orientation Index." *Primary Transit Network Study*. Portland, OR: Tri-Met, 1995, Chapter 3.

Newman, Michael. "Utopia, Dystopia, Diaspora." *Journal of The American Planning Association*, vol. 57, Summer 1991, pp. 344-347.

Newman, Peter W.G. and Jeffrey R. Kenworthy. "Gasoline Consumption and Cities: A Comparison of U.S. Cities With a Global Survey." *Journal of the American Planning Association*, vol. 55, Winter 1989, pp. 24-37.

Newman, Peter W.G. and Jeffrey R. Kenworthy. "Is There a Role for Physical Planners?" *Journal of the American Planning Association*, vol. 58, Summer 1992, pp. 353-362.

Newman, Peter W.G. and Jeffrey R. Kenworthy. "The Transport Energy Trade-Off: Fuel-Efficient Traffic Versus Fuel-Efficient Cites." *Transportation Research*, vol. 22A, 1988, pp. 163-174.

Articles (continued)

Noss, Reed F., Edward T. LaRoe III, and J. Michael Scott. "Endangered Ecosystems of the United States: A Preliminary Assessment of Loss and Degradation." Biological Resources Division, United States Geological Survey 4 (undated but available on the USGS web site, http:\\www.biology.usgs.gov, as of January 1998).

Novaco, Raymond, Daniel Stokols, J. Campbell and J. Stokols. "Transportation, Stress, and Community Psychology." *American Journal of Community Psychology*, no. 7, 1979, pp. 361-380.

Novaco, Raymond, Daniel Stokols and Louis Milanesi. "Objective and Subjective Dimensions of Travel Impedance as Determinants of Commuting Stress." *American Journal of Community Psychology*, vol. 18, 1990, pp. 231-257.

Ove, Torsten. "User Fees Replace Tax Increases: Municipalities Discover a Gold Mine in Charging for Government Services." *Pittsburgh Post-Gazette*, November 23, 1997, p. B-1.

"Pace Planning Expansion But Riders Still Shun Buses." *Chicago Sun-Times*, March 6, 1995.

Peirce, Neal R. "New Friends Plead the Case for Mass Transit." *The Baltimore Sun*, April 10, 1995, p. 9A.

Peiser, Richard B. "Density and Urban Sprawl." *Land Economics*, vol. 65, August 1989, pp. 193-204.

Peiser, Richard B. "Does It Pay to Plan Suburban Growth?" *Journal of the American Planning Association*, vol. 50, Autumn 1984, pp. 419-433.

Pettinico, George. "Civic Participation: Alive and Well in Today's Environmental Groups." *The Public Perspective*, June-July 1996.

Pochna, Peter and Clarke Canfield. "Growth Limits Clash with Landowner Rights; 'There Are No Easy Answers' as Southern Maine Municipalities Explore Various Strategies to Slow Growth and Its Costly Implications." *Portland Press Herald*, July 7, 1997, p. 1A.

Popenoe, David. "Urban Sprawl: Some Neglected Sociological Considerations." *Sociology and Social Research*, vol. 63, No. 2, January 1979.

Porter, Douglas R. "Impact Fees Come to Anne Arundel County." *Urban Land*, July 1988, pp. 34-35.

Presecky, William. "Ballot Issues Put Price Tags On Growth." *Chicago Tribune*, Metro Southwest Edition, January 19, 1996.

Presecky, William. "Peotone Airport Glows In Study—Third Regional Airport Is Called a Remedy to Sprawl." *Chicago Tribune*, August 24, 1996, p.5.

Presecky, William. "Regional Sprawl Linked to Higher Property Taxes." *Chicago Tribune*, January 30, 1995, p. 1N.

Pressler, Margaret Webb. "Toys R Us to Close 90 Stores." *The Washington Post*, September 17, 1998, p. C1.

Pressley, Sue Anne. "Atlanta's Booming Growth Is No Easy Ride." *The Washington Post*, December 4, 1998, p. A3.

Articles (continued)

Pucher, John. "Urban Passenger Transport in the United States and Europe: A Comparative Analysis of Public Policies." *Transport Reviews*, vol. 15, 1995, pp. 211-227.

Pucher, John. "Urban Travel Behavior as the Outcome of Public Policy: The Example of Modal-Split in Western Europe and North America." *Journal of the American Planning Association*, vol. 54, 1988, pp. 509-530.

Putnam, Robert D. "Bowling Alone: America's Declining Social Capital." *Journal of Democracy*, vol. 6, no. 1, January 1995.

Quintanilla, Ray. "Tollway No Longer Stopping Point for Annexations." *Chicago Tribune*, April 3, 1996, p.1.

Rebchook, John. "Costs of Urban Sprawl Estimated in Billions: High Density 'Villages,' Added Light Rail Seen as Needed Measures." *Rocky Mountain News*, May 15, 1997, p. 2B.

Redelmeier, Donald A. and Robert J. Tibshirani. "Association between Cellular-Telephone Calls and Motor Vehicle Collisions." *The New England Journal of Medicine*, vol. 336, no. 7, February 13, 1997.

Reich, Howard and Desiree Chen. "Sprawling Culture Scene Puts Suburbs In Starring Role." *Chicago Tribune*, August 5, 1996, p. 1.

Reid, Alice. "Work Patterns Shifting Commute, Traffic Study Says." *The Washington Post*, August 15, 1996, p. C1.

Resources for the Future. "Cross-Media Pollution and The Chesapeake Bay." *Resources*, vol. 124, Summer 1996, p. 20.

Rich, Michael. "The Reality of Welfare Reform: Employment Prospects in Metropolitan Atlanta." *Georgia Academy Journal*, Summer 1997.

Robinson, John. "Who's Doing the Housework?" *American Demographics*, vol. 10, no. 12, 1988.

Rodriguez, Alex. "Not Much 'Rush' In Rush Hour." *Chicago Sun-Times*, February 23, 1997, p. 8.

Rodriguez, Alex. "Transit Plan looks Ahead to 23 Years of Suburb Growth." *Chicago Sun-Times*, February 14, 1997, p. 3.

Romm, Joseph J. and Charles B. Curtis. "Mideast Oil Forever." *The Atlantic Monthly*, April 1996, pp. 57-74.

Rooney, Timothy S. "Traffic Jam Forms Against Route 53." *Chicago Daily Herald*, January 17, 1996, p. 1.

Rosenbloom, Sandra. "Travel by the Elderly." *1990 Nationwide Personal Transportation Survey: Demographic Special Reports*. Washington, DC: U.S. Department of Transportation, Federal Highway Administration, February 1995.

Rosenbloom, Sandra. "Travel by Women." *1990 Nationwide Personal Transportation Survey: Demographic Special Reports*. Washington, DC: U.S. Department of Transportation, Federal Highway Administration, February 1995.

Articles (continued)

Rothblatt, Donald M. "North American Planning: Canadian and U.S. Perspectives." *Journal of the American Planning Association*, vol. 60, Autumn 1994, pp. 501-507.

Rynkiewicz, Stephen, "Southwest Suburbs Witnessing a Boom." *Chicago Sun-Times*. January 27, 1995, p. 7.

Sanchez, Rene. "Population Increase Highest in Western States." *The Washington Post*, January 1, 1998, p. A14.

Sandoval, Greg. "Santa Clarita Makes Pitch to Lure Cruise Line to City." *Los Angeles Times*, April 23, 1997, p. B6.

Scenic America. "Principles for Conservation." http://www.scenic.org, December 17, 1998.

Schaeffer, M., S. Street, J. Singer and S. Baum. "Effects of Control on Stress Reactions of Commuters." *Journal of Applied Social Psychology*, vol. 18, 1988, pp. 944-957.

Schlar, Elliot and Walter Hook. "The Importance of Cities to the National Economy." *Interwoven Destinies: Cities and the Nation*, Henry Cisneros, ed. New York: W.W. Norton & Co., 1993.

Schwartz, J., D. Gold, D.W. Dockey, *et. al.* "Predictors of Asthma and Persistent Wheeze in a National Sample of Children in the United States." *American Review of Respiratory Disease*, no. 142, 1990, pp. 555-562.

Searcy, Dionne. "Barrington Area Goals Put To Test." *Chicago Tribune*, Metro Northwest Section, August 11, 1996.

Seley, J. "Spatial Bias: The Kink in Nashville's I-40." *Research on Conflict in Locational Decisions*. Philadelphia: Regional Science Department, University of Pennsylvania, 1970.

Seyfarth, J. and W. Bost. "Teacher Turnover and the Quality of Worklife in Schools: An Empirical Study." *Journal of Research and Development in Education*, vol. 20, 1986, pp. 1–6.

Shear, Michael D. "Prince William Shifts From Big to Small." *The Washington Post*, September 30, 1996, p. B1.

Sheppard, Stephen. "The Qualitative Economics of Development Controls." *Journal of Urban Economics*, vol. 24, 1988, pp. 310-330.

Sherrod, D. and S. Cohen. "Density, Personal Control, and Design." *Residential Crowding and Design*, J. Aiello and A. Baum, eds. New York: Plenum Press, 1979.

Shields, Todd. "On Edge." *The Washington Post Magazine*, February 16, 1997, p. 23.

Shore, William. "Recentralization: The Single Answer to More Than a Dozen United States Problems and a Major Answer to Poverty." *Journal of the American Planning Association*, vol. 61, 1995, pp. 496-503.

Simmons, Michael. "Rural England Lost In Concrete: Environmentalists fire warning shot at the Government as urban sprawl threatens to gobble up more and more of country-side." *The Guardian*, July 29, 1993, p. 3.

Sipress, Alan. "Widen the Roads, Drivers Will Come." *The Washington Post*, January 4, 1999, p. B1.

Articles (continued)

Smallwood, Lola. "Library Faces Threat of Red Ink." *Chicago Tribune*, July 8, 1998.

Soulé, Michael E. "Land Use Planning and Wildlife Maintenance." *Journal of the American Planning Association*, vol. 57, Summer 1991, pp. 313-323.

South Carolina Coastal Conservation League. "Getting a Rein on Runoff: How Sprawl and the Traditional Town Compare." *South Carolina Coastal Conservation League Land Development Bulletin*, no. 7, Fall 1995.

Span, Paul. "Auld Lang Syne on 42nd Street." *The Washington Post*, December 31, 1996, p. D1.

Spencer, Kyle York. "Cary Considers Stop-Work Orders on Construction Sites." *The News and Observer* (Raleigh, NC), August 20, 1997, p. B1.

Spencer, Le Ann. "Grayslake Project Sells Environment-Friendly Lifestyle." *Chicago Tribune*, Metro Lake Section, December 4, 1996.

Spinner, Jackie. "In Charles County, All Roads Lead to the Mall." *The Washington Post*, September 1, 1996, p. B1.

Spirn, Anne Whiston. "Urban Nature and Human Design: Reviewing the Great Tradition." *Classic Readings in Urban Planning*, Jay M. Stein, ed. New York: McGraw-Hill, 1995, pp. 475-495.

Stanek, Steve. "Some Fume As McHenry County Ups Its Gas Tax: Full Board Ignores Vote By Committee." *Chicago Tribune*, August 29, 1998.

Stegman, Michael A. and Margery Austin Turner. "The Future of Urban America in the Global Economy." *Journal of the American Planning Association*, vol. 62, Spring 1996, p. 157.

Steiner, Ruth L. "Residential Density and Travel Patterns." *Issues In Land Use and Transportation Planning, Models and Applications*. Washington, DC: Transportation Research Record No. 1466, 1994, pp. 37-43.

Stokols, Daniel, Raymond Novaco, J. Campbell and J. Stokols. "Traffic Congestion, Type-A Behavior, and Stress," *Journal of Applied Psychology*, vol. 63, 1978, pp. 467-480.

Stone, Deborah. "Does Business Development Raise Taxes?: A Commentary." *Public Investment*, March 1995, pp. 1-4.

Stouffer, Rick. "Incentive to Woo Business to Area Costs Taxpayers." *The Buffalo News*, November 12, 1995, p. 1A.

"Striking at the Heart of 'Beyond Sprawl." *BIA News*, vol. 19, no. 1, March 1996.

Sunde, Scott. "Urban Sprawl Turns Green to Brown as Tree Cover Shrinks." *Seattle Post-Intelligencer*, July 15, 1998, p. A1.

Surface Transportation Policy Project. *Transfer*, vol. 3, February 28, 1997.

Suro, Roberto. "Drop in Murder Rate Accelerates in Cities." *The Washington Post*, December 31, 1997, p. A1.

Tagliabue, John. "Europeans Agonize Over the Mall." *The New York Times*, September 10, 1996, p. D1.

Articles (continued)

Taylor, Brian. "Unjust Equity: An Examination of California's Transportation Development Act." *Transportation Research Record: Public Transit*, no. 1297, 1991, pp. 85-92.

Taylor, P. and C. Pocock. "Commuter Travel and Sickness: Absence of London Office Workers." *British Journal of Preventive and Social Medicine*, no. 26, 1972, pp. 165-172.

Thompson, Boyce. "Growing Smart: Whether you call it smart growth or sprawl, it's an important issue that we all need to address." *Builder*, National Association of Home Builders, July 1998.

Tidwell, Mike. "The Intercounty Connector. . . The Road to Ruin." *The Washington Post*, July 27, 1997, p. C3.

Timberg, Craig. "Budget Bust Follows Boom in Growth; 80s Suburban Sprawl is Drain on Schools, Services in 1990s," *The Baltimore Sun*, February 24, 1997, p. 1B.

Ulrich, Roger S., Robert F. Simons, *et al.* "Stress Recovery During Exposure to Natural and Urban Environments." *Journal of Environmental Psychology*, vol. 11, 1991, pp. 201-230.

U.S. Congress, Office of Technology Assessment. "Is the U.S. System Energy-Efficient? A Comparison with Europe." Chapter 3 in *Saving Energy in U.S. Transportation*. Washington, DC: U.S. Government Printing Office, July 1994.

U.S. Environmental Protection Agency. National Ambient Air Quality Standards for Ozone; Proposed Rule, *Federal Register*. vol. 61 (December 13, 1996), pp. 65715-65750.

"Using Car Phones Is as Dangerous as Driving Drunk." *Reuters/Fox* news report, February 13, 1997.

Van Biema, David. "A Social Emergency; In The Kind of Fiscal Crisis That May Soon Confront Others, Los Angeles County Considers Drastic Cuts." *Time*, July 3, 1995, p. 28.

Van Dyne, Larry. "Job Wars." *Washingtonian*, vol. 32, January 1997, p. 4.

Voith, Richard. "Central City Decline: Regional or Neighborhood Solutions." *Federal Reserve Bank of Philadelphia Business Review*, March/April 1996.

Warrick, Joby. "Earth at Its Warmest in Past 12 Centuries." *The Washington Post*, December 8, 1998, p. A3.

Warrick, Joby. "New Wetlands Guidelines, New Openings." *The Washington Post*, January 31, 1998, p. A1.

Warrick, Joby. "Opponents Await Proposal To Limit Air Particulates." *The Washington Post*, November 27, 1996, pp. A1, 14.

Wiewel, Wim. "The Fiscal Impact of Commercial Development." *Land Development*, vol. 6, Spring-Summer 1993, pp. 10-13.

Willen, Liz. "Swollen City Debt Nears Limit: State Legislation Needed to Avoid Cap." *Newsday* (New York, NY), December 10, 1998, p. A6.

Wilson, Scott. "Family Cemetery Is Threatened by Development." *The Washington Post*, October 16, 1997, D1.

Wilson, Scott. "In Howard, Opposition Builds to Rouse's Mixed-Use Development Plan." *The Washington Post*, January 19, 1998, p. B1.

Articles (continued)

Wilson, William Julius, "Appendix A: Perspectives on Poverty Concentration." *When Work Disappears: The World of the New Urban Poor.* New York: Vintage Books, 1996.

Wilson, William Julius, with Robert Aponte. "Appendix: Urban Poverty: A State-of-the-Art Review of the Literature." *The Truly Disadvantaged: The Inner City, the Underclass, and Public Policy.* Chicago, IL: University of Chicago Press, 1987.

Windsor, Duane. "A Critique of The Costs of Sprawl." *Journal of the American Planning Association*, vol. 45, 1979, pp. 279-92.

Ybarra, Michael J. "Putting City Sprawl on a Zoning Diet." *The New York Times*, June 16, 1996, section 4, page 4.

Yinger, John. "Access Denied, Access Constrained: Results and Implications of the 1989 Housing Discrimination Study." *Clear and Convincing Evidence: Measurement of Discrimination in America*, Michael Fix and Raymond J. Struyk, eds. Washington, DC: The Urban Institute Press, 1993.

Zinam, Oleg. "Quality of Life, Quality of the Individual, Technology and Economic Development." *American Journal of Economics and Sociology*, vol. 48, 1989, pp. 55-68.

About the Authors

F. Kaid Benfield is an environmental attorney and director of transportation and smart growth policy for the Natural Resources Defense Council in Washington, DC. He has also served the organization as director of its land program, director of its forestry and agriculture projects, and legal affairs coordinator. Prior to coming to NRDC, Kaid worked at the U.S. Department of Justice and in private legal practice. He is a graduate of Emory University and Georgetown University Law Center and the author of numerous publications related to environmental law and policy, including the book, *Reaping the Revenue Code: Why We Need Sensible Tax Reform for Sustainable Agriculture* (with Justin R. Ward and Anne F. Kinsinger: Natural Resources Defense Council, 1989). He is a member of several steering committees and boards relating to transportation and smart growth.

Matthew D. Raimi is a transportation policy analyst for the Natural Resources Defense Council in Washington, DC. He holds a master's degree in regional planning from the University of North Carolina at Chapel Hill and a BA from the University of Rochester. Prior to coming to NRDC, Matt worked for the Surface Transportation Policy Project, ICF Kaiser, and as a consultant to the University of North Carolina-Chapel Hill's Department of Transportation and Parking. Among his publications are *Five Years of Progress: 110 Communities Where ISTEA is Making a Difference* (with Joe DiStefano: Surface Transportation Policy Project, 1996), and several articles concerning transportation and land use.

Donald D.T. Chen manages research and directs the smart growth program for the Surface Transportation Policy Project (STPP), in Washington, DC. He has authored many reports on transportation pricing, public health, and the performance of public investments in transportation, including *The Going Rate: What It Really Costs to Drive* (World Resources Institute, 1992); *Roadmap Unfolding on Travel Efficiency* (Oak Ridge National Laboratory, 1994); *Getting A Fair Share: An Analysis of Federal Transportation Spending* (STPP, 1996); and *Mean Streets: Pedestrian Safety and Reform of the Nation's Transportation Law* (STPP and Environmental Working Group, 1997). Prior to his tenure at STPP, Don worked for years as a community organizer on issues relating to hunger and homelessness in New Haven, Connecticut. He holds a bachelor's degree in political science and master's degree in environmental studies from Yale University.